# W. H. AUDEN:
# The Far Interior

# W. H. AUDEN: The Far Interior

edited by
## Alan Bold

VISION
and
BARNES & NOBLE

Vision Press Limited
Fulham Wharf
Townmead Road
London SW6 2SB

and

Barnes & Noble Books
81 Adams Drive
Totowa, NJ 07512

ISBN (UK) 0 85478 056 4
ISBN (US) 0 389 20573 7

Printed and bound in Great Britain by
Unwin Brothers Ltd.,
Old Woking, Surrey.
Phototypeset by Galleon Photosetting,
Ipswich, Suffolk.
MCMLXXXV

# Contents

# Introduction

by ALAN BOLD

Of Auden's *Poems* (1930) an anonymous reviewer, in the *Times Literary Supplement* of 19 March 1931, wrote: 'instead of communicating an experience of value to us, it merely sets our minds a problem in allusions to solve.' Along with the impression of intellectual impenetrability went a suggestion of political commitment, and the volume passed into literary legend as a phenomenon 'new to English poetry, and appropriate for dealing with the new realities of 1930'.[1] Admittedly 'It was Easter as I walked in the public gardens' has references to 'anxiety at night', to a 'final war/ Of proletariat against police', to a teenage girl being shot and thrown 'down concrete stair', yet it also invokes a 'sullen valley where is made no friend' as an image of desolation. Similarly, though 'Consider this and in our time' has urgent phrases such as 'The game is up' and 'It is later than you think', it laments the fate of 'the ruined boys' of whom the young Auden was undoubtedly one since he considered the homosexuality that overwhelmed him 'indecent'.[2]

The idea of overcoming the sensation of ruin through the fulfilment of friendship is present in *Poems*, even if it is often buried beneath Auden's understandable desire to dazzle with his linguistic virtuosity. 'Control of the passes was, he saw, the key' offers lines about companionship:

> Woken by water
> Running away in the dark, he often had
> Reproached the night for a companion
> Dreamed of already.

'Since you are going to begin today' puts a sexual gloss on the quest for a companion:

7

You are the one whose part it is to lean,
For whom it is not good to be alone.
Laugh warmly turning shyly in the hall
Or climb with bare knees the volcanic hill,
Acquire that flick of wrist and after strain
Relax in your darling's arms like a stone
Remembering everything you can confess,
Making the most of firelight, of hours of fuss.

*Poems* included the charade *Paid on Both Sides* in which the poet fondly involves his friends. Dedicated to Cecil Day Lewis, it drops into the text the names of Edward [Upward], Stephen [Spender] and [Rex] Warner.

After the reception of *Poems* as a politically explosive volume, Auden had to live with a reputation as a revolutionary poet. It was not something he enjoyed, as he was an amiable individual who valued friendship more than fame. His two most celebrated political poems can be read, in retrospect, as attempts to deal with his own personality, as when, in 'A Communist to Others', he writes

Unhappy poet, you whose only
Real emotion is feeling lonely
When suns are setting.

or, in 'Spain', offers a blissful scenario:

To-morrow for the young the poets exploding like bombs,
The walks by the lake, the weeks of perfect communion;
Tomorrow the bicycle races
Through the suburbs on summer evenings. But to-day the
struggle.

Auden's career as a poet developed as he gradually acquired the courage to clarify the theme that was glimpsed in *Poems* and obscured in 'A Communist to Others' and 'Spain'. His ambition was, as Humphrey Carpenter says, 'to purge his poetry of false rhetoric and to make it serve the interests of truth, at whatever cost'.[3] In achieving this aim he was frequently misunderstood, but his persistence demonstrates one of the admirable qualities we most associate with the poems he produced.

Auden, it seems to me, is the only twentieth-century poet who has devoted a great talent to exploring exhaustively the theme of friendship by looking at all its manifestations from casual acquaintance to agape. All the confusion over Auden's early work, all the accusations that he abandoned deeply felt principles when he recovered his Anglican faith in 1939, amount to an assumption that the poet was once a passionately political creature who treacherously turned his back on his comrades. In fact, Auden never had comrades in the ideological sense but always had 'chums' (to use one of his favourite expressions) in the personal sense. The theme of friendship may not seem a major preoccupation for a poet, and indeed Auden has been slighted because 'he says what he has to say without much difficulty, and then, of course, he never has anything very difficult to say.'⁴ In literary theory friendship is considered a sentimental subject; as practised poetically by Auden it has social, theological and erotic overtones which is why it sustained him for a creative lifetime.

For critical orthodoxy, Auden's abiding theme is sufficiently unusual to present interpretative difficulties. Traditionally, poets have restricted themselves to expressions of love for *dead* friends and Milton's 'Lycidas', Shelley's 'Adonais' and Tennyson's *In Memoriam* were accepted as authentically poetic works because of their elegiac tone. Auden, however, wrote poems in praise of friends who were alive and he rejoiced in their vitality. The homosexual reputation of Auden may have prejudiced some critics against him as they possibly suspected that his poems about friendship were always sexual in origin. Yet Auden's concept of friendship was a broad one and included the notion of the Good Place, the basically domestic earthly paradise where he presided as symbolic mother. As a poet he could create literary offspring, but it was one of his great regrets that he could not father a child. His habit of referring to himself as 'Mother' in conversation—'No, dear, you take it from mother, *Pelléas* is shit'⁵—is surely significant.

Auden's first great friend was his own mother, Constance. Undoubtedly the young Auden was a mother's boy and in a sense he remained the eternal child craving maternal love even while, by his 'gift of double focus' (as he called it in *New Year Letter*), he himself enjoyed the rôle of mother. In his biography of Auden, Humphrey Carpenter describes how Auden loved Constance deeply:

9

but he felt that their close relationship had set up a great
tension in himself. . . . Looking back to his childhood, he felt
that he could ascribe almost everything in his adult character to
the relationship with his mother. . . . certainly he never got
away from his mother. As an adult he loved to invoke her
imaginary judgement on his own or other people's behaviour;
his usual phrase of criticism of any conduct that earned his
disapproval was 'Mother wouldn't like it.'[6]

More bluntly, Auden told Chester Kallman that 'Mothers
have much to do with your queerness and mine.'[7] When, in
1947, Kallman's promiscuity caused a crisis in Auden's life,
the poet wrote to Rhoda Jaffe about being 'anxious like a
momma'.[8] Inevitably, the landscapes that Auden admired had
maternal contours. As a schoolboy he had fallen in love with
the countryside in the north-western part of the Pennines. In
*New Year Letter* (1941), dedicated to mother-surrogate Elizabeth
Mayer, he wrote:

> In ROOKHOPE I was first aware
> Of Self and Not-self, Death and Dream:
> Adits were entrances which led
> Down to the Outlawed, to the Others,
> The Terrible, the Merciful, the Mothers;
> Alone in the hot day I knelt
> Upon the edge of shafts and felt
> The deep *Urmutterfurcht* that drives
> Us into knowledge all our lives,
> The far interior of our fate
> To civilize and to create.

For Auden the 'far interior' was the inner secret of his own
personality, the deepest part of him that had a motherly
capacity for giving and receiving friendship as well as creating
poems. 'In Praise of Limestone', from *Nones* (1951), reiterates
the maternal attraction of the limestone landscape.

> Mark these rounded slopes
> With their surface fragrance of thyme and beneath
> A secret system of caves and conduits; hear these springs
> That spurt out everywhere with a chuckle
> Each filling a private pool for its fish and carving
> Its own little ravine whose cliffs entertain
> The butterfly and the lizard; examine this region

>    Of short distances and definite places:
>    What could be more like Mother or a fitter background
>    For her son.

The narrator of *For the Time Being* (1944), the Christmas Oratorio Auden wrote 'In Memoriam Constance Rosalie Auden 1870–1941', likewise goes back to a poetic childhood haunted by 'The nursery bogey or the winecellar ghost' and states

>              We are afraid
>    Of pain but more afraid of silence; for no nightmare
>    Of hostile objects could be as terrible as this Void.
>    This is the Abomination. This is the wrath of God.

For Auden the process of maturing was the inventive attempt to fill the Void with friendship.

The life and art of Auden can be approached in terms of the assorted companions who comforted him at various stages of his career. His lifelong friendship with Christopher Isherwood began at prep school (St. Edmund's, Hindhead, Surrey), and by his own account it was when he was at Gresham's school, in North Suffolk, that he began to write poetry:

> I began writing poetry myself because one Sunday afternoon in March 1922, a friend [Robert Medley] suggested I should: the thought had never occurred to me. . . . At this time [Medley's] suggestion that I write poetry seemed like a revelation from heaven for which nothing in my past could account.[9]

In 'Letter to Lord Byron' (1937) the anecdote is phrased as follows:

>    But indecision broke off with a clean cut end
>      One afternoon in March at half past three
>    When walking in a ploughed field with a friend;
>      Kicking a little stone, he turned to me
>      And said, 'Tell me, do you write poetry?'
>    I never had, and said so, but I knew
>    That very moment what I wished to do.

As Auden dated his loss of his Anglican faith to 1922 it can be fairly inferred that the ritual of verse, suggested to him by a friend, took at that time the place of a religious routine.

More influential friends were made at Oxford where Auden

got to know C. Day Lewis, Stephen Spender and Louis MacNeice whose names were thereafter connected with the poetic School of Auden. Friends were the only kind of family Auden, as a homosexual, could gather about him. Hence the love of collaboration—with Isherwood (*The Dog Beneath the Skin, the Ascent of F6, On the Frontier, Journey to a War*), with MacNeice (*Letters from Iceland*), with Kallman (*The Rake's Progress, Elegy for Young Lovers, The Bassarids*). Hence the desire to salute his friends in dedications to poems and books so that *City Without Walls* (1969), for example, pays tribute to Peter Heyworth:

> At Twenty we find our friends for ourselves, but it takes Heaven
> To find us one when we are Fifty-Seven.

Auden's use of terms such as the Good Place and the Just City for his dream of Eden is a poetic projection of his personal search for the company of friends who alone could enhance his environment. It is interesting that when he was in Berlin in 1929 the poet frequented a homosexual bar in Zossenstrasse called the Cosy Corner. The name must have greatly appealed to him since a cosy corner is precisely what he wanted in life.

Auden's recovery of his Anglican faith, in November 1939, led not to a theological composition but to *New Year Letter* (1941) in which his disappointment with secular dogma is contrasted with his vision of an ideal community. Though the poem reaches out to the necessity of 'building the Just City now', its central affirmation presents a domestic situation not a civic utopia. In the third part of the poem Auden reminds Elizabeth Mayer, to whom the work is dedicated, of Christmas in her home on Long Island:

> Warm in your house, Elizabeth,
> A week ago at the same hour
> I felt the unexpected power
> That drove our ragged egos in
> From the dead-ends of greed and sin
> To sit down at the wedding feast,
> Put shining garments on the least,
> Arranged us so that each and all,
> The erotic and the logical,

> Each felt the *placement* to be such
> That he was honoured overmuch,
> And SCHUBERT sang and MOZART played
> And GLUCK and food and friendship made
> Our privileged community
> That real republic which must be
> The State all politicians claim,
> Even the worst, to be their aim.

The title poem of *Thank You, Fog* (1974)—the last collection of verse Auden assembled before his death on 29 September 1973—also celebrates the Good Place as a domestic 'privileged community'. In 1972 Auden left New York to return to England where he took the tenancy of the Brewhouse, a small cottage on the grounds of Christ Church, Oxford. He spent that Christmas near Salisbury at the house of James and Tania Stern. The other guest was Sonia Orwell, George Orwell's widow. According to Humphrey Carpenter, Auden was happiest when sealed in the house:

> He would not go further than the front door—'A *walk?* What on earth *for?*—and when a planned visit by car to the writer Christopher Sykes, who lived forty miles away, had to be cancelled because a blanket of fog had come down, he was visibly pleased, returning delightedly to the fire and his crossword.[10]

In 'Thank You, Fog' Auden affirms his faith in the 'privileged community' created by good companionship, addressing the fog as follows:

> how delighted I am
> that You've been lured to visit
> Wiltshire's witching countryside
> for a whole week at Christmas,
> that no one can scurry where
> my cosmos is contracted
> to an ancient manor-house
> and four Selves, joined in friendship,
> Jimmy, Tania, Sonia, Me.

Company was, for Auden, the perfect antidote to isolation.
    Auden's key experiences all persuaded him that humanity could only be apprehended by members of a like-minded

group gathered together in a Good Place, or 'privileged community', which might be a favourite bar or a living-room at Christmas or a church. In summer 1933, while teaching at the Downs School in Colwall, he had his Vision of Agape in the company of two women and one man and 'for the first time in my life I knew exactly . . . what it means to love one's neighbour as oneself.'[11] When he went to Spain as a Republican sympathizer in 1937 he was horrified by the harm done to the 'privileged community' of the churches of Barcelona:

> I found as I walked through the city that all the churches were closed and there was not a priest to be seen. To my astonishment, this discovery left me profoundly shocked and disturbed. . . . I could not escape acknowledging that, however I had consciously ignored and rejected the Church for sixteen years, the existence of churches and what went on in them had all the time been very important to me.[12]

When he regained his religious faith in 1939 the crucial moment came in a cinema in a German-speaking section of Manhattan when, watching a Nazi film on the conquest of Poland, he heard members of the audience shout 'Kill them!'[13] Relaxing outside a school, standing outside a shut church, sitting in a cinema— Auden always related to the atmosphere of the Good Place and was disturbed when its aura of tranquillity was shattered, as when the Barcelona churches were bereft of people and when the Manhattan cinema was transformed into the domain of a mob. 'A poet who wishes to improve himself should certainly keep good company',[14] Auden believed, which led to his distrust of the anonymity of the mob: 'A mob is active; it smashes, kills and sacrifices itself.'[15]

Introducing *The Dyer's Hand* (1963), Auden insisted that 'A poem must be a closed system.'[16] An examination of Auden's life and art suggests he applied this criterion to everything he encountered. Although he had his bouts of cruising for homosexual pickups, Auden's fundamental search was for a situation that would have the stability of a good marriage. When he met Chester Kallman, in April 1939, he was sure he had found his perfect mate and the relationship survived several crises. Auden used the term 'marriage' about his life with Kallman and 'possibly the two of them had sworn actual vows'.[17] Auden's wish to inhabit a 'closed system' with another led him to a formulation of his own principles of happiness in 'A Lullaby' from *Thank You, Fog*. Dismissing the Greek depiction of a youthful Narcissus as an error, Auden regards himself as a man with essentially motherly tendencies:

> For many years you envied
> the hirsute, the he-man type.
> No longer: now you fondle
> your almost feminine flesh
> with mettled satisfaction,
> imagining that you are
> sinless and all-sufficient,
> snug in the den of yourself,
> *Madonna and Bambino*:
> *Sing, Big Baby, sing lullay.*

The alternative images there—of 'he-man' and Madonna—are the two figures he scrutinized with his 'gift of double-focus'.

Auden's early obsession with the ideal of the leader—John Nower in *Paid on Both Sides*, the Leader in *The Orators* (1932)—has been treated as an ideological interest. Discussing *Paid on Both Sides*, Samuel Hynes suggests it asks

> an important question . . . and one that will preoccupy many writers: what is the good leader, the Truly Strong Man? what are his strengths and weaknesses? how does the leader recognize his destiny? how are leadership and freedom related?[18]

Ironically enough, the phrase 'the truly strong man' occurs first in the passage, composed in April 1939, beginning 'It was Easter as I walked in the public gardens':

> And recent particulars come to mind:
> The death by cancer of a once hated master,
> A friend's analysis of his own failure,
> Listened to at intervals throughout the winter
> At different hours and in different rooms.
> But always with success of others for comparison,
> The happiness, for instance, of my friend Kurt Groote,
> Absence of fear in Gerhart Meyer
> From the sea, the truly strong man.

15

Kurt Groote and Gerhart Meyer were boyfriends of Auden's in Berlin. When Auden met Meyer, the original Truly Strong Man, he was propositioned: 'Give me ten marks and I sleep with you tonight. . . . You can pay me on Tuesday.'[19]

So Auden's perception of the Truly Strong Man was homosexual in origin. We know, from John Layard's memoirs, that 'Wystan liked being beaten up a bit',[20] and it is instructive to compare Auden's Truly Strong Man with Quentin Crisp's analysis of a common homosexual fantasy, that of the Great Dark Man.

In *The Naked Civil Servant* (1968), Crisp writes:

> [The roughs] consciously tried to embody the myth of the great dark man which haunts the dreams of pathological homosexuals and is the cause of one of their dilemmas. . . . [Homosexuals] can clutch with both hands at the myth of the great dark man. Their choice, unless they suffer from some subsidiary kink, is guided by the desire to bolster up, with a number of contrasts, that dream of themselves which it is their one increasing purpose to maintain.[21]

Auden's most explicit statement of his sexual preferences, 'The Platonic Blow' (1948), is a variation on Crisp's Great Dark Man, for the poet's hero is a Great Blond Man. It is worth remembering, of course, that Auden himself, Chester Kallman, and Rhoda Jaffe—with whom Auden had a hetero-sexual affair in 1946—were blonds. Auden's 'The Platonic Blow' conjures up a Truly Strong Man:

> I glanced as I advanced. The clean white T-shirt outlined
> A forceful torso; the light-blue denims divulged
> Much. I observed the snug curves where they hugged the behind,
> I watched the crotch where the cloth intriguingly bulged.[22]

Over the years, as Auden indicated in 'A Lullaby', the Truly Strong Man was perceived as an aberration as the poet increasingly acknowledged the feminine principle of creativity in himself,

> The far interior of our fate
> To civilize and to create.

Seen in this context, the sequence 'Thanksgiving for a Habitat', from *About the House* (1965), can be appreciated as a thematic culmination of his art, not an opting out of social responsibilities. It is Auden's detailed description of the Good Place, the home he acquired in 1957 in Kirchstetten, Austria. The Just City he mentioned in 'Spain' and *New Year Letter* was an abstraction, whereas the Good Place, Auden's Eden, was a real home where he could receive friends. As the title poem of 'Thanksgiving for a Habitat' suggests, Auden had found the proverbial womb with a view:

> mine, a toft-and-croft
> where I needn't, ever, be at home to
>
> those I am not at home *with*, not a cradle,
>   a magic Eden without clocks,
> and not a windowless grave, but a place
>   I may go both in and out of.

Poem by poem, the sequence maps out the territory of this particular Good Place. It was, as he says in 'For Friends Only', 'a shrine to friendship—something he had spent years searching for. Ultimately 'a shrine to friendship' is what Auden meant by Eden, which is why the Good Place was a smaller unit than the Just City. In 'Vespers', from 'Horae Canonicae', he had admitted as much by juxtaposing one against the other: 'You can see, then, why between my Eden and his New Jerusalem, no treaty is negotiable.' Whereas Auden's early poetry is vitiated by abstraction, his mature work is rich in particulars.

More than most modern poets, Auden was in the habit of punctuating poems with pronouncements on the status and purpose of poetry. When he said, in 'In Memory of W. B. Yeats', that 'poetry makes nothing happen' he was rationalizing his position in 1939, consciously casting off the political label that had been attached to him throughout the 1930s. When he said, in 'The Cave of Making'—his tribute to his late friend Louis MacNeice in 'Thanksgiving for a Habitat'—that 'to stink of Poetry/ is unbecoming', he was evidently weary of his own reputation as a public poet. Though Auden said that 'among the many functions of the poet, preaching is one',[23] he was never really happy with the role of political prophet. His rejection of political poems such as 'A Communist to Others' and 'Spain' as 'trash'[24] demonstrates his acute embarrassment at their schematic treatment of morality. A genuinely political poet of the 1930s, Hugh MacDiarmid, never took Auden seriously as a committed writer. Realizing that the School of Auden, in the 1930s, comprised chums rather than comrades, MacDiarmid undermined the whole foundation of 'British Leftish Poetry, 1930–1940' in these terms:

> Auden, MacNeice, Day Lewis, I have read them all,
> Hoping against hope to hear the authentic call . . .
> And know the explanation I must pass is this
> —You cannot light a match on a crumbling wall.

Against that devastating critique we can set another poem, 'W. H. Auden' by Christy Brown, which takes a sympathetic look at the man

> speaking your verse in a tired unlit voice
> as if you wanted to close the door and be gone
> to where you might at last pin down peace
> drink unending wine and converse with friends
> till all the sacred cows came home

It may not seem much to claim Auden as the great modern poet of friendship, an author at his most characteristic in lines like these, from 'Since':

> Of what, then, should I complain,
> pottering about
> a neat suburban kitchen?
> Solitude? Rubbish!
> It's social enough with real
> faces and landscapes
> for whose friendly countenance
> I at least can learn
> to live with obesity
> and a little fame.

Yet it is only literary fashion that claims, in the 1930s, that a poem must be political; in the 1940s, that a poem must be rhetorical; in the 1950s, that a poem must be conversational; in the 1960s, that a poem must be confessional. In the everyday world that Auden applauded in his art, friendship is a crucial and life-enhancing reality. He said, in the dedication (to Michael and Marny Yates) of *Thank You, Fog*,

## Introduction

> None of us are as young
> as we were. So what?
> Friendship never ages.

Auden communicated this conviction through poems that are, thanks to his marvellous metrical gifts, built to last.

*Acknowledgements*: extracts from the works of W. H. Auden—specifically *The Dance of Death* (London: Faber and Faber, 1933); *The Dog Beneath the Skin*, with Christopher Isherwood (London: Faber and Faber, 1935; New York: Random House, 1935); *The Dyer's Hand* (New York: Random House, 1962; London: Faber and Faber, 1963); *Collected Poems*, edited by Edward Mendelson (London: Faber and Faber, 1976; New York: Random House, 1976); *The English Auden*, edited by Edward Mendelson (London: Faber and Faber, 1977; New York: Random House, 1978)—are reprinted by permission of the publishers Faber and Faber Ltd., London, and Random House, Inc., New York. Acknowledgement is also gratefully made to Edward Mendelson, Literary Executor of The Estate of W. H. Auden.

### NOTES

1. Samuel Hynes, *The Auden Generation* (London: Faber, 1976), p. 57.
2. Humphrey Carpenter, *W. H. Auden: A Biography* (London: Allen and Unwin, 1981), p. 49.
3. Ibid., p. 454.
4. A. Alvarez, *The Shaping Spirit* (1958; rept. London: Arrow Books, 1963), p. 88.
5. Charles Osborne, *W. H. Auden: The Life of a Poet* (London: Eyre Methuen, 1979), p. 315.
6. Carpenter, pp. 11–12.
7. Ibid., p. 258.
8. Ibid., p. 315.
9. W. H. Auden, *The Dyer's Hand* (London: Faber, 1963), p. 34.

10. Carpenter, p. 445.
11. W. H. Auden, *Forewords and Afterwords* (London: Faber, 1973), p. 69.
12. Cited in Hynes, *The Auden Generation*, p. 251.
13. Carpenter, p. 282.
14. Auden, *The Dyer's Hand*, p. 37.
15. Ibid., p. 82.
16. Ibid., p. xii.
17. Carpenter, p. 312.
18. Hynes, p. 54.
19. Carpenter, p. 98.
20. Cited in ibid., p. 90.
21. Quentin Crisp, *The Naked Civil Servant* (1968; rept. London; Fontana, 1977), pp. 62–3.
22. There are various versions of 'The Plantonic Blow'; this text comes from a six-page pamphlet (London, 1967), entitled 'A Gobble Poem'. Though Auden publicly denied authorship of the poem, Charles Osborne (*W. H. Auden: The Life of a Poet*, p. 283) says that 'privately he was quite proud of it.'
23. W. H. Auden and Christopher Isherwood, *Journey to a War* (1939; revd. London: Faber, 1973), p. 7.
24. Cited in Robin Skelton (ed.), *Poetry of the Thirties* (Harmondsworth: Penguin, 1964), p. 42.

# Part One:
# GOSPEL OF THE MUSE

I bring my gospel of the Muse
To fundamentalists, to nuns,
To Gentiles and to Jews

—Auden, 'On the Circuit'

# 1

# Auden as Christian Poet

## by CHARLES OSBORNE

Poetry is made not of ideas, but of words. No major poet of the present century has known this more clearly and consistently than W. H. Auden, who on several occasions reiterated his belief in the poem as a well-made object and his rejection of the idea of poetry as self-expression or as the vehicle through which religious, political or philosophical beliefs could or should be propagated. Yet political themes do lie scattered throughout his verse of the '30s, and philosophical ideas are certainly not absent from his post-war verse. And, although for Auden words may have been primarily tools or ingredients, they can never—even for a virtually mindless 'sound poet'— be entirely objective. An intelligent man's thoughts on philosophy and religion will therefore necessarily colour his choice of words, whether or not he chooses to write overtly on political or religious topics. W. H. Auden may have been a Christian who wrote poetry, or he may have been a Christian poet. Let us consider both possibilities.

Was Auden a Christian? We are all, in a sense, Christians, in that we have been born in what one might call the light of Christ: born into a Christian tradition, into a world whose morals are Judeo-Christian. Even the Jews are Christians. Those of us who do not accept this position have to opt out of it, like trade unionists unwilling to pay their dues to the Labour Party. We have to label ourselves as agnostics or atheists, or take up one of the crankier religions, or pretend to be Muslims or whatever. Very few of us, if we think of these matters at all seriously, remain stuck with the same attitude for our entire lives. Many people brought up as Christians drift away from the church, others leap out of the Catholic frying pan into the Communist fire or *vice versa*, others waver back and forth, while some, content to believe nothing for most of their lives, baulk at regularizing this into a belief in Nothing, and send for a priest at the last moment.

Was Auden a Christian? When was he a Christian? How was he a Christian? He certainly accepted the concept of a Christian mind, as distinct from or opposed to a Greek mind. To Auden, the Christian and Jewish minds were essentially one:

> Christendom was a product of Jewish historical religious experience and Gentile speculation upon and organization of that experience. The Greek mind is the typically Gentile mind, and it is at odds with the Jewish consciousness. As a Greek the Christian is tempted to a seesaw between worldly frivolity and a falsely spiritual other-worldliness, both of them, *au fond*, pessimistic; as a Jew he is tempted to the wrong kind of seriousness, to an intolerance which persecutes dissenters as wicked rather than stupid. The Inquisition was a product of a Gentile interest in rationality and a Jewish passion for truth.[1]

Auden goes on to make the point that the Crucifixion was actually performed by the Romans 'for the frivolous reason that Jesus was a political nuisance', and that those Jews who demanded it 'did so for the serious reason that, in their opinion, Jesus was guilty of blasphemy, i.e., of falsely claiming to be the Messiah'. Every Christian, Auden concludes, is both Pilate and Caiaphas. Both Roman and Jew.

This is not the attitude of a conventionally devout Christian. Auden, however, came from a conventionally devout Anglican family. Both parents were themselves the children of Anglican vicars, but it was Auden's mother who supplied most of the devotion, while his father tempered it with convention. Mrs. Auden insisted on family prayers being held daily, in which the household servants participated, and took her children to High Mass at an Anglo-Catholic church on Sundays. Auden was later to recall that his first experience of religion was neither spiritual nor intellectual but aesthetic.

Comparing his early years, for the purpose of a book review, with those of Leonard Woolf and Evelyn Waugh, the adult

Auden noted: '1920, period of ecclesiastical Schwärmerei. 1922, discovers that he has lost his faith.'² This discovery was made at the age of 15. Auden's hiatus of unbelief was to last a good eighteen years. Indeed, whether he ever returned to the unquestioning faith of his childhood years is highly doubtful. His was essentially a questioning, sceptical temperament.

The rationalist faced with a mystical experience can incorporate it into his rational view of the world, or he can use it as a way into religion. That Auden chose to use the one significant mystical experience of his young adulthood as a way back to the church is suggested by the account of it which he wrote thirty years later:

> One fine summer night in June 1933 I was sitting on a lawn after dinner with three colleagues, two women and one man. We liked each other well enough but we were certainly not intimate friends, nor had any one of us a sexual interest in another. Incidentally, we had not drunk any alcohol. We were talking casually about everyday matters when, quite suddenly and unexpectedly, something happened. I felt myself invaded by a power which, though I consented to it, was irresistible and certainly not mine. For the first time in my life I knew exactly— because, thanks to the power, I was doing it—what it means to love one's neighbour as oneself. I was also certain, though the conversation continued to be perfectly ordinary, that my three colleagues were having the same experience. (In the case of one of them, I was able later to confirm this.) My personal feelings towards them were unchanged—they were still colleagues, not intimate friends—but I felt their existence as themselves to be of infinite value and rejoiced in it.
>
> I recalled with shame the many occasions on which I had been spiteful, snobbish, selfish, but the immediate joy was greater than the shame, for I knew that, so long as I was possessed by this spirit, it would be literally impossible for me deliberately to injure another human being. I also knew that the power would, of course, be withdrawn sooner or later and that, when it did, my greed and self-regard would return. The experience lasted at its full intensity for about two hours when we said good-night to each other and went to bed. When I awoke the next morning, it was still present, though weaker, and it did not vanish completely for two days or so. The memory of the experience has not prevented me from making use of others, grossly and often, but it has made it much more

difficult for me to deceive myself about what I am up to when I do. And among the various factors which several years later brought me back to the Christian faith in which I had been brought up, the memory of this experience and asking myself what it could mean was one of the most crucial; though, at the time it occurred, I thought I had done with Christianity for good.[3]

This experience led not to an immediate return to religion but to a poem celebrating not even the mystical nature of that summer night experience but instead a sensuous, physical well-being:

Out on the lawn I lie in bed,
Vega conspicuous overhead
  In the windless nights of June;
Forests of green have done complete
The day's activity; my feet
  Point to the rising moon.

Later stanzas of the poem contrast somewhat guiltily the poet's life of ease with the imminence of war or revolution, but the solution appears to lie in human relationships rather than in religion. In fact, though Auden retained an amused fondness for the church and its ritual, and delighted in hymn-singing on occasions both suitable and unsuitable, for most of the '30s he paid a half-hearted lip service to Marxism. Unlike many of his friends, however, he stopped short of joining the Communist party. And when, in 1937, he went to Spain to support an anti-clerical Republican Government, he was distressed to find all the churches closed and not a priest to be seen:

To my astonishment, this discovery left me profoundly shocked and disturbed. The feeling was far too intense to be the result of a mere liberal dislike of intolerance, the notion that it is wrong to stop people from doing what they like, even if it is something silly like going to church. I could not escape acknowledging that, however I had consciously ignored and rejected the Church for sixteen years, the existence of churches and what went on in them had all the time been very important to me.[4]

Despite his reaction to the closure of the churches in Spain, it was not until 1940 that Auden began regularly to go to church again. In October of that year, he rejoined the Anglican Communion. Commentators on Auden have made much of this conversion or return to Christianity, and the poet himself wrote about it at length in his contribution to the volume, *Modern Canterbury Pilgrims*, in which he described his Anglo-Catholic upbringing, his gradual loss of interest in religion as he grew to manhood, and his realization that behind his devout phase 'lay a quite straightforward and unredeemed eroticism'.[5]

Growing away from a Christian family into an intellectual world where most people, certainly most of the writers of his circle, were atheists or agnostics, Auden had for years found himself ceasing to think about religion. But the beliefs of his childhood were still embedded within him, and it is hardly surprising that when, in his early thirties, he came to examine himself and his beliefs, he should discover that the faith drilled into him as a child had by no means died. He had, in any case, never lost his taste for abstruse theological discussion, and shortly after his visit to Spain he had met, in a publisher's office, an Anglican layman,

> and for the first time in my life felt myself in the presence of personal sanctity. I had met many good people before who made me feel ashamed of my own shortcomings, but in the presence of this man—we never discussed anything but literary business—I did not feel ashamed. I felt transformed into a person who was incapable of doing or thinking anything base or unloving.[6]

The man, whom Auden did not name, was Charles Williams, and the literary business they discussed was *The Oxford Book of Light Verse*. But if Spain, Williams, and, as one will see later, Kierkegaard had begun to lead Auden's thoughts back to the church, it was a mystical experience, apparently the opposite of that blissful communion on an English lawn in 1933, which brought a degree of urgency to his feelings about the subject. This second experience, which he must have undergone sometime during 1939, is recorded in a deliberately vague paragraph in the *Modern Canterbury Pilgrims* essay:

> So, presently, I started to read some theological works, Kierkegaard in particular, and began going, in a tentative and

experimental sort of way, to church. And then, providentially—
for the occupational disease of poets is frivolity—was forced to
know in person what it is like to feel oneself the prey of demonic
powers, in both the Greek and the Christian sense, stripped of
self-control and self-respect, behaving like a ham actor in a
Strindberg play.

What is most interesting about Auden's 'conversion' is that
he remained very much as he had formerly been. He had been
an extremely eccentric Marxist, and he now became an
equally eccentric Christian, one in whom the Audenish
outweighed the Christian elements. He was able to accept
Christian dogma more easily than Marxist dogma, or at least
to pay greater lip-service to it, because it was, as dogma, less
dangerous. It would seem that what Auden sought, after an
experience which had frightened him, was a set of rules to
which he could cling and which would protect him against
unknown terrors. He had always, like most liberal humanists,
accepted the moral tenets of Christianity. Now he was
prepared to swallow its supernatural aspects as well, for the
sake, one might say, of a quiet life.

Whether a quiet life produces better poetry than a turbulent
life is debatable. Auden chose not to debate the issue, but to
regard it as a challenge to his powers as a poet. If he changed
at all as a result of officially becoming a Christian, it was a
change in the direction of dogmatism and illiberality, though it
would hardly be fair to lay the blame for this entirely upon the
Church, for Auden encouraged the ageing and hardening
process, and began to play the rôle of the inflexible old fogy for
years before he had any right to it.

Asked solemnly by a friend to state his theological position,
Auden replied:

> Liturgically, I am Anglo-Catholic, though not too spiky, I hope.
> As for forms of church organization, I don't know what to think.
> I am inclined to agree with de Rougemont that it will be back to
> the catacombs for all of us. As organizations, none of the
> churches look too hot, do they? But what organization ever
> does?[7]

He did not allow his religion to interfere with his pleasures,
and was, for instance, quite happy both to consider homo-

sexuality a sinful state and to indulge in homosexual acts regularly for the rest of his life. He never finally or completely surrendered either to politics or to religion, but took from each precisely as much as he wanted, and no more. He needed to have an official stance from which to view the world, and was certainly more content with the trappings of Anglo-Catholicism than with those of Marxism. But, for all that he liked to indulge in theological and liturgical small-talk, no one who knew him at all well in the last twenty years of his life could truthfully call Auden a devoutly religious man. What he had lost in his teens was not faith but childhood acceptance of what his elders had passed down to him; what he regained at the age of 33 was, again, not faith: he merely thought himself back into an organization with a reassuring ritual. He liked to be as tidy in large, abstract matters as he was untidy in small, personal ones, creating thus a kind of balance.

During the years of his 'hiatus of unbelief', years in which the chief concerns of Auden's poetry were social and political, moral issues nevertheless continued to engage his thought. In a 1929 notebook, he compiled a glossary of Christian and psychological terms. Two or three years later, he added a third column of social terms:

| *Social terms* | *Christian terms* | *Psychological terms* |
| --- | --- | --- |
| Society, the happy | Heaven | The Unconscious |
| Matter | Earth | The Conscious Mind |
| Society, the unhappy | Hell | The repressed unconscious |
| The revolution | Purgatory | The consulting-room |
| The collective | The Father ⎧ Body? ⎫ | The Ego-instincts. The self ideal |
| The individual | The Son ⎩ Mind? ⎭ | The Death-instincts. The not-self ideal |
| History | The Holy Ghost | The Libido. The relation between these two opposites |
| Nature | The Madonna | Nature |
| The Communist Party | The Four Archangels | The four great ganglia of the body |
| The capitalist system | Satan | The Censor |
| The ruling classes | The Devils | The repressed instincts |
| Starvation, war, unemployment | Hell-Fire | Unhappiness, disease and mania |
| The appearance of class distinction | The Fall of Man | The advent of self-consciousness |

29

## W. H. Auden: The Far Interior

Though his poetic imagery continued for some years to be drawn more frequently from the first and the third columns than from the second, the possibility that the solutions to society's problems and the cures for its ills might not be found in either Communism or Psychiatry lurks in many of Auden's poems of the '30s. If one's morals have to be Judeo-Christian, the poet seems often to be saying, perhaps one's beliefs should be, as well: if, that is, one must have beliefs.

If politics failed him, it is probably equally true to say that Auden failed politics. What he wanted from Communism was a strict discipline, but what he was able to give the working class to which he romantically aspired was not the best or the deepest of his art. Often, indeed, it was as inept poetically as it was politically. And, if he and Psychology failed each other, it was because Auden was willing only to select from its tenets, and to reject whatever he found unpalatable. The way back to religion as a theme for poetry came for Auden through love.

Love is a major theme of Auden's poetry in the years up to the outbreak of World War II. Ignored by Marx and misunderstood by Freud, love was the force, both moral and creative, which was to transform society by changing men's hearts. Auden's 'love', however, changes its nature from poem to poem, and is at its best somewhat vague. It is goodwill to all men, it is the selflessness of the lover's feeling for the beloved, it is a positive force for good, and it is a biologically natural urge. But it is also selfishly possessive:

> Love had him fast but though he fought for breath
> He struggled only to possess another,
> The snare forgotten in their little death,
> Till you, the seed to which he was a mother,
> That never heard of love, through love was free,
> While he within his arms a world was holding,
> To take the all-night journey under sea,
> Work west and northward, set up building.
>
> Cities and years constricted to your scope,
> All sorrow simplified though almost all
> Shall be as subtle when you are as tall:
> Yet clearly in that 'almost' all his hope
> That hopeful falsehood cannot stem with love
> The flood on which all move and wish to move.[8]

30

This is clearly not that love of which the Old Testament psalmist sings, or which Christ enjoins us to feel for all mankind, but a love caught in snares of its own making. The Christian concept of love is still some years away from the poet. It makes its most telling appearances in Auden's poetry neither in the '30s when the poet was an anxious politically and socially orientated moralist, nor in the '50s and later when he had become the pure and secular singer of songs, but in his American decade, the '40s, the years of the long poems: *New Year Letter, For the Time Being, The Sea and the Mirror* and *The Age of Anxiety*.

It is also to be found in a number of shorter poems of the '40s and '50s. In 'The Riddle' (actually written in June 1939), the duality of man's relationship to God is examined. The first four of the poem's five stanzas present the argument; the duality of the first stanza is that of freedom and necessity:

> Underneath the leaves of life,
> Green on the prodigious tree,
>     In a trance of grief
> Stand the fallen man and wife:
> Far away a single stag
> Banished to a lonely crag
> Gazes placid out to sea,
> While from thickets round about
> Breeding animals look in
>     On Duality,
> And small birds fly in and out
>     Of the world of man.

Later, 'Even orators may speak/ Truths of value to the weak.' But oratory is a lie and truths that are of value to the weak are, perhaps, of no use to the strong. The final truth resorted to by the poet is set forth in the fifth stanza which also reveals the poem to be a love poem, addressed to a 'beloved':

> Nowhere else could I have known
> Than, beloved, in your eyes
> What we have to learn,
> That we love ourselves alone:
> All our terrors burned away
> We can learn at last to say:

'All our knowledge comes to this,
That existence is enough,
That in savage solitude
    Or the play of love
Every living creature is
    Woman, Man and Child.'

The act of love, even of love for oneself, is contrasted with the soldiers who judge and the orators who speak. 'Necessary acts are done/ By the ill and the unjust', but 'the Judgment and the Smile,/ Though these two-in-one/ See creation as they must,/ None shall reconcile.'

John Fuller has pointed out[9] that the idea of the poem can be found in two sentences in Auden's essay in *Modern Canterbury Pilgrims*:

> As a spirit, a conscious person endowed with free will, every man has, through faith and grace, a unique 'existential' relation to God, and few since St Augustine have described this relation more profoundly than Kierkegaard. But every man has a second relation to God which is neither unique nor existential: as a creature composed of matter, as a biological organism, every man, in common with everything else in the universe, is related by necessity to the God who created that universe and saw that it was good, for the laws of nature to which, whether he likes it or not, he must conform are of divine origin.

In a poem dating from 1940, 'In Sickness and in Health', the duality or division in man's relationship to his creator has become the starting point of man's way of examining experience. Love is no longer even a partial answer to the questions to be posed, nor have the questions themselves remained the same:

> Let no one say I Love until aware
> What huge resources it will take to nurse
>     One ruining speck, one tiny hair
> That casts a shadow through the universe:
> We are the deaf immured within a loud
> And foreign language of revolt, a crowd
> Of poaching hands and mouths who out of fear
> Have learned a safer life than we can bear.

Ten years later, Auden was to write[10] that 'A purely existential attitude, since it has no conception of the universal

32

or the eternal, cannot be Christian, to whom the existential is only one, admittedly very important aspect of his situation.' Twenty years later, however, he would have retreated again from this position. In 1940 he is still warning himself against the difficulties of loving. The formal solutions of the church are not, at this time, of any help to him. His is the essentially Protestant attitude, and all he can depend upon is an ambivalent individual conscience.

Almost as important to the Christian as love is sin, and it is with sin that Auden is concerned in a 1949 poem, 'Memorial for the City'. The City, of course, is the Christian community, and it is in a woeful condition. 'The crow on the crematorium chimney/ And the camera roving the battle/ Record a space where time has no place.' Ideas derived not only from Charles Williams to whose memory the poem is dedicated but also from Kierkegaard and Reinhold Niebuhr are to be found in this poem whose qualified optimism is vitiated somewhat by the didacticism of its presentation. The argument is in the poetry, whereas the argument should *be* the poetry.

The most successful of the poem's four sections is the second which John Fuller[11] has described as 'an adroit potted history of Christendom'. In it Auden surveys the Christian scene from Pope Gregory to Napoleon, but it is Martin Luther who, according to the poet, perceives the unbridgeable gap between the 'Sane City' in which 'scribes and innkeepers prospered' and the Sinful City:

> In a sandy province Luther denounced as obscene
>   The machine that so smoothly forgave and saved
> If paid; he announced to the Sinful City a grinning gap
>   No rite could cross; he abased her before the Grace:
> Henceforth division was also to be her condition;
>   Her conclusions were to include doubt,
> Her loves were to bear with her fear; insecure, she endured.

Many of Auden's shorter poems in the '40s are secular poems attempting to be Christian. A natural agnostic who yearned for the Cross, Auden found himself from poem to poem attempting 'to rescue Jerusalem from a dull god' and inevitably failing as a theologian though as often as not succeeding as a poet. 'Horae Canonicae', a sequence of seven poems written at various times between 1949 and 1954, perhaps comes closest to success on both levels. Based on the canonical hours, those hours emblematic of the events of Good Friday which are set aside by the church for meditation and prayer, the poems deal with guilt, sin, and the limits imposed upon individual action and responsibility by the ritual of the church. In 'Prime', the focus is on the moment of awakening—

> Holy this moment, wholly in the right,
>     As, in complete obedience
> To the light's laconic outcry, next
>     As a sheet, near as a wall,
> Out there as a mountain's poise of stone,
>     The world is present, about,
> And I know that I am, here, not alone . . .

—but the soul's innocence of the morning gives way to the worldliness of the day, and in 'Terce',

> After shaking paws with his dog
> (Whose bark would tell the world that he is always kind),
>     The hangman sets off briskly over the heath. . . .

6 a.m. and then 9 yield to 12 noon in 'Sext', the high noon of a civilization in which

> Few people accept each other and most
> will never do anything properly,
>
> but the crowd rejects no one, joining the crowd
> is the only thing all men can do.

The hour of 'Nones', 3 p.m., is the time when, following the crucifixion, a great darkness covered the earth. It is also a modern Mediterranean siesta-time when men dream away their guilt, their responsibility for 'the deed'. By 6 p.m. and 'Vespers' (a prose poem), the Christian community has recovered its equilibrium and is taking refuge in good works. But whose definition of 'good' is most acceptable to God?:

> You can see, then, why, between my Eden and his New Jerusalem, no treaty is negotiable.
>
> In my Eden a person who dislikes Bellini has the good manners not to get born: In his New Jerusalem a person who dislikes work will be very sorry he was born.

In my Eden we have a few beam-engines, saddle-tank locomotives, overshot waterwheels and other beautiful pieces of
obsolete machinery to play with: In his New Jerusalem even
chefs will be cucumber-cool machine minders.

In my Eden our only source of political news is gossip: In his
New Jerusalem there will be a special daily in simplified spelling
for non-verbal types.

In my Eden each observes his compulsive rituals and super-
stitious taboos but we have no morals: In his New Jerusalem the
temples will be empty but all will practice the rational virtues.

The New Jerusalem which Auden here despises is that Just
City which, in those simpler far-off days of the thirties, he so
desperately wanted to build.

In 'Compline', at 9 p.m., the hour of sleep has arrived: a
sleep preceded by traditional prayers. The poet prays for 'dear
C' and for 'all poor s-o-b's who never/ Do a thing properly'.
The final poem of the sequence, 'Lauds', returns one cyclically
to the morning hours and the first prayer of the day. The poet
retreats into the liturgy, the voice becomes less personal:

> Already the mass-bell goes ding-dong;
> The dripping mill-wheel is again turning:
> *In solitude, for company.*

> God bless the Realm, God bless the People;
> God bless this green world temporal:
> *In solitude, for company.*

> The dripping mill-wheel is again turning;
> Among the leaves the small birds sing:
> *In solitude for company.*

Though these shorter poems present interesting aspects of
Auden's attempts to adopt a Christian position, it is to his four
long poems of the '40s that one must turn to understand fully
the extent and nature of the poet's religious stance.

*New Year Letter* (whose American edition was called *The
Double Man*) was written in America throughout most of
1940. Cast in the form of a letter to Auden's friend Elizabeth
Mayer, the poem is in three parts, the first of which deals with

the artist's relationship to society, the second with the war which had just broken out in Europe, and the third with the problems of living in the present, of reconciling New Year in Manhattan with the death of an old world on the other side of the Atlantic, and on the other side of history. The poem has attached to it eighty pages of notes in verse and prose.

It was in October 1940, shortly after completing *New Year Letter*, that Auden began going to church again every Sunday morning, regularly attending Holy Communion at his local Episcopalian church. *New Year Letter* represents the poet's attempt to find a system of belief by which he could live, his earlier flirtation with a watered-down socialism having failed him just as socialism had failed Europe.

Auden expected to be able to find that system of belief in Christianity, and in *New Year Letter* he argues himself into an acceptance of the Christian faith, though he seems never to have acquired that faith on which Christianity is ostensibly based. What he accepted is perhaps better described as the Christian attitude. He took the sensible view that, if something works, it is therefore, in a sense, true. Christian morality, as distinct from Christian hypocrisy, Christian militancy and Christian ferocity towards other religions, was based on that self-interested love ('Do unto others as you would that they should do unto you') which had always been attractive to Auden's temperament. Returning to Christianity was for him a question not so much of believing as of deciding. Order is what he sought, both in life and in art:

> To set in order—that's the task
> Both Eros and Apollo ask;
> For Art and Life agree in this
> That each intends a synthesis,
> That order which must be the end
> That all self-loving things intend
> Who struggle for their liberty,
> Who use, that is, their will to be.

In the second part of the poem, secular liberalism and Communism's totalitarian morality are both dismissed:

> We hoped: we waited for the day
> The State would wither clean away,

36

Expecting the Millenium
That theory promised us would come:
It didn't.

The man who wrote these lines is on the way to becoming
the first, perhaps the only one, of a new breed: the Rational
Christian. His Devil is a modern sophisticate whose favourite
strategy is to 'Induce men to associate/ Truth with a lie, then
demonstrate/ The lie' and thus 'treat babe and bath-water the
same'. This is the Devil who hoaxed the early Christians and
even fooled Wordsworth into thinking that the French Revolution was the Second Coming.

In the concluding section of the poem, Auden arrives at the
door of his rational church and settles for something less than
perfection. The entrance to this temple to compromise is on
top of a hill whose summit keeps retreating:

> We cannot, then, will Heaven where
> Is perfect freedom; our wills there
> Must lose the will to operate.
> But will is free not to negate
> Itself in Hell; we're free to will
> Ourselves up Purgatory still,
> Consenting parties to our lives,
> To love them like attractive wives
> Whom we adore but do not trust;
> We cannot love without their lust,
> And need their stratagems to win
> Truth out of time. In Time we sin.

The poem ends with an obliquely phrased prayer for guidance, but the poet understands with a bleak clarity that
guidance will come not from God but from one's friends, from
'Dear friend Elizabeth' to whom the poem is addressed:

> We fall down in the dance, we make
> The old ridiculous mistake,
> But always there are such as you
> Forgiving, helping what we do.
> O every day in sleep and labour
> Our life and death are with our neighbour,
> And love illuminates again
> The city and the lion's den,
> The world's great rage, the travel of young men.

The notes to *New Year Letter* reveal the extent of Auden's indebtedness to, amongst others, Kierkegaard, Blake, Nietzsche, Rilke, Goethe and Charles Williams. They are a kind of commonplace book in miniature. Indeed, the entire poem is a kind of self-communing in the guise of a letter, an argument with the self which ends with Ego persuading Id to accept a socially useful Christianity with the supernatural element removed or, at least, ignored.

Of all Auden's commentators, Richard Hoggart[12] most accurately describes *New Year Letter*:

> Auden does not seem to be, at this point, at ease in his belief. That unease is reflected in the tricks of technique (some of the images gloss over a problem rather than clarify it). The 'Letter' is not a religious poem; it is an argument in verse, perceptive, careless, suggestive, bookish, vivid, almost everywhere competent, and in places brilliant and moving.

Written between October 1941 and July 1942, 'For the Time Being', which Auden subtitled 'A Christmas Oratorio', is a more explicitly Christian poem than *New Year Letter* in which the poet was feeling (or rather thinking) his way back to the church. For the argument of the earlier poem, 'For the Time Being' substitutes acceptance or attitude. Using the form of the Protestant oratorio, for it was originally his intention to write a text to be set to music by Benjamin Britten, Auden for the only time in his life used Christianity as a direct subject for poetry; the poem tells the story of the annunciation and the birth of Christ in nine sections, most of which correspond to the traditional division of the nativity story in medieval religious drama. That Auden, even an Auden who had newly re-discovered Christianity, should have used such a subject is surprising, for he held the view that religion was no fit subject matter for art:

> There can no more be a 'Christian' art than there can be a Christian science or a Christian diet. There can only be a Christian spirit in which an artist, a scientist, works or does not work. A painting of the Crucifixion is not necessarily more Christian in spirit than a still life, and may very well be less.[13]

In the first section of the poem, 'Advent', Auden confronts the problem of belief:

For the garden is the only place there is, but you will not
     find it
Until you have looked for it everywhere and found nowhere
     that is not a desert;
The miracle is the only thing that happens, but to you it
     will not be apparent,
Until all events have been studied and nothing happens that
     you cannot explain;
And life is the destiny you are bound to refuse until you
     have consented to die.

Belief brings with it its concomitant doubt, and in the third
section, 'The Temptation of St. Joseph', Joseph is even led to
doubt Mary's virginity:

*Joseph*

My shoes were shined, my pants were cleaned and pressed,
And I was hurrying to meet
     My own true love:
But a great crowd grew and grew
Till I could not push my way through,
     Because
A star had fallen down the street;
     When they saw who I was,
The police tried to do their best.

*Chorus* (off)

*Joseph, you have heard*
*What Mary says occurred;*
*Yes, it may be so.*
*Is it likely? No.*

It is in 'The Meditation of Simeon', the seventh section and
entirely in prose, that Auden states his own personal belief
most fully. This Simeon is not the Biblical character who cries
'Lord, now lettest thou thy servant depart in peace', but a
modern man in search of a soul. His meditations are interrupted by comments from a chorus: at first he dwells on man's
present condition:

*Simeon*

As long as there were any roads to amnesia and anaesthesia still
to be explored, any rare wine or curiosity of cuisine as yet
untested, any erotic variation as yet unimagined or unrealized,

39

any method of torture as yet undevised, any style of conspicuous waste as yet unindulged, any eccentricity of mania or disease as yet unrepresented, there was still a hope that man had not been poisoned but transformed, that Paradise was not an eternal state from which he had been forever expelled, but a childish state which he had permanently outgrown, that the Fall had occurred by necessity.

*Chorus*

*We danced in the dark but were not deceived.*

However, the birth of Christ redefines man's situation:

*Simeon*

By the event of this birth the true significance of all other events is defined, for of every other occasion it can be said that it could have been different, but of this birth it is the case that it could in no way be other than it is. And by the existence of this Child, the proper value of all other existences is given, for of every other creature it can be said that it has extrinsic importance but of this Child it is the case that He is in no sense a symbol.

*Chorus*

*We have right to believe that we really exist.*

These, it must be observed are not the insights of a poet but the (to a non-believer) meaningless assertions of a Christian apologist. The poet's lapse into triviality and clumsy satire in Herod's speech in 'The Massacre of the Innocents'—

Why should he dislike me so? I've worked like a slave. Ask anyone you like. I read all official dispatches without skipping. I've taken elocution lessons. I've hardly ever taken bribes. How dare he allow me to decide? I've tried to be good. I brush my teeth every night. I haven't had sex for a month. I object. I'm a liberal. I want everyone to be happy. I wish I had never been born.

—and skittishness in 'Soldiers' ('George, you old debutante,/ How did you get in the Army?') are hardly redeemed by the pious banality of the final chorus:

He is the Way.
Follow Him through the Land of Unlikeness;
You will see rare beasts, and have unique adventures.

He is the Truth.
Seek him in the Kingdom of Anxiety;
You will come to a great city that has expected your return
    for years.

He is the Life.
Love Him in the World of the Flesh;
And at your marriage all its occasions shall dance for joy.

In its subject matter the most completely Christian of Auden's poems, in its cynical, cheap tone—

Come to our old-world desert
Where everyone goes to pieces;
You can pick up tears
For souvenirs
Or genuine diseases

—'For the Time Being' is one of the least pleasing, least valuable of his longer works.

Critical opinion of Auden is most divided on the subject of 'The Sea and the Mirror' which, together with *For the Time Being* which preceded it and *The Age of Anxiety* which was to follow, contains long stretches of prose as well as verse. Described by its author as 'A Commentary on Shakespeare's *The Tempest*', it has been denounced by Joseph Warren Beach as for the most part 'a long-winded disquisition in prose on literary-art-in-an-age-of-naturalistic-unbelief',[14] and praised by several other critics for its abundant technical skill as well as for its witty though serious argument.

Framed by a preface and a postscript, the work consists of three sections: the first, in which Prospero addresses Ariel; the second, in which the 'supporting cast', i.e. Antonio, Ferdinand, Stephano, Gonzalo, Alonso, Sebastian, Trinculo, Miranda, Adrian and Francisco, Master and Boatswain, contribute in turn; and the third, a long prose section entitled 'Caliban to the Audience'. The basic theme of the poem is the relationship of the poetic imagination to the problems of existence and belief in the modern world, a theme which emerges most clearly in the *tour de force* of Caliban's speech, written in a superb pastiche blending the style of late Henry James with the tone of Oscar Wilde:

41

Such are the alternative routes, the facile glad-handed highway or the virtuous averted track, by which the human effort to make its own fortune arrives all eager at its abruptly dreadful end. I have tried—the opportunity was not to be neglected—to raise the admonitory forefinger, to ring the alarming bell, but with so little confidence of producing the right result, so certain that the open eye and attentive ear will always interpret any sight and any sound to their advantage, every rebuff as a consolation, every prohibition as a rescue—that is what they open and attend for—that I find myself almost hoping, for your sake, that I have had the futile honour of addressing the blind and the deaf.

Art as decoration of life, or escape from life, is weighed in the balance and found wanting, and so, too, is the audience with such a view of art. But art of deeper significance is suspect, for

if the intrusion of the real has disconcerted and incommoded the poetic, that is a mere bagatelle compared to the damage which the poetic would inflict if it ever succeeded in intruding upon the real.

Life is a spiritual journey in which art can be nothing more than a diversion upon the way. It is that 'Wholly Other Life' to which man must aspire. This real and true life, Auden asserts, can be found only in acceptance of 'the real Word' through the Church.

The smugness of his stance in 'The Sea and the Mirror' could not have been maintained for ever, and in *The Age of Anxiety*, the last of his four major poems, written between July 1944 and November 1946, Auden can already be seen retreating from that certainty of tone to join the uncertain and the lost again. He returns from the imagined worlds of Bethlehem (*For the Time Being*) and Shakespeare's *The Tempest* (*The Sea and the Mirror*) to the contemporary New York of 'New Year Letter'. Retaining the dramatic form of 'For the Time Being' and 'The Sea and the Mirror', he sets his four characters, Quant, Malin, Rosetta and Emble, in a Greenwich Village bar on the night of All Souls.

Quant is an Irish-American clerk in a shipping office, Malin a Medical Intelligence Officer in the Canadian Air Force, Rosetta a buyer for a big department store, and Emble a young Mid-Westerner who had enlisted in the Navy. Their private reveries are interrupted by a radio broadcast with its recital of familiar horrors and banal activities:

> Now the news. Night raids on
> Five cities. Fires started.
> Pressure applied by pincer movement
> In threatening thrust. Third Division
> Enlarges beachhead. Lucky charm
> Saves sniper. Sabotage hinted
> In steel-mill stoppage. Strong point held
> By fanatical Nazis. Canal crossed
> By heroic marines. Rochester barber
> Fools foe. Finns ignore
> Peace feeler. Pope condemns
> Axis excesses. Underground
> Blows up bridge. Thibetan prayer-wheels
> Revolve for victory. Vital crossroads
> Taken by tanks. Trend to the left
> Forecast by Congressman. Cruiser sunk
> In Valdivian Deep. Doomed sailors
> Play poker. Reporter killed.

The four, hitherto strangers to one another, fall to talking and, in the second part of the poem, leave their bar-stools and move to the 'quieter intimacy of a booth', where they discuss their own contributions to, and their own situations in, the human predicament. They forget their surroundings and their sense of time until, in part three, they share in a dream-like mystical search for happiness, before, in part four, making their way 'through half-lit almost empty streets' to Rosetta's apartment where, in part five, they continue to talk, over sandwiches and drinks. In part six, leaving Emble and Rosetta in the apartment, together but alone (for Emble has passed out in Rosetta's bedroom), Malin takes the subway south while Quant walks home in an eastward direction. The spiritual pilgrimage of the night has left them as separate and alone as before they began to speak to one another.

The poem's style is, in places, as inaccessible and remote as the world to which the poet condemns his characters:

> Come, peregrine nymph, display your warm
> Euphoric flanks in their full glory

Of liberal life; with luscious note
Smoothly sing the softer date of an
Unyielding universe, youth, money,
Liquor and love; delight your shepherds
For crazed we come and coarsened we go
Our wobbling way: there's a white silence
Of antiseptics and instruments
At both ends, but a babble between
And a shame surely. O show us the route
Into hope and health; give each the required
Pass to appease the superior archons;
Be our good guide.

Elsewhere, it lapses into the familiar irrelevance and triviality:

QUANT had now reached the house where he lived and, as he started to climb the steps of his stoop, he tripped and almost fell. At which he said:

Why, Miss ME, what's the matter? *Must* you go woolgathering?
Once, I was your wonder. How short-winded you've gotten.
Come, Tinklebell, trot. Let's pretend you're a thoroughbred.
Over the hill now into Abraham's Bosom.

Malin is the intellectual of the four, and it is his final long speech which encapsulates the poem's central theme, the quest for a way to live. Malin, representing the poet Auden, makes the Christian choice, but with little of that sense of joy or certainty which is supposed to accompany the Christian faith, at least in its moment of acquisition:

In our anguish we struggle
To elude Him, to lie to Him, yet His love observes
His appalling promise; His predilection
As we wander and weep is with us to the end,
Minding our meanings, our least matter dear to Him,
His Good ingressant on our gross occasions
Envisages our advance, valuing for us
Though our bodies too blind or too bored to examine
What sorts excite them are slain interjecting
Their childish Ows and, in choosing how many
And how much they will love, our minds insist on
Their own disorder as their own punishment,

44

His question disqualifies our quick senses,
His truth makes our theories historical sins,
It is where we are wounded that is when He speaks
Our creaturely cry, concluding His children
In their mad unbelief to have mercy on them all
As they wait unawares for His World to come.

The poem concludes with two bleak paragraphs of prose:

So thinking, he returned to duty, reclaimed by the actual world where time is real and in which, therefore, poetry can take no interest.

Facing another long day of servitude to wilful authority and blind accident, creation lay in pain and earnest, once more reprieved from self-destruction, its adoption, as usual, postponed.

Judging *The Age of Anxiety* to be 'poetically a failure', Richard Hoggart identifies what he sees as the chief defect of the poem:

What distresses most is that Auden worries his themes, that he seems not to have the patience to let them emerge, but has to thrust them at the reader. The Seven Stages, for example, which forms the core of the book, is altogether too consciously developed: the symbols rarely do anything to reinforce and extend the meaning; after a lot of effort we recognise, or think we recognise, what they are meant to signify—but our response is not deepened.[15]

It may well be that this failing is but a reflection of Auden's failure to accept, on the deepest level, the Christianity which he was consciously so eager to embrace. His response to Christianity and to the Church seems not to have been deep, but to have lain on the surface of his thoughts. The essential nature of his poetry is not religious but humanist, and what can the poet do but observe and accept the nature of his art, which springs from his real being?

Auden himself seems to have accepted that this is so. The most telling, though somewhat oblique, comment on the Christian element in his poetry and the most illuminating revelation of the essentially unreligious nature of his religious belief is to be found in this passage from a sermon Auden preached in Westminster Abbey in 1966, many years after he had emerged from the turbulent quasi-religious years of the '40s:

> Those of us who have the nerve to call ourselves Christians will do well to be extremely reticent on the subject. Indeed, it is almost the definition of a Christian that he is somebody who *knows* he isn't one, either in faith or morals. Where faith is concerned, very few of us have the right to say more than—to vary a saying of Simone Weil's—'I believe in a God who is like the True God in everything except that he does not exist, for I have not yet reached the point where God exists.' As for loving and forgiving our enemies, the less we say about that the better. Our lack of faith and love are facts we have to acknowledge, but we shall not improve either by a morbid and essentially narcissistic moaning over our deficiencies. Let us rather ask, with caution and humour—given our time and place and talents, what, if our faith and love were perfect, would we be glad to find it obvious to do?

### NOTES

1. Introduction to *The Portable Greek Reader* (New York, 1948).
2. Review of *A Little Learning* by Evelyn Waugh and *Beginning Again* by Leonard Woolf (*New Yorker*, 3 April 1965).
3. Introduction to *The Protestant Mystics*, ed. Anne Fremantle (Boston, 1964).
4. From Auden's contribution to *Modern Canterbury Pilgrims*, ed. James A. Pike (New York, 1956).
5. Ibid.
6. Ibid.
7. Quoted by Ursula Niebuhr in *W. H. Auden: A Tribute*, ed. Stephen Spender (London, 1974).
8. 'Meiosis', Auden, *Collected Poems* (London, 1976).
9. In John Fuller, *A Reader's Guide to W. H. Auden* (London, 1970).
10. In 'Religion and the Intellectuals' (*Partisan Review*, February 1950).
11. Fuller, *A Reader's Guide*.
12. Richard Hoggart, *Auden, An Introductory Essay* (London, 1951).
13. In *The Dyer's Hand* (New York, 1962).
14. Joseph Warren Beach, *The Making of the Auden Canon* (Minneaopolis, 1957).
15. Hoggart, *Auden, An Introductory Essay*.

# 2

# Auden's Political Vision

## by WALTER PERRIE

With minor qualifications, Auden was an old-fashioned liberal—in other terms, a bourgeois individualist—for whom politics were subsidiary to moral sense. As he said himself in 'Letter to Lord Byron' (1936):

> I hate pompositas and all authority;
> Its air of injured rightness also sends
> Me shuddering from the cultured smug minority.
> 'Perpetual revolution', left-wing friends
> Tell me, 'in counter-revolution ends.
> Your fate will be to linger on outcast
> A selfish pink old liberal to the last.'

For Auden that moral sense was fundamentally the voice of Protestant conscience with all its perfectionist demands. That said, Auden was an extremely complicated character of acute intellect, and his views were seldom, if ever, simple. Alongside his individualism one has to place what seems to have been a healthy sensualism and the fact that he absorbed at least some of the lessons of the Marxist stress on history and material conditions as determining factors in social life. His political Marxism may never have been very secure—he was too sharp to be satisfied by the kind of simplistic Marxism available in the '30s—but: 'When he wrote about poetry, a subject in which he was more secure of his knowledge, he was steady, even exuberant, in his materialist approach.'[1]

Auden was not just a complicated character but, very often, a self-divided and contradictory one, and it was in the dialectic of the individual and society, which runs through so much of Auden's writing, that he explored some of those contradictions. The evolution of Auden's political vision is inextricable from his overall development. He was prolific in both poetry and prose and, especially in the '30s, did not hesitate to spell out in detail his views on a wide range of social issues. To follow that development in detail would be beyond the scope of an essay but what is clear, from the prose and poetry alike, is that Auden's starting point—that complex of attitudes and impulses which has to be taken as given—was that of a moralist: 'Auden is, from first to last, a moralist who wants his poems to arouse his audience into critical self-awareness and to incite them to reform.'[2]

Auden had a respectable, upper middle-class English upbringing with, inevitably, its accent on religion, patriotism and duty. Auden quickly learned that his inherited attitudes were inadequate to the world he actually had to inhabit:

> We were the tail, a sort of poor relation
> To that debauched, eccentric generation
> That grew up with their fathers at the War,
> And made new glosses on the noun Amor.[3]

Auden, like so many of his contemporaries, found himself cut off from traditional attitudes for they could hardly but see that the status quo was unacceptable. He was, therefore, a dislocated moralist who, though he saw that the world was far from perfect, could not, as a young man, accept that it was not perfectible. The concept of perfectibility which underlay so much of Auden's early work, had as its corollary the rejection of existing realities, not only personal and literary but also social and political. By the close of the '30s Auden had come to reject all notions of perfectibility to replace them with the need to accept the fallen-ness of the world, that is, its imperfection and, perhaps, imperfectibility. That was the basic shift in Auden's development and it was more or less complete by 1940. It enabled him to accept and—a crucial term for Auden—to *pardon* himself and the world to a greater extent than ever before. That acceptance was never complete nor ever without its tensions, for he lost little of the urgency of his moral sense.

Auden's acceptance of the world's fallen-ness did not tempt him—as it did Eliot—to world-rejection. He continued to insist that the world remained the proper sphere of moral struggle, for, if not perfection, at least goodness lay within the individual's reach:

> Evil is unspectacular and always human,
> And shares our bed and eats at our own table,
> And we are introduced to Goodness every day. . . .[4]

Throughout his career Auden portrayed his desires and dilemmas in terms of the quest for the Good Place and the Just City. The house divided against itself, and the house he might 'go both in and out of' were fundamental images of fallen-ness and healing. The fact that he did not reject either side of his dialectic—between the duty to accept and pardon a Self and world both fallen on one hand and, on the other, a recognition of the extent of that world's evil—makes him, in a broad sense, a deeply political poet. Of his peers, only Yeats was able to sustain a comparable dialectic.

Not surprisingly, Auden's development has been much misconstrued and critical platitudes can be as difficult to dislodge as any elderly dictator. This one spends much time lamenting the disappearance of the Auden of its revolutionary youth (1931–38) and deplores the treacherous frivolity of its former hero whom it understands to have sold out to Anglicanism and a complacent triviality. A fair example of this automatism was enacted in a recent review of Humphrey Carpenter's *W. H. Auden*. The notice was headed 'Faith found but the cause lost' and continued of Auden's work after 1944: 'apart from "In Praise of Limestone", "The Cave of Making", and a handful of other poems the bulk are deliberately minor-technical experiments, word-games, occasional poems, aphorisms and so on. I find it sad.'[5] It is less sad than simply untrue but, as Clive James remarks: 'It is a common opinion among the English literati that Auden's later work is a collapse.'[6]

The reasons for such a crass and widespread misreading of both the texts and of Auden's life are complex. They have something to do with the degree to which he was lionized as a Byronic radical in the '30s—which was itself something of a misreading. They have to do with the fact that he was

thought to have—whether out of cowardice or complacency—
fled to America in 1939. They have to do with a kind of
automatism about religion on the part of the Left. More
subtly, though, they have something to do with the deep roots
put down by Romanticism in the English critical tradition. It
sometimes seems as though Auden has been assimilated to a
kind of Wordsworth archetype whereby the fiery young
radical turns into the boring old reactionary with a consequent
loss of poetic power. In fact, if Auden is to be compared with
any of the Romantics, Byron is a more suitable candidate. Like
Byron, Auden's early work was more psychological than
political in its concerns. Both were moralists who thought of
poetry as having an educative function, and both were, in that
respect, more at home with the Augustans than with the
Romantics. Above all, both sought an effective middle voice in
which to talk about a wide range of social issues:

> I want a form that's large enough to swim in,
> And talk on any subject that I choose,
> From natural scenery to men and women,
> Myself, the arts, the European news. . . .[7]

As a consequence, both have suffered from the apparently
inherent prejudice in English criticism in favour of lyric
romanticism.

Cleared of the débris of prejudice, the facts of Auden's life
and work have now been placed beyond question by Carpenter's
biography and by Mendelson's *Early Auden*. The pattern which
emerges is one of wholesale dislocation, literally, a being-out-
of-place. That dislocation had several aspects. To many of
Auden's Oxford contemporaries the bourgeoisie, from whose
loins most of them sprang, were by 1930 politically taboo.
Additionally, Auden's sexual and emotional impulses were
under complete social interdict. The heritage of liberalism was
seen to have been catastrophically inadequate and, finally, the
conventions of Eliotean modernism made finding a language
in which to express social issues all-but impossible.

Many of Auden's generation not only saw the Great War as
having exposed the weaknesses and hypocrisies of liberal
ideology but as having, at least in part, been brought about by
the rhetoric of that ideology, and few thought that fascism and

mass unemployment could be halted or reversed by liberalism. Auden himself summed it up at the close of the '30s when he wrote that

> The most obvious social fact of the last forty years is the failure of liberal capitalist democracy, based on the premises that every individual is born free and equal, each an absolute entity independent of all others; and that a formal political equality, the right to vote, the right to a fair trial, the right of free speech, is enough to guarantee his freedom of action in his relations with his fellow men. The results are only too familiar to us all. By denying the social nature of personality, and by ignoring the social power of money, it has created the most impersonal, the most mechanical and the most unequal civilisation the world has ever seen, a civilisation in which the only emotion common to all classes is a feeling of individual isolation from everyone else, a civilisation torn apart by the opposing emotions born of economic injustice, the just envy of the poor and the selfish terror of the rich.[8]

His sense of isolation and self-division preoccupied Auden and, in part at least, derived from his attitude to his homo-sexuality. He regarded his sexuality as profoundly flawed and seems, in late 1929, to have made some attempt at having himself 'cured' by psychoanalysis.[9] The many references in his early writing to crooks and crookedness are sexual rather than political references. Auden continued to think of his sexuality as flawed throughout his life, though after 1939 his attitude to it changed in other respects. The important point for his early work is that he saw it as something which isolated him from other persons and from the possibility of any secure or enduring love and, certainly, from any socially integrated relationship. That this sense of isolation was fundamental is clear from an essay he wrote on 'Writing' in 1932 when he suggests that 'The urge to write, like the urge to speak, came from man's growing sense of personal loneliness, of the need for group communication.' And again: 'Since the underlying reason for writing is to bridge the gulf between one person and another, as the sense of loneliness increases, more and more books are written. . . .'[10] As will be seen, at this stage Auden psychologizes social issues and continued to do so until well into the '30s. His reason was that, at this stage, social issues

51

were subordinate to his sense of his own self-divisions. Obviously, to believe oneself to be flawed in something as fundamental as one's sexuality gives urgency to the quest for something that will heal one's divisions and self-doubts and very often produces an apparent but superficial politicization which is little more than a projection of one's personal obsessions. So, in some measure, it was for Auden, until at least 1932.

Auden's first impact on the literary world came with *Poems* (1930). In it he seems to deal, albeit in non-specific terms, with political themes. However, as Mendelson illustrates with reference to those which appear to deal with the social crises of 1929 and 1930:

> Each poem acknowledges the political aspects of the approaching crisis, and each acknowledges economics by alluding to the distance between places where money is made and where it is spent. But in writing these poems Auden lays claim to the crisis as a proper subject for psychological analysis and cure, as if he intended to rescue political problems from the political mind. . . .[11]

Duchêne takes a similar view: 'The cosmogony of the *Poems* is, in the last resort, the dramatisation of a personal predicament.'[12] Although in the period 1930–32 Auden began to make explicit reference to capitalism, his serious reading in Marxism was still some way off and intellectually he was still under the sway of D. H. Lawrence, Homer Lane, Groddeck, Layard and Freud. In 1932 when he seemed to be flirting with Communism, he was describing its appeal for the bourgeoisie in terms of its 'demand for self-surrender from those who, "isolated, feel themselves emotionally at sea" '[13] and in 'A Communist to Others' (1932) the apparent spokesman for the Party is a ventriloquist's dummy for Auden's psychologistic diagnoses. As Mendelson says:

> The Party would not be pleased to learn that its stalwart orator found this vision (of mystical brotherhood) in the final pages of Gerald Heard's *Social Substance of Religion*, where Heard explicitly rejects a Marxist economic communism. . . .[14]

What many saw as political stances in his poetry of this period were, in fact, parables for his own condition for which he simply omitted to provide the interpretative key, thereby leaving the poems open to a variety of interpretations, including the political. That is not to say that political interpretations are wrong, only that they are unhelpfully limited in their usefulness because they do not genuinely reflect Auden's concerns at the time. It is only with recent work by Mendelson and others on the early poems that much of their notorious obscurity can be cleared up and the results do not support narrowly political interpretations. That, however, is not to dispute Auden's very generalized political interests at the time.

Some of his motivation may be better understood if we bear in mind that with the rising tide of the Depression and the collapse of the Labour Party in 1931, there seemed nothing to put between Europe (including Britain) and a general fascism except solidarity with the only remaining organized opposition and that meant the still untarnished Communist Party. So at least Spender, Day Lewis, Edward Upward and many more of Auden's contemporaries believed at the time. As Samuel Hynes says: 'Clearly by 1933 Auden was a larger-than-life figure in a movement that was political in general intention but was religious in tone, and literary in its manifestations.'[15] For Auden, though, the commitment was more in the eyes of his admirers than in reality, though he did nothing to discourage it. His sense of his own self-divisions may have chimed in peculiarly aptly with the growing divisions in Europe, but Auden 'knew that he was too much of a bourgeois ever to join the Communist Party or ally himself directly with the working class. His politics remained a matter more of attitude than action.'[16] As he recorded himself much later: 'Looking back, it seems to me that the interest in Marx taken by myself and my friends . . . was more psychological than political. . . .'[17] Auden felt alienated from his own class but, unlike Upward, he was under no illusion that he might join another.

Auden remained a moralist and, as such, was intent on becoming a genuinely public poet. Riven by loneliness and self-doubt the last thing he wanted was a poetry of 'self-expression', that is, organized around his own self-divisions. His concern for a moral-didactic poetry, however, was taboo to modernism. Like Brecht both chose didactic manners suitable for irony and celebration. Both taught through parables. Where modernism had used innovative forms to speak of historical necessity, Auden and Brecht adopted traditional forms to speak of freedom and choice.[18] Politics and sociology offered adequate rhetoric for the arguments he wanted to make: what he needed was a way of incorporating this rhetoric into a memorable language for poetry. He began to recognise that the literary manner he inherited from his modernist predecessors had rendered practical social issues invisible by assimilating all experience into a private introspective order.[19]

Byron had solved a comparable difficulty in *Don Juan* and it is no accident that from about 1933 the influence of Yeats and Byron supplanted that of Hardy and Eliot. Yeats seemed indeed to have developed a viable public voice, though Auden under-estimated the degree to which Yeats's manner was specific to Yeats's different cultural milieu. Auden's continued interest in Byron throughout the '30s was symptomatic of his need to find an effective middle-style: one which did not fall, at the one extreme, into surrealist farce (as the early dramas tended to), and at the other, into a Miltonic pomposity. It was to take him until 1945 to solve the problem adequately.

Effectively stripped of all anchors Auden must have felt abysmally isolated and insecure. However, from 1933 there began a gradual change which was to take another six years to work itself through but which was of decisive importance for Auden's future development. In the mystical experience of goodness and love, of a fleeting and spontaneous but powerful sense of communion with others which he records in 'A Summer Night' and which can be dated to June of 1933, Auden had an intimation that his overwhelming sense of alienation was not inevitable. Mendelson distinguishes two stages in the development of the early Auden:

> While in his earliest work (to 1933) Auden had no hope of altering the divisive loneliness that was his main subject, in his work after June 1933 he both explored his division and sought to resolve it.[20]

Thereafter, until he settled in America in 1939, Auden went from idea to idea and country to country in an effort to locate the Good Place: that intellectual, emotional, geographic and

linguistic nexus where his loneliness might be assuaged and
his divisions healed:

> Where does this journey look which the watcher upon the
> quay,
> Standing under his evil star, so bitterly envies,
> As the mountains swim away with slow calm strokes
> And the gulls abandon their vow? Does it promise a juster
> life?
>
> Alone with his heart at last, does the fortunate traveller find
> In the vague touch of a breeze, the fickle flash of a wave,
> Proofs that somewhere exists, really, the Good Place,
> Convincing as those that children find in stones and holes?[21]

The rest of the poem has no definite answer and, in 1938,
Auden was still full of self-doubt and near to despair. In the six
years between 1933 and 1939 Auden's political development is
very confused and often self-contradictory. The important
point for an understanding of the later poetry is that he was
not who his political admirers took him for.

Few poets have been as peripatetic as Auden in the '30s: 'He
carried his isolation everywhere. . . . His constant subject
became the journey; and his constant frustration the journey's
failure to take him someplace different from his starting
point.'[22] Short visits to Denmark, Germany and Belgium were
succeeded by full-scale expeditions to Iceland, Spain and
China. Throughout this troubled period he showed himself a
consistent opponent of fascism and greatly deepened his
knowledge of Marxism. As Stephen Spender wrote of him: 'He
had a firmer grip of Marxist ideology, and more capacity to
put this into good verse than many writers who were closer to
communism.'[23] He remained, however, primarily a moralist
with strong interests in psychology and his criticisms of
Marxism—as he understood it—were those of someone whose
fundamental standpoint was individualist. He expressed his
views on Marxism in 1935 in an essay entitled 'The Good Life'
where he suggests that

> Psychology and Communism have certain points in common:
> (1) They are both concerned with unmasking hidden conflicts.
> (2) Both regard these conflicts as inevitable stages which must
> be made to negate themselves.

(3) Both regard thought and knowledge not as something spontaneous and self-sufficient, but as purposive and determined by the conflict between instinctive needs and a limited environment. . . .

(4) Both desire and believe in the possibility of freedom of action and choice, which can only be obtained by unmasking and making conscious the hidden conflict.

The hostility of Communism to psychology is that it accuses the latter of failing to draw correct conclusions from its data. Finding the neurotic a product of society, it attempts to adjust him to that society, i.e. it ignores the fact that the neurotic has a real grievance. . . . The failure to say this has reduced psychology to a quack religion for the idle rich.[24]

Auden then goes on to deal with the hostility of Communism to religion and finds that 'In fact Communism is the only political theory that really holds the Christian position of the absolute equality in value of every individual, and the evil of all State restraint. . . .'[25] He then goes on to treat of Social Democracy which

claims to achieve the same end as the Communist, by non-violent means and with religious tolerance; it is questionable, however, whether its behaviour in Europe, its pretence that it uses no violence, or its assumption that the possessing classes, however ready to make concessions, will ever voluntarily abdicate, can much longer convince.[26]

This would seem to take Auden a good part of the way towards Marxism but, in fact, his position was still full of contradictions, as was to become evident in his subsequent suppression of 'Spain' and other poems of the period.

Though Auden constantly stresses individual moral choice in his work, during much of the '20s and '30s he also wanted to suggest that people are often the unconscious victims of forces larger than the individual. In his early poetry he sees people simply as instruments of the Life Force or evolution—sometimes called *Love*—who, when they no longer serve its purposes are discarded by it. Auden absorbed this view from Groddeck, D. H. Lawrence and others, and it was not a large step in the mid-'30s to deck it out in a new costume and call it the *Force of History*. Auden retracted this fatalist element from his writings but did keep the materialism he had absorbed from his readings in Marxism and never went back on the general view he stated in 1938 that:

> Man has always been a social animal living in communities. This falsifies any theories of Social Contract. The individual *in vacuo* is an intellectual abstraction. The individual is the product of social life; without it, he would be no more than a bundle of unconditioned reflexes. Men are born neither free nor good. Societies and cultures vary enormously. On the whole, Marx seems to me correct in his view that physical conditions and the forms of economic production have dictated the forms of communities. . . .[27]

Auden's reconciliation of that materialism with a religious outlook was to occupy him for much of the '40s.

Marxism, however, was not, for Auden, an adequate account of the world and he had certainly never accepted the Leninist view of the historical rôle of the Communist Party. He had never lost his interest in religion and of his time in Spain recorded almost nothing beyond the detail of his sudden awareness that he was shocked by the closed churches. By late 1938 Auden was weary of his quest and near to despair. He had come to suspect again that his loneliness was inescapable. His experiences in Spain, China and elsewhere had convinced him, if he ever needed convincing, that there was no natural goodness in man. Not only had he rejected any messianic illusions he may once have nourished about himself, he had rejected most of the thinkers in whom he had been interested over the past decade. By 1939 the novelty of the Soviet Union had worn off for many West-European intellectuals. Stalin was no longer a hero-figure and the signing of the Molotov-Ribbentrop pact disillusioned many would-be communists. In the context of political events in 1938–39, despair was perhaps a not unreasonable response and there is nothing surprising in Auden's withdrawal at that time from any active political position. Like many others in that period when a general European War had come to seem inevitable and when literature had been shown over an entire decade to be politically ineffectual, Auden realized that the values which poetry represents have nothing to do with the stridency and exhortation of active political struggle. And, in any case, by 1938 Hitler and Mussolini had cornered the market in stridency. Hynes attributes that general withdrawal by many British writers to a growing sense of the impotence of literature in the face of world events and that seems correct. Auden's attitude at the time is best represented by a handful of poems—including some of his greatest—which recognize the realities of the world situation but which, in the face of those realities, insist on affirmation. With *Two Cheers for Democracy* E. M. Forster articulated what seems to have been a widespread feeling and Auden's sonnet sequence 'In Time of War' is dedicated to him. It opens:

> Here, though the bombs are real and dangerous,
> And Italy and King's are far away,
> And we're afraid that you will speak to us,
> You promise still the inner life shall pay.

One of the turning points of the sequence is Sonnet XIII in which Auden sounds the first affirmative note:

> Certainly praise: let the song mount again and again
> For life as it blossoms out in a jar or a face,
> For the vegetable patience, the animal grace;
> Some people have been happy; there have been great men.

The affirmation is tentative and we are immediately reminded of actualities: 'But hear the morning's injured weeping', and that 'The Good Place has not been'. Nevertheless the affirmation grows, through Sonnet XXIII and its summoning of the spirit of Rilke 'Who through ten years of silence worked and waited'. In Sonnet XXV Auden renounces once and for all his fatalism, 'Nothing is given: we must find our law', for

> We have no destiny assigned us:
> Nothing is certain but the body; we plan
> To better ourselves; the hospitals alone remind us
> Of the equality of man.

The note of affirmation was sounded again in 'September 1, 1939' and, most powerfully, in 'In Memory of W. B. Yeats':

> In the nightmare of the dark
> All the dogs of Europe bark,
> And the living nations wait,
> Each sequestered in its hate;

despite which Auden asks that the poet 'Still persuade us to rejoice' and

> In the deserts of the heart
> Let the healing fountain start,
> In the prison of his days
> Teach the free man how to praise.

This affirmative note had never been wholly absent from Auden. The partial celebration of imperfection, which can be found as early as 1937 in 'Lay your sleeping head, my love', is now much more explicit and complete. It is also accompanied by a public renunciation of the Yeatsian rhetoric, and, with it, all claims for the political relevance of poetry.

Auden's denial of any immediate political function for poetry was stated explicitly in 'The Public v. the late Mr. W. B. Yeats' (1939) and reinforced in *New Year Letter*. His view was, and remained, unequivocal and a note he wrote for a commonplace book in 1970 restates it in almost identical terms:

> By all means let a poet, if he wants to, write *engagé* poems, protesting against this or that political evil or social injustice. But let him remember this. The only person who will benefit from them is himself; they will enhance his literary reputation among those who feel as he does. The evil or injustice, however, will remain exactly what it would have been if he had kept his mouth shut.[28]

Whether or not one agrees with Auden's fairly extreme statement of his view, it was fundamental to his later work. It should be kept in mind, though, that Auden's target is directly political poetry and that he is *not* denying *any* social function to poetry. Indeed, he continued to think of it as having an educative function, albeit in the negative sense of something which can disintoxicate and disenchant.

Clearly, between 1938 and 1940 some radical transformation had taken place for Auden but it was one for which the whole of the later '30s was a preparation. In late 1938 he had begun to read Kierkegaard. By 1940 he had rejoined the church and, perhaps most importantly, had fallen in love and had that love returned.

From Marx and Freud to Kierkegaard is a shorter step than some of Auden's detractors have thought, but why take the step at all? Auden had realized that his divisions could not be healed by an act of will or by their submergence in any external force, whether a group, an ideology or a career, but simply had to be accepted. Accepting his own imperfect nature he learned, however painfully, to accept others, warts and all:

> Throughout the 1930s he had hoped for some political or visionary or predestined end to division. It could not happen. In America, when he had given up his last hopes for Utopia, he learned instead to 'honour the fate you are', with all its incorrigible divisions, 'Travelling and tormented,/ Dialectic and bizarre.'[29]

He began to believe that life, once accepted and despite its absurdity, could be celebrated and this transformation is the key to the later poetry: 'He had thought he could love for a faithless moment, before beauty and vision died, now he knew that he might love faithfully if he accepted imperfection and change.'[30] Kierkegaard, the intellectual peg on which Auden hung his new coat, was, at the least, convenient: 'In Kierkegaard he not only found philosophical reasons for accepting life, but a theology insisting that it must be accepted.'[31] And, for all the apoplexy of his critics, 'in reality the leap had been only a small hop, and, in retrospect at least, anything but surprising.'[32] Kierkegaard insists that God is wholly beyond the reach of human knowledge. Therefore, the worldly realms— the ethical and aesthetic—have to be confronted on their own terms and within those realms man has free will to choose either good or evil. This view enabled Auden to retain his whole materialist analysis of economic and literary history with which to approach the world, but rooted now in his assurance that his values of truth and love were ultimately validated in his religious experience. Auden was very much a rationalist on worldly topics, but that his religious foundations should be beyond the reach of rationality suited him very well.

Auden's attitude to the Good Place underwent a similar transformation. It was no longer somewhere to be looked for but somewhere to be made. Auden's work deals consistently with moral choice, the capacity which Auden understood to distinguish man from animal. Now the Good Place was to be created by appropriate moral choices, and because such choices are something given afresh for each individual, history is no longer seen as a linear progress:

> Now he represents all human time as the irresolute divided middle realm between two unified realms that lie beyond history. . . . This *homeostatic* vision of time, the opposite of cataclysmic, sees all human history as fallen and divided, with Eden and Utopia as imaginary ideals outside of time, and that can be neither remembered by nostalgia nor realised by revolution.[33]

Because men can choose good or evil, they must not allow themselves to be misled by fantasies of past and future if that entails any sacrifice in the real present of the virtues of love and truth. This shift in attitude places the accent very firmly back on the individual and on subjectivity. Auden came now to a new determination to live in the present, a determination revealingly evident in a letter he wrote to E. R. Dodds in 1940 about his decision to live in the United States: 'At least I know what I am trying to do, which most American writers don't, which is to live deliberately without roots. . . .'[34]

The conclusion that Auden felt strengthened to undertake such a course by the fact that he felt, at last, that he was loved and could love, is inescapable given the power with which the new note is sounded in his poetry:

> For now I have the answer from the face
> That never will go back into a book
> But asks for all my life, and is the Place
> Where all I touch is moved to an embrace,
> And there is no such thing as a vain look.[35]

And again:

> Restored! Returned! The lost are borne
> On seas of shipwreck home at last:
> See! In a fire of praising burns
> The dry dumb past, and we
> Our life-day long shall part no more.[36]

It is this assurance of love which enables him to fully accept the implications of imperfection:

Nowhere else could I have known
Than, beloved, in your eyes
What we have to learn,
That we love ourselves alone:
All our terrors burned away
We can learn at last to say:
'All our knowledge comes to this,
That existence is enough. . . .'[37]

From 1940 until nearly the end of the decade Auden
sought to learn to celebrate life and to find an appropriate
language in which to do so. The kind of overt political
references which had appeared in his poems throughout the
'30s stopped and it was widely assumed that Auden had
become a non-political or even an anti-political and private
poet. His rejection of political and poetic interest in a programme for Utopia was final, for:

> What is implicit in this, and willl soon become manifest in
> Auden's writings, is his recognition that a *voluntary errand* does
> not merely ignore suffering but causes it. All acts of will, all
> errands that have somewhere to get to, exert force over a
> person or object outside the self. There is always someone who
> gets in the way. . . .[38]

Now, for Auden, the Just City and the Good Place can be
created only by a measure of realism, charity and pardon in
our personal lives coupled to a defence of rationality. Auden
thought of the world as fundamentally hostile to the individual:
not only nature, but the social-historical world as well since,
for both, the individual is disposable. The Good Place is
wherever we can be left in peace enough to get on with
creating it. The metaphor of the journey was not discarded but
its significance changed: 'All the long works of the 1940s after
*New Year Letter* are dialectical landscapes dramatizing the
journeys men make to get across frontiers separating Aesthetic,
Ethical and Religious existence—Kierkegaard's dialectical
triad.'[39] For Auden it was a difficult journey frequently punc-
tuated by despair, but now the despiar was kept private.
Gradually, however, Auden did find an increased capacity for
acceptance and by the end of the decade he had learned not
just to accept life but to praise it:

The works of the 1940s all show that the human world is blessed in a religious sense. God made it. But its earthly satisfactions, while considerable, never quite deserve 'blessed' as a secular epithet. After 1950 they do, and Auden will then not only affirm the need to accept secular life but will celebrate the joy of doing so.[40]

After the transformations which Auden experienced in 1939–40 he did not stop changing. His development through the 1940s, '50s and '60s is as complex as that through the '20s and '30s, and it would need a further essay to follow it through all its twists and turns. Its broad outline, however, is relatively clear in that Auden continued to develop his capacity to celebrate life. It is this Auden who is so often accused of complacency and triviality. Nothing could be further from the truth and the evidence is in the poems. If political poetry means party-political poetry, then Auden after 1940 was not a political poet but, then, he never had been. If, however, that narrow view of politics is put aside and politics can be understood to mean a vision of the *polis*, of human society and its workings, then the late Auden seems to me the most deeply political of English poets of the twentieth century. His politics may be somewhat bleak, but it would be a peculiarly uninformed attitude to find them reactionary.

From 1940 onwards the obscurity bred by private context and reference disappears from Auden's work, and he draws increasingly on the discourse of the physical sciences, history and anthropology for his references. It is a quintessentially public poetry organized around and consistently implying social value-judgements. It would be misleading to describe it as Augustan, for nothing quite like it existed in English hitherto, but in its rootedness in a value-structure which encompasses social as well as personal life, rather than in the ephemera of mood and feeling, it is closer to the Augustans than to romantic modernism. What seems to have misled some critics is Auden's comic technique, mistaking comedy for triviality. The vision of the later Auden of the comic absurdity of life might be trivial if it did not know about suffering, but suffering is the continual context and background in which it operates. Justin Replogle makes the point well:

> In effect, he had to learn how to make poems that mocked poetry, and how to believe in something that laughed at the pretensions

of belief. When he learned how to do both, he made some extraordinarily beautiful poems. They were profound, moving, skilful—and comic.[41]

Auden's personal unhappiness is not directly relevant to his texts if we are prepared to look at them objectively, but since some critics have failed to do so, it is perhaps worth a sentence or two to refute the idea that Auden's later poems were written out of a sense of personal contentment. Auden's determination to praise life was as much despite as because of his personal life. Of course, he did find Good Places: Ischia, where he spent his summers in the early '50s, and, above all, his house at Kirchstetten in Lower Austria where he spent his summers from 1958 until loneliness and ill-health prompted his return to Oxford. But if Kirchstetten was the Good Place about which he told Spender that

> sometimes he stood in the garden with tears of gratitude and surprise that he possessed a house of his own; and he looked forward with increasing eagerness each year to the moment when he could leave New York and return to 'my beloved Kirchstetten'[42]

that has to be measured against the background out of which such gratitude had grown. In February 1943 he wrote to his friend Elizabeth Mayer:

> There are days when the knowledge that there will never be a place which I can call home, that there will never be a person with whom I shall be one flesh, seems more than I can bear. . . .[43]

Later still, Auden coped with his loneliness by adhering to a rigid routine which enabled him to work in the mornings and drink himself into nightly oblivion. As he said: 'Drinking, of course, can be a bid for affection, for absolute tolerance. It's certainly connected with getting stuck or sold out, emotionally.'[44] In 1969 he proposed marriage to Hannah Arendt simply in the hope of companionship.

Auden's later essays on social themes show that he continued to try to elaborate his position with regard to literature and politics into a general and coherent *Weltanschauung*. Auden seems always to have had a powerful rationalistic element in his make-up which shows in his later work as an insistence that the ethical and aesthetic realms are subject not just to moral choice but to rational moral choice. At its worst, it becomes a rather Aristotelian love of categories proliferated without much regard for their relevance. Rather than examine those essays in any detail—for which there is no space here—some inkling of the later Auden's political vision can best be indicated by looking, briefly, at one of his late poem-sequences of which *About the House* seems to me to be the most powerful.

*About the House* was first published in the U.K. in 1966—1965 in America. It was composed between 1962 and 1964 when Auden was spending his summers at Kirchstetten. The collection is divided into two parts: 'Thanksgiving for a Habitat' and 'In and Out'. The former celebrates his house at Kirchstetten and consists of twelve poems, a total of just under a thousand lines. Its structure is straightforward: a prologue, general thanksgiving, a poem for each room, and a concluding poem 'The Common Life', dedicated to Chester Kallman. Unusually for Auden, each poem is dedicated to a friend, thereby establishing a community which cuts across time and space. Each poem is formally an ode, but Auden displays great skill in varying the tone and form from poem to poem. The house was Auden's most enduring image for both the individual and for society at large. In his later work Auden made much use of external objects, persons or events around which to weave his reflections. These are a kind of occasional poem but a rather special kind in that an external object or event can provide a ready-made relation between the personal and public worlds, so that Auden can write personally without being private. This allows him an intimacy of tone which would not otherwise be possible and which presupposes on the part of both poet and audience a common familiarity with the kind of cultural reference Auden will use. His political accent on the personal and the individual—the particular—finds its literary equivalent in his refusal to be an impersonal voice speaking to no one in particular.

Poems in praise of a house may sound like middle-age at its most self-satisfied but, in fact, the sequence is, though funny, deeply moving; an all-but unique achievement in English. Auden manages this by means of two related techniques. Firstly, his subject matter is serious, though the vocabulary with which he talks about it is funny, and, secondly, across the diverse formal schemes which shape each poem (syllable and word-counting in some, syllable-counting and rhyme in others) he runs elaborate but informal speech-rhythms which create the underlying tone of the poems. As Replogle observes, the speakers in *About the House* 'have moved even further in the direction of love. The impulse to praise sacred objects is stronger than ever.'[45] Those voices, though oratorical and highly various, are essentially direct and, in a broad sense, lyrical in the intensity of feeling they create. Though an analysis of the syntactic and lexical devices Auden uses to create that tone would have to be very complex, the effect is one of an underlying simplicity of conversational speech.

Although the odes have as their ostensible subjects the rooms of his house, their real contents are extended meditations on the meaning of the ideas of home and community, of what it is to be specifically human. To that end Auden draws his lexicon from virtually all the sciences, history and, above all, anthropology. 'Thanksgiving for a Habitat', for example, opens with just such a reference:

> Nobody I know would like to be buried
> with a silver cocktail shaker,
> a transistor radio and a strangled
> daily help . . .

and similar references are scattered in profusion throughout the sequence. Auden has composed a set of serious and even solemn meditations and arguments which he has decked out in the most gaudy colours. They are no less serious for that, but much more lively.

It would be impossible in a few pages adequately to summarize Auden's thought in these poems, not just because it is subtle and there is a lot of it, but because what he is saying is as much in *how* he says it as in any extractable content—as is only proper in poetry. It is, however, worth commenting on one or two of the poems in illustration of the range of Auden's concerns. The opening poem 'Prologue: The Birth of Architecture' is a meditation on time: appropriately enough, for it originally belonged to his sequence of history poems in *Homage to Clio* (1960). He begins by distinguishing time as experienced by the individual from time on a natural or historical scale:

> From gallery-grave and the hunt of a wren-king
> to Low Mass and trailer camp
> is hardly a tick by the carbon clock, but I
> don't count that way nor do you:
> already it is millions of heartbeats ago
> back to the Bicycle Age,

with the implication that our experience of time-present is the reality on which we have to base our lives. He then goes on to assert how problematic we find our time-present in the world into which we are thrown. That world is non-human, for nature knows nothing of conscious choice and whatever human world there is to be, we have to build:

> . . . No world
> wears as well as it should but, mortal or not,
> a world has still to be built
> because of what we can see from our windows,
> that Immortal Commonwealth
> which is there regardless: It's in perfect taste
> and it's never boring but
> it won't quite do.

because:

> . . . to construct
> a second nature of tomb and temple, lives
> must know the meaning of *If*.

In the second poem, 'Thanksgiving for a Habitat', Auden sketches in the general conditions in which the human world has to be built, arguing that the world is basically hostile to the individual. History, like nature, is rife with mindless violence. If personal dignity and privacy are to have any chance to develop, then it will be in a context in which we must create the conditions for them, among which are a respect for the sacredness of life and an intelligent tolerance:

> . . . Linnaeus recoiled from the Amphibia
> as a naked gruesome rabble,
> Arachnids give me the shudders, but fools
> who deface their emblem of guilt

67

are germane to Hitler: the race of spiders
shall be allowed their webs. I should like
to be to my water-brethren as a spell
of fine weather: many are stupid,

and some, maybe, are heartless, but who is not
vulnerable, easy to scare,
and jealous of his privacy? . . .

The third poem, 'The Cave of Making', is among the most beautiful and moving Auden wrote. Dedicated 'In Memoriam Louis MacNeice' it is, of course, the poem for Auden's study and in it he meditates on his craft, on its place in the modern world, on friendship, loneliness and mortality. It is an extremely complex poem but at its centre is the line of thought that develops around this passage:

> . . . More than ever
> life-out-there is goodly, miraculous, lovable,
> but we shan't, not since Stalin and Hitler,
> trust ourselves ever again: we know that, subjectively,
> all is possible.

If the sequence can be said to have a dominant motif, then it is of the need for personal moral choice in the face of social evil for, as he wrote in a much earlier poem:

> For the present stalks abroad
> Like the past and its wronged again
> Whimper and are ignored,
> And the truth cannot be hid:
> Somebody chose their pain,
> What needn't have happened did.[46]

Each poem in the sequence develops these ideas further, but the close of the sequence is marked by a distinct change of mood which comes first in the eighth poem 'Grub First, Then Ethics (Brecht)'. In this, his kitchen poem, Auden meditates on the relations between the material conditions of life and ethical and aesthetic values, poking gentle fun at anyone who thinks any sort of decent society can be built without first attending to the provision of adequate material conditions:

> ...Jew, Gentile or pigmy,
> he must get his calories
> before he can consider her profile or
> his own, attack you or play chess,
> and take what there is however hard to get down. . . .

Auden is well aware that, as he says in 'The Cave of Making':

> ... (It's heartless to forget about
> the underdeveloped countries,
> but a starving ear is as deaf as a suburban optimist's:
> to stomachs only the Hindu
> integers truthfully speak.) . . .

and is led to consider the only kind of community he thinks possible for the artist and his audience in the modern world:

> the houses of our City
> are real enough but they lie
> haphazardly scattered over the earth,
> and her vagabond forum
> is any space where two of us happen to meet
> who can spot a citizen
> without papers. So, too, can her foes. Where the
> power lies remains to be seen,
> the force, though, is clearly with them. . . .

Auden believes that the Just City, the Good Place where love and truth are the lights by which some men at least choose to live is worth defending, if necessary even to the extent of personal destruction. Though the manner may be comic, Auden is at this point utterly serious and was enough of a classicist not lightly to refer to that marvellous passage of Herodotus's (VII, 225–26) which he echoes here without a full awareness of how central Herodotus's telling is to ideas of heroism in the European literary tradition:

> ... perhaps only
> by falling can She become
> Her own vision, but we have sworn under four eyes
> to keep Her up—all we ask for,
> should the night come when comets blaze and meres break,
> is a good dinner, that we
> may march in high fettle, left foot first,
> to hold her Thermopylae.

Auden closes the sequence with gratitude for the love he has experienced and the home he does have. Against a background of evil and violence 'every home should be a fortress', not just to keep out nature but also 'The Dark Lord and his hungry animivorous chimeras', and concludes thus:

> . . . *The ogre will come in any case*:
> so Joyce has warned us. Howbeit,
> fasting or feasting, we both know this: without
> the Spirit we die, but life
>
> without the Letter is in the worst of taste,
> and always, though truth and love
> can never really differ, when they seem to,
> the subaltern should be truth.

Auden's strategy in these poems is to create a comic effect by highlighting life's absurdities, which he does by juxtaposing incongruous lexical elements: incongruous because the discourses from which they are lifted are so seemingly diverse and incompatible. Thus, a scientific term may be juxtaposed with a conventional or slangy idiom as in 'Arachnids give me the shudders', or 'Low Mass and trailer camp'. Auden extends this juxtaposition into line contrasts using it as a deflationary technique so that the spectacular rhetoric of 'when comets blaze and meres break' is immediately followed by the very mundane 'is a good dinner'. In the hands of a craftsman as skilled as Auden, these absurdities highlight rather than destroy the serious intent of the comedy. Carpenter reports some remarks made by Auden to Spender: 'The ideal at which I aim is a style which shall combine the drab sober truthfulness of prose with a poetic uniqueness of expression.'[47] In the best of the late poetry and especially in *About the House* he achieved that, and the effect is one of great power and subtlety.

Auden's gift to literature in his later work is a poetically effective language in which to talk about a great range of social experience in a very direct way. That is not so different from the aims set for themselves by such obviously political poets as MacDiarmid, Brecht and Neruda.

## NOTES

Where only titles are given the reference is to a *poem* by Auden.

1. E. Mendelson, *Early Auden* (London, 1981), p. 307.
2. J. G. Blair, *The Poetic Art of W. H. Auden* (Princeton, 1965), p. 6.
3. *Letter to Lord Byron.*
4. *Herman Melville.*
5. W. Keir; the review appeared in the *Sunday Standard* of 28 January 1981.
6. C. James, *At the Pillars of Hercules* (London, 1979), p. 37.
7. 'Letter to Lord Byron'.
8. W. H. Auden, 'The Public v. the Late Mr. William Butler Yeats' (1939). Printed in: E. Mendelson (ed.), *The English Auden* (London, 1977), pp. 392–93.
9. E. Mendelson, *Early Auden*. See pp. 54–9.
10. E. Mendelson (ed.), *The English Auden*. 'Writing', pp. 305 and 312.
11. E. Mendelson, *Early Auden*, p. 89.
12. F. Duchêne, *The Case of the Helmeted Airman* (London, 1972), p. 45.
13. E. Mendelson, *Early Auden*, p. 130.
14. Ibid., p. 144.
15. S. Hynes, *The Auden Generation* (London, 1976), pp. 111–12.
16. E. Mendelson, *Early Auden*, p. 137.
17. Ibid., quoted on p. 307.
18. Ibid., p. XXI.
19. Ibid., p. 131.
20. Ibid., p. 178.
21. 'A Voyage: I. Whither?'
22. E. Mendelson, *Early Auden*, p. 243.
23. J. G. Blair, op. cit. Quoted on p. 23.
24. E. Mendelson (ed.), *The English Auden; The Good Life*, pp. 351–52.
25. Ibid., p. 353.
26. Ibid., p. 354.
27. Ibid., 'I Believe' (1939), p. 373.
28. W. H. Auden, *A Certain World* (London, 1971), p. 87.
29. E. Mendelson, *Early Auden*, p. 359.
30. E. Mendelson, *Early Auden*, p. 235.
31. J. Replogle, *Auden's Poetry* (London, 1969), p. 50.
32. Ibid.
33. E. Mendelson, *Early Auden*, p. 235.
34. H. Carpenter, *W. H. Auden* (London, 1981). Quoted on pp. 288–89.
35. 'The Prophets'.
36. 'Twelve Songs: III'.
37. 'The Riddle'.
38. E. Mendelson, *Early Auden*, p. 364.
39. J. Replogle, op. cit., p. 61.
40. Ibid., p. 70.
41. Ibid., p. 99.
42. H. Carpenter, op. cit. Quoted on pp. 392–93.

43. Ibid., quoted on p. 316.
44. H. Griffin, *Conversations with Auden* (San Francisco, 1981), p. 41.
45. J. Replogle, op. cit., p. 172.
46. 'A Walk After Dark'.
47. H. Carpenter, op. cit. Quoted on p. 419.

# 3

# Goebbels and Goblins: Politics and the Fairy-Tale in Auden's Poems

by JAN MONTEFIORE

> You never were an Isolationist;
>    Injustice you had always hatred for,
> And we can scarcely blame you, if you missed
>    Injustice just outside your lordship's door:
>    Nearer than Greece were cotton and the poor.
> To-day you might have seen them, might indeed
> Have walked in the United Front with Gide
>
> Against the ogre, dragon, what you will:
>    His many shapes and names all turn us pale,
> For he's immortal, and to-day he still
>    Swinges the scaly horror of his tail.
>    Sometimes he seems to sleep, but will not fail
> In every age to rear up to defend
> Each dying force of history to the end.[1]

This quotation from 'Letter to Lord Byron' (*Letters from Iceland*, 1937) is an excellent instance in miniature of the ways Auden's poetry, especially in the 1930s, uses fairy-tale motifs to carry political analysis and meditation. The first thing to be said of this approach is that it is plainly eccentric. Dragons and ogres, like the dream-symbolism to which they are closely related, have an obvious appropriateness as images of the mind's own processes: an insight which Auden elaborates in the essays 'Grimm and Anderson' and 'The Quest Hero',[2] but they constitute an unlikely political vocabulary. Nothing would seem less suitable for articulating the international catastrophes of the '30s than these irrational fairy-tale monsters; and yet Auden created a public poetry which still has the power to move and excite out of this unsuitable material—or rather out of the edgy relationship between such overtly subjective symbolism and the threatening external world of Fascism and the United Front which the poetry seeks to grasp and explain. This relation is not merely a tension of opposites (or, a hostile critic might say, of irrelevancies). Although politics, in the sense of causes and elections, do matter to Auden's poems,[3] he was always less interested in these than in 'the heart's invisible furies'[4]; this has been documented by his biographer[5] and is evident even in the brief quotation above: the nightmare dragon is charged with excitement, while the 'United Front' has none. But this is not to say that the poetry is therefore essentially unpolitical; as those writers[6] who have argued the relationship of psychoanalysis and ideology have shown, it would be a dangerously ignorant political analysis that made no connexion between the popularity of Fascism and those invisible furies. Auden's poems, especially those written during the '30s, explore and dramatize that connexion. Their fairy-tale elements evoke and articulate the relationship between the isolated individual and the political crises which he perceives, fears, suffers (mostly indirectly) and desires, but which he does not control and hardly even influences. While this has the obvious limitation of claiming a universal status for an onlooker's dilemma, it can also embody a cogent understanding of the fantasies by which such an onlooker/victim negotiates—or denies—the gap between himself and the world of political significance. (Yes, there is another obvious limitation implied in calling the person experiencing humanity's dilemma 'he'. The Oedipal complications which these poems explore do imply a masculine subject; and while there is no need to labour this point, one should not ignore Auden's sexism.)

Not that this fairy-tale imagery represents inner desires in a straightforward way; an element of play is evident in that

'Letter to Lord Byron' passage, partly in the poet's obvious pleasure in his power of improvised illustration and in the incongruous brilliance of his use of dream-material—or something near it—to represent serious political realities, partly in the sophisticated game that is set up between poem and readers. The description of the Dragon invites you not only to identify it as a misquotation from Milton's 'Ode on the morning of Christ's Nativity' (in which the Devil 'Swindges the scaly horror of his folded tail') but to pick up its simultaneously phallic and castrating symbolism, which is emphasized by the metrically necessary excision of 'folded' from Milton's line. The Dragon, that is, who in Auden represents a brute authority, represents also a threatening paternal imago who 'comes in dreams at puberty to man/ To scare him back to childhood if he can'[7]—a nuance that must be recognized if the line is to be savoured. This is a knowing poetic method which demands equally sophisticated readers; as Randall Jarrell writes of Auden in a related context, 'The poem exists on two levels, like counterpoint—that is, like a counterpoint in which one of the levels has to be supplied by its hearer.'[8] But the Freudian understanding demanded of the reader is more than a game; there is a rank excitement discernible through the sophistication with which the primitive fairy-tale imagery is handled in order to make a historical point about the persistence of authoritarian brutality. This combination of rank excitement and knowledgeable exploration of the ways in which the worlds of political materialism and the unconscious inhabit one another is characteristic of the best of Auden's poetry in the '30s, which it is this essay's purpose to examine.

I am not arguing that Auden's poetry in the '30s uses an exclusively or even predominantly fairy-tale symbolic language, or that the fairy-tale elements in Auden's entire poetic *oeuvre* are all clustered in his '30s work. Both propositions are demonstrably unsound. True, Randell Jarrell finds that in this period 'the fundamental structural picture underneath the poems is that of the fairy-tale Quest'[9]; but 'underneath' is the right word here. Heroes and monsters go almost unmentioned in the famous political poems 'Spain' and 'To a Writer on his Birthday' and are conspicuous by their absence in 'The Malverns', 'A Communist to Others', and 'A Summer Night'.

And while references and allusions to fairy-tales are scattered throughout Auden's poetry from 'The Silly Fool' in *Poems* (1930)[10] to 'August 1968' and 'Song of the Ogres' in *City Without Walls* (1969), it is rare for any of Auden's poems to be dominated by this material, and still rarer for a poem to be organized around it. The quotation above from 'Letter to Lord Byron' is fairly representative of Auden's method, at least in the '30s: it is an exposition which the dragon enters as a vivid illustration; this takes over the argument, but can be dropped when Auden wishes to resume it. Those exceptional poems which are entirely organized around fairy-tale material are of two kinds. Some are expository allegories—shorter, neater versions of the 'Letter to Lord Byron' method. Sonnet XII in the sequence 'Sonnets from China' is an allegory of this kind, about the failures of rationalism:

> And the age ended, and the last deliverer died
> In bed, grown idle and unhappy; they were safe:
> The sudden shadow of the giant's enormous calf
> Would fall no more at dusk across the lawns outside.
>
> . . . The vanquished powers were glad
> To be invisible and free; without remorse
> Struck down the sons who strayed into their course,
> And ravished the daughters, and drove the fathers mad.[11]

Alternatively, a poem may inhabit the world of fairy-tale in order to identify and dramatize the moment of crisis in an individual's or a generation's history as with the 'Epilogue' to *The Orators*—' "Where are you going?" said reader to rider' and 'Autumn Song ('Starving through a leafless wood/ Trolls run scolding for their food').[12] But of course, 'The Quest' (1941) which is Auden's most sustained treatment of fairy-tale material, does not date from the '30s at all, nor is it political. This sonnet sequence is a series of short ingenious allegories of key moments, mainly, though not entirely, of Conversion and Grace, in various lives. If one is collecting fairy-story allusions in Auden's poems, 'The Quest' is a rich source; but what is to me remarkable about these poems, in which heroes, dragons and magical obstacles unproblematically represent a purely inner life, is how uninteresting they are compared with the numinous, exasperating work of the '30s. Their wit, ingenuity and technical accomplishment are admirable, but as one of the heroes in 'The Quest' discovers, 'the terrible adventure is a little dull.'[13] Auden's representation of ogres and bogies keep their primitive terror best in those poems, like 'Now the leaves are falling fast', or the late 'August 1968', which attempt to get a purchase on contemporary history. As Randall Jarrell perceptively noted, Auden's poems *needed* their politics. His argument deserves to be quoted in full:

> At the ultimate compulsive level of belief most of his Marxism drops away (and, in the last few years, *has* dropped away [this was published in 1941]); his psychoanalytical, vaguely medical beliefs are so much more essential to Auden—'son of a nurse and doctor, loaned a dream'—that the fables he may have wanted to make Marxist always turned out to be psycho-analytical. But Marxism as a source of energy, of active and tragic insight, was invaluable; it was badly needed to coun-teract the passivity, the trust in Understanding and Love and God, that are endemic in Auden.[14]

This is a brilliant insight; Jarrell's two devastatingly per-ceptive critiques of Auden are among the subtlest and most intelligent readings that his poems have ever had. They have been very little noticed by English critics (too leftish? too Freudian?) but any serious critique of Auden still needs to take account of Jarrell's arguments. They apply particularly to Auden's fairy-tale material, but before going further with this argument it is necessary to examine just how this fairy-tale material functions in Auden's poems, and what psycho-analytical meanings it carries.

### 'The life of the psyche'

Auden has described fairy-tales as a kind of universally intelligible dream-language: 'Broadly speaking, and in most cases, the fairy-tale is a dramatic projection of the life of the psyche.'[15] In 'The Quest Hero' Auden elaborates on the ways in which fairy-tales symbolize 'our subjective experience of life'[16]:

> (1) Many of my actions are purposive; the *telos* towards which they are directed may be a short-term one, like trying to write a sentence which shall express my present thoughts accurately, or

a lifelong one, the search to find true happiness or authenticity of being, to become what I wish or what God intends me to become. What more natural image for such a telos than a beautiful Princess or the Waters of Life?

(2) I am conscious of time as a continuous irreversible process of change. Translated into spatial terms, this process becomes, naturally enough, a journey.

(3) I am conscious of myself as unique—my goal is for me only—and as confronting an unknown future—I cannot be certain in advance whether I shall succeed or fail in achieving my goal. The sense of uniqueness produces the image of the unique hero; the sense of uncertainty, the images of successful rivals.

(4) I am conscious of contradictory forces in myself, some of which I judge to be good and others evil, which are continually trying to sway my will this way or that. The existence of such forces is given. I can choose to yield to a desire or to resist it, but I cannot by choice desire or not desire.

Any image of this experience must be dualistic, a contest between friends and enemies.

On the other hand, the quest provides no image of our objective experience of social life.[17]

These cogent interpretations are readily applicable to those poems in which dragons, heroes and wishing wells represent elements of the psyche and nothing more—they could easily stand as a commentary on 'The Quest'. They do however present a problem for my suggestion that Auden's political poems use fairy-tale material to symbolize unconscious thought processes (in particular, the repression and authority-worship Auden associates with the Right), since Auden's interpretations define fairy-tale as a model of *conscious* experience: having certain aims, being aware of oneself as unique and as subject to impulse. If the poet wants to write about the mind's dark interior, isn't the obvious solution not fairy-tale but what Freud called the 'royal road to the unconscious': namely the dream? Certainly, dreams and their

Freudian interpretations are important in Auden's work in the '30s: In 'Now through night's caressing grip', dreams are expounded through their own mechanisms of inversion and displacement:

> Just and unjust, worst and best
> Change their places as they rest:
> Awkward lovers lie in fields
> Where disdainful beauty yields:
> While the splendid and the proud
> Naked stand before the crowd.[18]

Or, as in 'Dear, though the night is gone', a dream is interpreted even as it is related:

> O but what worm of guilt
> Or what malignant doubt
> Am I the victim of;
> That you then, unabashed,
> Did what I never wished.
> Confessed another love;
> And I, submissive, felt
> Unwanted and went out?[19]

Another love-poem, 'The earth turns over', has a condensed witty version of this method; dreams contain paradoxical disguises which can be penetrated by anyone (that is, poet and reader) who knows his Freud:

> There move the enormous comics, drawn from life;
> My father as an Airedale and a gardener,
> My mother chasing letters with a knife:
> You are not present as a character,
> —Only the family have speaking parts.—
> You are a valley or a river-bend,
> The one an aunt refers to as a friend,
> The tree from which the weasel racing starts.[20]

All of these poems, which are incidentally among Auden's most beautiful, insist on the dream's character of disguised wish-fulfilment; the dreams are riddles to which the poet thinks he knows the answers, which somehow retain their mystery even after decoding. But the most outrageously 'Freudian' of Auden's dreams is not, presumably, his own at all—the nightmare of the unfortunate repressed Miss Gee:

> She dreamed a dream one evening
> That she was the Queen of France,
> And the Vicar of St. Aloysius
> Asked Her Majesty to dance,
>
> But a storm blew down the place,
> She was biking through a field of corn,
> And a bull with the face of the Vicar
> Was charging with lowered horn,
>
> She could feel his hot breath behind her,
> He was going to overtake.
> And the bicycle went slower and slower
> Because of that back-pedal brake.[21]

You hardly need to have heard of Freud to interpret this fruity example of wish-fulfilment and censorship from a poem that is itself a kind of parabolic gloss on Auden's famous line 'the distortions of ingrown virginity'.[22] A stereotypically plain pious spinster transforms herself into a Queen of France (where fashionable clothes come from) courted by the vicar on whom she's fixated; sexual desire, even in the acceptably disguised form of being asked for a dance, is so disturbing as to be felt as a 'storm' that destroys her fantasy 'palace', and the Vicar becomes a monstrous phallic bull, his 'horn' getting additional emphasis from the rhyme-scheme. Obvious diagnosis: unconscious repression plus possible repressed father-fixation (St. Aloysius suggests a Roman Catholic or High Church parish, whose Vicar would be 'Father' X). Yet Miss Gee's dream, like those in the love-poems, remains a riddle, though one easily solved; the differences lie in the tone of heartless comedy, and the turning of the dream into a sophisticated irony at the expense of the dreamer. Also, of course, in the narrative form that gives details of her daily life (dowdy clothes, attendance at St. Aloysius, bicycle) which the dream-work turns into symbols of desire and discontent. (Dreams characteristically work up material from everyday life and consequently can only rarely be discussed in isolation from the dreamer's own life and circumstances without losing their significance; even Miss Gee's dream gets part of its parabolic significance from her eventual death from cancer, the outlet for her 'foiled creative fire.) It is significant that all of these poems about dreams are either love-poems or about sexuality in and out of disguise. This makes them recalcitrant material for poems about politics, especially if the political analysis is of the mechanics of repression. Dreams as Freud understood them after all represent the action of the pleasure principle, disguised from unconscious censorship and repression—and the more rigid the censorship, the more elaborate and complex is the symbolism of the dream. If fairy-tale constitutes difficult material for a political discourse, dreams are hopelessly esoteric. They may be the royal road to the unconscious, but fairy-tales are much more legible signposts. Moreover, while psychoanalysis is not common knowledge, fairy-tales are, and can therefore be used much more straightforwardly as common ground between poet and readers.

In 'September 1st, 1939' Auden uses this potent and readily intelligible symbolic vocabulary to define contemporary crisis in a way that brings immediate conviction:

> Faces along the bar
> Cling to their average day;
> The lights must never go out,
> The music must always play . . .
> Lest we should see where we are,
> Lost in a haunted wood,
> Children afraid of the dark
> Who have never been happy or good.[23]

The childishness of fairy-tales is admitted here and made part of the poem's analysis of human inadequacy. A similar fairy-tale image of children deserted in a treacherous world surfaces in 'Now the leaves are falling fast':

> Starving through a leafless wood
> Trolls run scolding for their food
> And the nightingale is dumb
> And the angel will not come.[24]

The image of children misled by their guardians in a desolate world also dominates the end of 'The Capital' with its implied prediction of the probable fate of those lured by the city:

81

> But the sky you illumine, your glow is visible far
> Into the dark countryside, the enormous, the frozen
> Where, hinting at the forbidden like a wicked uncle,
> Night after night to the farmer's children you beckon.[25]

It is characteristic of Auden's allusion to fairy-tale that although they are easy to recognize, it is impossible to say exactly which fairy-tale is being referred to. Here the allusions are possibly to 'Hansel and Gretel', more probably to 'The Babes in the Wood', with maybe a touch of Dante. What is needed is that readers should understand, be moved by the images, and recognize them as drawn from the register of fairy-tale, but it does not really matter which fairy-tale. They are allusive reinterpretations, but not re-tellings. Similarly, the beautiful 'Enter with him/ These legends, love' refers to the *kind* of fairy-tale in which the hero gets magical assistance on his quest; it is an allegorical reading of fairy-tale material, in general, not of any particular story:

> Enter with him
> Those legends, love
> For him assume
> Each diverse form
> As legend simple
> As legend queer
> That he may do
> What these require
> Be, love, like him
> To legend true.[26]

Even in the sonnets of 'The Quest', Auden does not seem interested in fairy-tale narrative for its own sake. The poems are allegorical interpretations of Quest-stories in general; readers only need to know enough to recognize the archetypes to which Auden alludes. It is taken for granted that readers already know the story:

> They noticed that virginity was needed
> To trap the unicorn in every case
> But not that, of those virgins who succeeded,
> A high percentage had an ugly face.[27]

In a way related to the admission of childishness in 'September 1st, 1939', the poem admits the fact that fairy-tale

has an element of cliché and turns this to account; the cliché is
in the minds of the subjects.

> Now everyone knows the hero must choose the old horse,
> Abstain from liquor and sexual intercourse,
>
> And look out for a stranded fish to be kind to. . . .
>
> Forgetting that his information comes mostly from married
> men
> Who liked fishing and a flutter on the horses now and then,
>
> And how reliable can any truth be that is got
> By observing oneself and then just inserting a Not?[29]

Auden uses fairy-tale as a universally intelligible symbolic
shorthand; he is not interested in what particular stories mean
but in the way their material carries meaning. The way his
poems deploy their fairy-tale material is therefore at the
opposite pole from the way this same fairy-tale material is
handled by, for instance, the women poets, writing today.
(Interest in the fairy-tale and myth is so common with us that
it almost amounts to an obsession.) Women poets, like Auden,
understand fairy-tales as representations of 'the life of the
psyche'. But whereas Auden takes as 'given' the structures
which assign purposive choosing and action to the man and a
passive destiny of waiting and being chosen to the woman
('what more *natural* [my emphasis] image for . . . a telos than a
beautiful Princess or the Waters of Life?'),[30] these poets direct
their aims at transforming these assumptions. And not only
poets; the American critics Sandra Gilbert and Susan Gubar
underpin their readings of nineteenth-century fiction in *The
Mad Woman in the Attic* with a fable of creativity that is itself a
revised version of 'Snow White' in which the Wicked Queen
becomes a doomed heroine rebelling against patriarchy.[31] Liz
Lochhead's 'The Grimm Sisters' and the revised versions of
Grimm in Olga Broumas's *Beginning with O* re-tell these stories
and sometimes change their punch-lines in order to deconstruct
what is taken as 'natural'; fairy-tales in these poems therefore
almost always take the form of narrative fable.[32] The difference
between these women poets' and Auden's uses of fairy-tale is
that theirs is a narrative poetry which understands, to use the

overworked but handy slogan, that 'the personal is political' and for whom the specificity of each story that describes the inner life is very important, while Auden's lyrical and/or expository poems explore the ways in which the worlds of 'the political' and 'the personal' inhabit one another.

Auden is anyway not at his best as a storyteller (except for his gruesome cautionary ballads like 'Victor' and 'Miss Gee'). His lack of interest in narrative is plain in the poem 'The Witnesses' ('You dowagers with Roman noses'). The early versions of this poem[33] tell a story, which Auden rightly scrapped in the version printed in *Collected Poems*; its Part ii relates the life of Prince Alpha who surpasses every expectation and dies because he knows his life is pointless. He has adventures:

> Where did he travel? Where didn't he travel?
> Over the ice and over the gravel
> and the sea;
> Up the fevered jungle river
> Through haunted forests without a shiver
> he wandered free.
>
> What did he do? What didn't he do?
> He rescued maidens, overthrew
> ten giants
> Like factory chimneys, slaughtered dragons
> Though their heads were larger than railway wagons,
> tamed their defiance.[34]

These adventures are—to indulge a structuralist's pun—merely perfunctory; what makes them enjoyable is Auden's gay parody of conventional heroics. The only real point of Prince Alpha's story is its ending—i.e. his discovery that nothing fails like success—'No, I am not the truly strong man/ O let me die.'[35] This cannot interest or convince because there is no connection between the adventures and the failure. Isherwood, of course, has a version of this same fable in *Lions and Shadows*:

> The Truly Strong Man travels straight across the broad America of normal life, taking always the direct, reasonable route. But 'America' is just what the truly weak man, the neurotic hero, dreads. And so, with immense daring, with

84

infinitely greater expenditure of nervous energy, time, money, physical and mental resources, he prefers to attempt the northern circuit, the laborious, terrible north-west passage, and his end, if he does not turn back, is to be lost for ever in the blizzard and the ice.[36]

The difference is plain here, between Isherwood who cares for the fable and Auden who cares for the revelation which the fable carries. Because the story in 'The Witnesses' is so sketchy, it is left vague whether Prince Alpha fails merely because of inner weakness or because history has no longer room for heroes, so that like the speaker of 'I have a handsome profile', he lives in, or rather dies, because of 'a world that has had its day'.[37] Where the poem really comes to life is in Part iii (the only surviving part of the original in the *Collected Poems*), in which the nightmare forces which doomed the hero introduce themselves: 'On your left and on your right,/ In the day and in the night,/ we are watching you.'[38] The Witnesses are demons of human limitation, close relatives of, if not identical to the 'Lords of Limit' in a contemporary poem, 'training dark and light/ And setting a tabu 'twixt left and right' . . . Whose sleepless presences endear/ Our peace to us with a perpetual threat.'[39] They manifest themselves only to punish in a scene instinct with the kind of threatening horrors that pursue us in nightmares:

> The sky is darkening like a stain
> Something is going to fall like rain,
>     and it won't be flowers.

> When the green field comes off like a lid,
> Revealing what was much better hid,
>     unpleasant;
> And look! behind you without a sound
> The woods have come up and are standing round
>     in deadly crescent.

> The bolt is sliding in its groove,
> Outside the window is the black remov-
>     ers van.
> And now with sudden swift emergence
> Come the women in dark glasses, the humpbacked surgeons
>     and the scissor man.[40]

These are avengers whose powers cannot be abolished by any act of human will, and whom no act of Parliament can eradicate. John Fuller interprets them as Necessity and Time ('You are the town and we are the clock')[41]. I construe them differently as the ways in which we falsely represent Necessity to ourselves. In their power to negate human will ('you have to obey but you don't have to like it')[42] they resemble Kipling's Gods of the Copybook Headings, the eternal principles of Limit on which man's hubris will always be wrecked:

> As it will be in the future, it was at the birth of man—
> There are only four things certain since Social Progress
> began—
> That the Dog returns to his Vomit and the Sow returns to
> her Mire
> And the burnt Fool's bandaged Finger goes
> wabbling back to the Fire,
>
> And that after this is accomplished, and the brave new
> world begins
> When all men are paid for existing, and no man must pay
> for his sins,
> As surely as Water will wet us, as surely as Fire will
> burn,
> The Gods of the Copybook Readings with terror and
> slaughter return![43]

Whereas Kipling insists, with aggressive satisfaction, that 'Social Progress' will always disintegrate into dirt, injury and 'terror and slaughter', Auden recognizes the element of fantasy in the punishment promised to the transgressors of Limit. The penalties the Witnesses threaten us with are unreasonably, fantastically severe, but despite their final warning 'This could happen any day/ So be careful what you say and do',[44] there is no indication that they can do more than frighten. But of course they do not need to; in the fantasy world of the poem, they are supreme, just as they are in the mind's unconscious.

Like Kipling's Gods, these Witnesses are a lethal conflation of reality-principle and incredibly severe super-ego. They also, I think, double as imagos of both parents in their malign aspects:

> You are the town and we are the clock,
> We are the guardians of the gate in the rock,
> the Two.[45]

This contradictory doubling which is typical of dream-logic, also helps to explain why the Witnesses' first appearance in 'The year of my youth' was as 'two old men' with the punning names 'Titt and Tool'.[46] The kinds of unconscious fantasies that underly Kipling's hard-headed 'realism' are in Auden's poem made to declare themselves; but whereas with 'the burnt Fool's bandaged Finger . . . wabbling' the castration-allusion is plainly not intentional, when Auden's Witnesses climax their horrible threats with the 'scissor-man' (out of *Struwwelpeter*), the allusion is nearly as overt as the phallic bull in Miss Gee's dream.

'The Witnesses' lies at the subjective extreme of a poetic that expounded and dramatized the relation between the nightmare of the dark and the factual terrors of totalitarian Europe. This is not just a matter of drawing analogies between the arbitrary cruelties committed in fantasy by a punishing super ego and those performed at the will of an oppressive dictator. Auden's poetry explores the complex processes of collusion and self-betrayal, whereby human minds not only fear that if they are disobedient the 'Gods . . . with terror and slaughter return' but actually want them to—and turn that wish into a false 'knowledge'. It is this wish for domination and cruelty that gives the fascist dictator his chance. Not, of course, that 'The Witnesses' says all that. It is not a political poem at all, except in the important sense that it enables the reader consciously to experience the emotional mechanism of obedience towards a terrorizing authority.

*Mythologies and symptoms*

> No one knows . . .
> What ugly feast may village band be celebrating[47]

As we have seen, the world of fairy-tale overlaps readily with the world of *The Interpretation of Dreams*, and not only because Freud was interested in *Märchen*. Fairy-tales, as Bruno Bettelheim[48] has expounded, are the versions of dreams that we learn

87

childhood and pass on to our children. Both fairy-tale and dream are narrative mythologies, the one being a common-or-garden version of the esoteric other. Auden's '30s poetry draws not only on these narrative mythologies but on mythologies of the kind discovered and classified by Roland Barthes—that is, representations charged with glamour and importance that seem to us natural but which are themselves the bearers of ideology.[49] One such mythical world in the '30s poetry is the English rural idyll: that is, the patriotic dream of an unchanging countryside and unspoilt village symbolizing England's immemorial stability. (This was especially topical in the '30s; shepherds on horseback and the 'immemorial' tasks of ploughing and reaping were favourite subjects for newspaper photographs.)[50] Auden is clear about the rôle nostalgia plays in such representations of pastoral England:

> We would show you an English village: You shall choose
> its location
> Wherever your heart directs you most longingly to look:
> you are loving towards it
> Whether north to Scots Gap or Bellingham where the black
> rams defy the panting engine
> Or West to the Welsh marches; to the lilting speech and
> the magicians' faces.
> Wherever you were a child or had your first affair
> There it stands amid your darling scenery:
> A parish bounded by the wreckers' cliff; or meadows where
> browse the Shorthorn and the maplike Friesian
> As at Trent Junction the Soar comes gliding: out of green
> Leicestershire to swell the ampler current.[51]

But Pressan Ambo, the Good Place invoked in this loving psalm of the English countryside, is a poisoned idyll: the dream village always turns out to be a nest of vampires. An obvious source for this nightmare pastoral is 'Mortmere' the fantasy-world created by Isherwood and Upward[52], a grotesque surrealist parody the familiar English dream of an unspoilt pastoral village; but I think Auden also comes to it via detective fiction. The detective-story with a rural country-house setting, inhabited by a cast of county 'types', is typical of the inter-war 'Golden Age' of detective-story.[54] Auden's late essay 'The Guilty Vicarage' explains the compulsive readability of detective-stories through the reader's need for organized fantasies of crime and revenge; the poem 'Detective Story' (1936) has the same theme: 'Someone has to pay for/ Our loss of happiness, our happiness itself.'[56]

Certainly the cast of village characters in *The Dog Beneath the Skin* could come straight out of a parodied detective story. As well as this dream turned nightmare of the nasty pastoral, Auden invokes the world of school especially in *Poems* and in *The Orators*, his language mimicking Bulldog Drummond:

> Are you sure you're our Saviour? We're certain you smell,
> All of us itching in every nerve
> To give you the thrashing you richly deserve.[57]

The language evoking the world of school[58] in Auden's poetry is more an undertone than a theme and shades off into boyish insouciance and camp humour. However, what dream villages, detective stories, school stories, 'real' dreams and fairy-tales all have in common is that they are all non-realist representations: mythologies* visibly powered by the pleasure principle. To put this in simpler terms, they are all ways in which people at once understand and evade understanding their own and others' lives by fantasizing about them. These mythologies invoked or parodied in Auden's poetry, fairy-tales are extremely important. Unlike the nostalgic dream of rural England, their significance is not so subliminally felt as to need a Roland Barthes to point it out; and unlike 'real' dreams, they are not too obscure or too esoteric to be easily intelligible. This does

---

* I am using Roland Barthes's term 'mythologies' rather than Samuel Hynes's well-known description of the '30s Audenesque mode as 'parable-art'[59] because Hynes's term applies to narrative. A parable is a story with a multiplicity of meanings, any or all of which may be understood by its listeners/readers. Though Auden mines the narrative mythologies, fairy-tale and dream for poetic symbols, his art is lyric and expository, not narrative; nor, as I have argued above, are all the myths he draws on narrative ones. To call poems parables because their symbolism is drawn from a mythical world would mean stretching the term 'parable' to mean not much more than 'non-realistic representation'. It is difficult not to fudge here: I am aware of stretching Barthes's usage in the opposite direction, to cover narrative fantasies. I still think Barthes's analysis of myth and ideology makes his term 'mythology' an appropriate description of Auden's dramatizations of fantasy, illusion and wilful blindness.

not prevent the fairy-tale material from having a symptomatic status:

> The crumbling lighthouse is circled with moss like a muff;
> The weasel inhabits the courts and the sacred places;
> Despair is in our faces.
>
> For the Dragon has wasted the forest and set fire to the
>     farm;
> He has mutilated our sons in his terrible rages
> And our daughters he has stolen to be victims of his
>     dissolute orgies;
> He has cracked the skulls of our children in the crook of his
>     arm,
> With the blast of his nostrils he scatters death through the
>     land
> We are babes in his hairy hand.
>
> O, when shall the deliverer come to destroy this dragon?
> For it is stated in the prophecies that such a one shall appear
> Shall ride on a white horse and pierce his heart with a spear;
> Our elders shall welcome him home with trumpet and organ,
> Load him with treasure, yes, and our most beautiful
>     maidenhead
> He shall have for his bed.[60]

This chorus from the *Ascent of F6* articulates the particular human weakness of defining evil as something outside oneself which one needs take no responsibility for. The speakers imagine the decay of their country as the work of the 'Dragon'—an uncontrollable, bestial evil which they can do nothing to prevent. To say 'The Dragon has wasted our forests . . . we are babes in his hairy hand' is to abjure responsibility. They need the nightmare Dragon so that they will not have to wake and do what must be done in the day. In their passive wish for a Leader to solve their problems, they are like Aesop's frogs, and are lucky not to get the would-be King Stork of 'It's farewell to the drawing-room's civilised cry', who sees himself as just the fairy-tale hero for which a sick world is waiting:

> For I, after all, am the Fortunate One,
> The Happy-Go-Lucky, the spoilt Third Son;
> For me it is written the Devil to chase
> And to rid the earth of the human race.

90

> The behaving of man is a world of horror,
> A sedentary Sodom and slick Gomorrah;
> I must take charge of the liquid fire
> And storm the cities of human desire.
>
> .　　.　　.
>
> For it's order and trumpet and anger and drum
> And power and glory command you to come;
> The graves shall fly open and let you all in,
> And the earth be emptied of mortal sin.[61]

This poem dramatizes the need to dominate and punish: the converse of the need of the speakers in 'Chorus' to be dominated. Just as they imagine coping with catastrophe as anyone's job but their own, this speaker thinks himself the lucky hero, the 'spoilt third son' destined to 'rid the earth of the human race',[61] and imagines evil everywhere except in himself, the destroyer. Both poems implicitly diagnose the pathology of fascism in the symbiotic need that leaders and led have for one another; the leader is eventually going to destroy his followers as well as their 'enemy'— that is, independent humanity. Auden elaborates the diagnosis of the appeal of fascism to the powerless in 'Letter to Lord Byron', portraying world view of the little man, 'the bowler hat who straphangs on the tube/ And kicks the tyrant only in his dreams.'[62] His condition is even worse than that of the weak who want a deliverer: he needs his tyrant:

> 'I am like you,' he says, 'and you, and you.
>     I love my life, I love the home-fires, have
> To keep them burning. Heroes never do.
>     Heroes are sent by ogres to the grave.
>     I may not be courageous, but I save.
> I am the one who somehow turns the corner,
> I may perhaps be fortunate Jack Horner.
>
> 'I am the ogre's private secretary;
>     I've felt his stature and his powers, learned
> To give his ogreship the raspberry
>     Only when his gigantic back is turned.
>     One day, who knows, I'll do as I have yearned.
> The short man, all his fingers on the door.'
> With repartee shall send him to the floor.'

91

> One day, which day? O any other day,
>   But not to-day. The ogre knows his man.
> To kill the ogre—that would take away
>   The fear in which his happy dreams began,
>   And with his life he'll guard dreams while he can.
> Those who would really kill his dream's contentment,
> He hates with real implacable resentment.[63]

As an analysis of *petit-bourgeois* attraction to fascism and of the way people at once need and hate authority, this deserves to go alongside Fromm or Reich.[64] It is also a marvellously alive, flexible and witty poetry of argument. But a poetry of political analysis posed in psychological terms has obvious drawbacks, especially when the mechanisms dramatized are identification and submission. It can and sometimes does lead to muddle of the kind incurred by the poem 'Where do They come from? Those whom we so much dread' written in 1939. The imminent threat of fascism and war is identified with the bad dreams of the fortunate:

> Terrible Presences that the ponds reflect
> Back at the famous, and when the blond boy
>
> Bites eagerly into the shining
> Apple, emerge in their shocking fury.[65]

'They' are the enemy: at once representing the real dispossessed (like 'the gathering multitudes outside/ Whose glances hunger worsens' in another poem[66]) and 'our' own fantasies. 'They' are like evil spirits whom 'our' carelessness has summoned—'O we conjured them here like a lying map . . . Our money sang like streams on the aloof peaks.'[67] 'They' are also 'our' destined fate:

> . . . though all our whiteness shrinks
> From the hairy and clumsy bridegroom
> We conceive in the shuddering instant.[67]

'We' are at once guilty of 'their' existence, and innocent of their wickedness, while needing them to seduce and/or execute us. In fact, it is impossible to find out by the end of the poem what if any objective status 'our' guilt has; the poem gets stuck in the processes of identification it is supposed to analyse.

*Goebbels and Goblins: Politics and the Fairy-Tale in Auden's Poems*

*Dragons, swastikas and sickles*

I do not want to make too much of the failure of 'Where do They come from?', which after all Auden dropped from later editions of his poetry. But the muddle visible in that poem does raise a question which this essay has so far avoided asking: are these 'mythologies' really effective as the language of a politically analytic poetry? Fairy stories may generate poetic intensity and be signposts to the world of the unconscious, but can they really mediate realities as hard and threatening as fascism and class oppression? Do they in fact justify their presence in a political poetry?

The value of mythology, and especially of fairy-tale as symbol, depends crucially on the interpretations of them offered by the poem—interpretations which may include acknowledgement of their shortcomings. Fairy-tale material can undoubtedly make for silliness, cosiness or whimsy. Yet such fairy-tale figures as dragons and ogres can derive a paradoxical strength from mediating real threats; and if they simplify these in one way, they can be used to make a subtle analysis in another. Similarly, the poet's own awareness that his symbols are not wholly appropriate to the things they represent can work to make the poem more subtle or to turn it into a game of ingenious evasion. The shifts and turns of the poet's attitude can be seen at their best if we resume the passage with which I began this article: the stanzas defining the 'dragon' of fascism against which Lord Byron might have fought. Here is the continuation:

> Milton beheld him on the English throne
>
> And Bunyan sitting in the Papal chair;
> The hermits fought him in their caves alone,
>     At the first Empire he was also there,
>     Dangling his Pax Romana in the air.
> He comes in dreams at puberty to man
> To scare him back to childhood if he can.
>
> Banker or landlord, booking-clerk or Pope,
>     Whenever he's lost faith in choice and thought
> When a man sees the future without hope,
>     Whenever he endorses Hobbes' report

'The life of man is nasty, brutish, short',
The dragon rises from his garden border
And promises to set up law and order.

He that in Athens murdered Socrates
    And Plato then seduced, prepares to make
A desolation and then call it peace
    To-day for dying magnates, for the sake
Of generals who can scarcely keep awake,
And for that doughy mass in great and small
That doesn't want to stir itself at all.

The first of these stanzas is splendid—a direct but sophisticated poetry of statement. Auden sketches human history
through a series of heroes celebrated for their courage in the
cause of progress. The history given is simple (possibly
Marxist but also consistent with a Whig interpretation), but
the thought is not. Auden is not saying that the Dragon *is*
reaction but that he represents it; he is the symbol by which
revolutionaries and rebels have imagined their enemies
('Milton beheld him . . . the hermits fought him'). Hence the
logically shaky but emotionally convincing analogy on the last
couplet between the adolescence of the (male) individual and
the life of nations. The following stanza, while never less than
pleasurable, witty and penetrating, is not so good. Its first line
is agreeably vigorous, but its list of social types sounds random—
all except the 'booking clerk' are wealthy and powerful; does
this mean they like the humble *petit-bourgeois* are possible
recruits for a Popular Front, or just that the alliterations and
inverted stresses sounded good? Similarly, though the introduction of the Hobbes quotation is pleasurably ingenious,
Auden's different versions of the temptation to despair are not
like an argument defining itself with increasing precision but
like a slightly random list of variations on the same theme
('Whenever . . When . . Whenever'), governed more by rhyme
than by logic. Real vigour returns with the last couplet, in
which history gives way to comedy, with the comic surrealism
of the dragon appearing, djinn-like, in the suburban garden.
This incongruous containment of the monster within the
'garden border' is counterpointed by the ingenious technique
through which the rhyme 'border/law and order' gets the

cliché—'law and order' to dance to the poet's tune. The couplet hovers on the edge of whimsy but does not fall.

When in the third stanza Auden returns to a serious vein, the argument and language coarsen slightly. The quick summary of Athenian intellectual life is well enough, but the Tacitus allusion[69] and its indictment of imperialism is a bit too slick, while the Capitalist masters of the Dragon—'dying magnates' and dozing generals—are too vaguely and comically sketched to be taken seriously. The Right were, and are, a lot more formidable than *that*. To make the controllers of the Dragon ludicrous is a way of avoiding the problem of defining them and their relationship to the brutality which the Dragon represents. This political/psychological diagnosis underlying the argument is not without subtlety: it runs, roughly 'authoritarian brutality in general and fascism in particular is, as it has always been, the servant of the ruling classes—as of now, the capitalist Right; and its allies are despair and inertia.' The subtlety and precision of this diagnosis are all directed at the forces of the mind; the actual material enemies are cartoon-figures, objects of the poet's comic ingenuity. This crudity is partly a matter of the poet's own attitude; the gay, serious intelligence of Auden's expository method begins to curdle like a mayonnaise, separating out into the solemn ('He that in Athens murdered Socrates') and the inappropriately light-hearted ('generals who can scarcely keep awake'). This separation is complete in the following stanzas, which alternate complete seriousness ('And every man in every generation/ Tossing in his dilemma of his bed/ Cries to the shadows of the noble dead'[70]) and slightly camp cosy humour ('I must write home or mother will be vexed/ So this must be continued in our next.')

But the difficulty with Auden's representation of history by fairy-tale and dream is not only a question of how this is interpreted and presented to the reader; it is also inherent in the material. Dragons, ogres and heroes *are* oversimplified representations of history.

This is apparent in the ogre's very last appearance in Auden's poems—the short poem 'August 1968',[71] arguably Auden's best single political poem:

The ogre does what ogres can,
Deeds quite impossible to Man,
But one prize is beyond his reach,
The ogre cannot master Speech.
About a subjugated plain,
Among its desperate and slain,
The ogre stalks with hands on hips
While drivel gushes from his lips.[71]

Unlike Auden's Popular Front poems of the '30s where it is not always clear if the enemy is fascism or the capitalists, the political target of this poem is plain: the Russian invasion of Czechoslovakia and the crushing of 'Dubcek democracy'. The poem's opposing of human language to idiot 'drivel' defines the ogre as subhuman. He does 'deeds quite impossible to Man' because he is superhumanly strong and subhumanly cruel, also imbecile. 'Drivel gushes from his lips' conflates saliva with a torrent of meaningless words; an implied definition of state socialist propaganda as decayed meaningless speech which is familiar from Orwell's *Nineteen Eighty-four*[72] and which is made particularly vivid by the disgusting image of the ogre's dribbling mouth. What he does—'what ogres can'—is of a piece with what he is, crushing men into 'desperate and slain' because that is the nature of his uncomprehending brutality. The U.S.S.R., Auden seems to say, really *does* represent idiot evil. Not that 'August 1968' can be dismissed as cold-warrior propaganda; the crushing of democracy *is* brutally stupid, and Auden's epigrammatic fable can apply to other occasions when tanks grind over human freedom.

This is, clearly, a very successful political poem. And yet paradoxically its fable precludes any political explanations of the event it records, or rather alludes to (just as 'Letter to Lord Byron' had no explanation of the ascendancy of the 'dragon' of reaction except the inertia of 'dying magnates'). To speculate on the Politburo's reasons for sending in the tanks would be to concede human intelligence to the ogre; he would remain a nasty bit of work, but not an imbecile. And yet the drivelling giant 'stalking' among his victims is such a haunting image because he is a genuinely nightmare figure, as horrible as Kipling's 'blind face that cries and can't wipe its eyes'.[73] The nightmare at once supplies the power in the poem and limits its discourse.

*Goebbels and Goblins: Politics and the Fairy-Tale in Auden's Poems*

This may suggest that the difficulties inherent in using the language of fairy-tale and dream are, simply, insuperable. Yet the poems I have discussed do not seem to me failures. Auden's strength as a poet was inseparable from his understanding that nightmares are not confined to sleep.

NOTES

To make reference easier, all quotations from poems are identified in the notes by the first line or title of the poem quoted. All but one quotation are from Auden's *Collected Poems*, ed. Mendelson (Faber, 1976) and *The English Auden*, ed. Mendelson (Faber, 1977). I have abbreviated these titles to C.P. and E.A.

1. W. H. Auden, 'Letter to Lord Byron', Part II, E.A., p. 180.
2. W. H. Auden, 'Grimm and Anderson', collected in *Forewords and Afterwords* (Faber, 1973), pp. 198–208, and 'The Quest Hero', *Texas Quarterly* IV, May 1962, reprinted in *Tolkien and the Critics*, ed. Neil D. Isaacs and Rose A. Zimbardo (University of Notre Dame Press, 1968), pp. 40–61.
3. For contrary views, see Frederick A. Buell, *W. H. Auden as a Social Poet*, and Justin Replogle, *Auden's Poetry* (Methuen, 1969); and most influentially, the essay on Auden in John Bayley's *The Romantic Survival* (Constable, 1957), pp. 127–85.
4. 'The Capital', E.A., p. 236.
5. Humphrey Carpenter, *W. H. Auden: A Biography* (Allen and Unwin, 1981), Chapters 6 and 7; Carpenter discusses Auden's Marxism in detail on pp. 147–57, insisting that this was always skin-deep: 'even at this time he seems not to have held Communist views with any seriousness' (p. 152).
6. See R. Coward and J. Ellis, *Language and Materialism* (Routledge, 1977) and R. Barthes, *Mythologies* (Paladin, 1973) and *Image-Music-Text* (Fontana, 1977).
7. 'Letter to Lord Byron', E.A., p. 181.
8. Randall Jarrell, 'Changes of Attitude and Rhetoric in *Auden's Poetry*', collected in *The Third Book of Criticism* (Faber, 1969), p. 145.
9. R. Jarrell, 'Freud to Paul: The Stages of Auden's Ideology', *Third Book of Criticism*, p. 157.
10. See 'The youngest son, the youngest one/ was certainly no wise one/ Yet could surprise one', E.A., p. 34; this invokes the character of a 'youngest son', thought a simpleton, who succeeds where his older brothers fail, as in 'The Golden Goose' and 'The Waters of Life'.
11. 'And the age ended', E.A., pp. 255–56.

97

12. "O where are you going?", E.A., p. 110; 'Now the leaves are falling fast', E.A., p. 159.
13. 'Suppose he'd listened to the erudite committee', W. H. Auden, C.P., p. 229.
14. Jarrell, 'Changes of Attitude', *Third Book of Criticism*, p. 118.
15. W. H. Auden, 'Grimm and Anderson', *Forewords and Afterwords*, p. 197.
16. W. H. Auden, 'The Quest Hero', *Tolkien and the Critics*, pp. 44–5.
17. Ibid., p. 45.
18. 'Now through night's caressing grip', E.A., pp. 283–84.
19. 'Dear, though the night is gone', E.A., p. 161.
20. 'The earth turns over', E.A., p. 145.
21. 'Miss Gee', E.A., pp. 214–15.
22. 'Sir, no man's enemy', E.A., p. 36.
23. 'September 1st, 1939', E.A., p. 246.
24. 'Now the leaves are falling fast', E.A., p. 159.
25. 'The Capital', E.A., p. 236.
26. 'Enter with him', E.A., p. 114.
27. 'They noted that virginity was needed', C.P., p. 227.
28. 'Fresh addenda are published every day', C.P., pp. 228–29.
29. See Anne Sexton, *Transformations* (Oxford, 1970); Liz Lochhead, *The Grimm Sisters* (Next Editions, 1980), Olga Broumas, *Beginning with O* (Harper, 1977). For a survey of women poets who take mythical subjects, see Alicia Ostriker, 'The Thieves of Language: Women Poets and Revisionist Myth-making', *Signs*, Autumn 1982, Vol. 8, No. 1.
30. See n. 16.
31. See S. Gilbert and S. Gubar, *The Madwoman in the Attic* (Yale, 1979), pp. 1–42; also Mary Jacobus' review, *Signs* (Spring 1981), 517–23.
32. See 'Tam Lin' and 'Ariadne', Liz Lochhead, op. cit; 'Cinderella', O. Broumas, op. cit.; Anne Sexton, 'Briar Rose', op. cit.
33. This poem first appeared as part of the long narrative poem 'In the year of my youth' (1932), printed in the *Review of English Studies* (Autumn 1978).
34. 'The Witnesses', E.A., p. 128.
35. Ibid.
36. Christopher Isherwood, *Lions and Shadows* (Signet, 1970), 128.
37. 'I have a handsome profile', E.A., p. 123.
38. 'The Witnesses', E.A., p. 128.
39. 'Now from my windowsill', E.A., pp. 115–16.
40. 'The Witnesses', E.A., p. 130.
41. John Fuller, *A Reader's Guide to W. H. Auden* (Thames and Hudson, 1970), pp. 83–4.
42. 'The Witnesses', E.A., p. 129.
43. R. Kipling, *Definitive Edition of Kipling's Verse* (Hodder, 1941), p. 793.
44. 'The Witnesses', E.A., p. 130.
45. Ibid., p. 129.
46. See MacDiarmid, 'In the year of my youth', R.E.S., p. 295; also Carpenter, op. cit., pp. 146–47.
47. 'Who will endure', E.A., p. 54.

48. Bruno Bettelheim, *The Uses of Enchantment: The meaning and Importance of Fairy Tales* (Peregrine, 1976).
49. R. Barthes, *Mythologies* (Paladin, 1970).
50. See Ian Jeffrey, 'A Feeling for the Past: Photojournalism' in the catalogue to The 'Thirties Exhibition (Arts Council publications, 1980), pp. 109–20.
51. 'The Summer holds', E.A., pp. 282.
52. Isherwood, op. cit., pp. 60–72.
53. A point made by Bernard Bergonzi in *Reading the Thirties* (Macmillan, 1978), pp. 18–19.
54. See Colin Watson, *Snobbery with Violence* (Eyre & Spottiswoode, 1971). Agatha Christie's *The Murder of Roger Ackroyd* is a classic in this genre.
55. Auden 'The Guilty Vicarage', *The Dyer's Hand* (Vintage Books, 1968), pp. 146–58.
56. 'Detective Story', E.A., p. 204.
57. 'Beethameer, Beethameer, bully of Britain', E.A., p. 87.
58. Again, Bernard Bergonzi has a full discussion of the Audenesque obsession with school in the chapter 'Men among boys, boys among men', *Reading the Thirties*, pp. 10–37.
59. Samuel Hynes, *The Auden Generation* (Faber, 1976), p. 14.
60. 'Let the eye of the traveller', E.A., p. 287.
61. 'It's farewell to the drawing-room's civilized cry', E.A., p. 208.
62. 'Letter to Lord Byron', Part II, E.A., 179.
63. Ibid.
64. Erich Fromm, *The Fear of Freedom* (Routledge, 1944); Wilhelm Reich, *The Mass Psychology of Fascism*, tr. V. R. Carfagno (Farrar, Straus and Giroux, 1979).
65. 'Where do They come from', E.A., p. 243.
66. 'Out on the lawn I lie in bed', E.A., p. 137.
67. 'Where do They come from', E.A., p. 243.
68. 'Letter to Lord Byron', Part II, E.A., 181.
69. 'They make a desert and call it peace', Tacitus, *Agricola* 30.
70. 'Letter to Lord Byron', E.A., p. 181.
71. 'August 1968', C.P., p. 104.
72. Cf. the appendix on Newspeak in *Nineteen Eighty-four*; also the essay 'Politics and the English Language' collected in *Inside the Whale and other essays* (Penguin, 1964).
73. Kipling, 'At the end of the passage', *Life's Handicap* (1907), p. 204.

# 4

# Auden's Images

## by WILLIAM LOGAN

*1*

Like so many elements of his practice, Auden's imagery
deserves a book, though both his attitude and his compulsion
might be more honoured, and more accommodated, by an
encyclopedia. Those whose tastes enforce a division between
his poems early and late, or between the English Wystan and
the American Auden, respond to a difference of which the
image is necessarily a part. One may prefer early Auden for his
tropes and later Auden for his mind without suggesting that the
mind earlier or the images later were commonplace or insub-
stantial. In the early poems, however, the images are conspicuous for the ideas they enact; in the later poems they often
merely support or uphold what the mind wishes to call
attention to, once leading actors reduced to pages and footmen,
if not footnotes.[1]

Auden's verse is characteristically mechanical; its very
facility marks its calculation. Poem after poem, the lines are
bodied forth with the effusive cleverness of the schoolboy or the
sour enthusiasm of the don, but these are masks more than true
manners—a coldness underlies them. The lines spew forth as if
utterly interchangeable, one image for another, one rhyme for
another, like the moralizing couplets of Shakespeare's sonnets.[2]
It would not be surprising if either poet found in his agility a
kind of disgrace; the honesties and warmth we impute to their
poems may have been alien to their makers. Auden's early

100

preoccupation with machinery was incarnated in the stamping dies that minted his images. He seems less a craftsman, at home with his leather belt and bench, than the owner of a vast factory, less Fabergé than Henry Ford.

Consider the list. The list may derive from a preciseness, even a prissiness, that must tyrannize in order to suggest ('Moraine, pot, oxbow, glint, sink, crater, piedmont, dimple') or from an inventive faculty that cannot suffer the *bon mot* when *bon mots* will do ('when any world is to be wrecked,/ Blown up, burnt down, cracked open,/ Felled, sawn in two, hacked through, torn apart'). There is something faintly comic in the seriousness of a list, an inadequacy of language only over-adequacy will satisfy.[3]

Auden's habits were cumulative, not integrative; he did not develop the Shakespearean instinct for shuffling through metaphors like cards. If his imagination was clerkly, it had to account for experience in such emphases as the list allowed. By its very accumulation the list may rummage through human acquisition ('under the eaves, in bulging boxes,/ Hats, veils, ribbons, galoshes, programs, letters/ Wait unworshipped'). It may scrupulously articulate a progression ('A word, a laugh, a footstep, a truck's outcry') that would otherwise require a street of extras or an army of adjectives. At best a list's elements exist in delicate tension ('The roads, the illegitimates, the goats', 'Yes-man, the bar-companion, the easily-duped'); at worst they collapse into a rag-bag of metre and meaning ('an important decision made on a lake,/ An illness, a beard, Arabia found in a bed,/ Nanny defeated, Money', 'Nocturnal trivia, torts and dramas,/ Wrecks, arrivals, rose-bushes, armies,/ Leopards and laughs'). The list may become so long that it strangles its function; it may become merely a listing, its co-ordinates unco-ordinated.

One cannot escape, however, the playfulness and utter wilfulness of a world arranged by threes and fours: 'The physician, bridegroom and incendiary'; 'The dog, the lady with parcels, and the boy'; 'dandruff, night-starvation, or B.O.'; 'motor-bikes, photography, and whales'; 'A judge, a landscape, and a wife'; 'Orchid, swan, and Caesar'; 'Enigmas, executioners and rules'; 'gendarmes, banks/ And aspirin'; 'temples, tombs, and terminal god'; 'surf-riding, claret, sex';

'drains, bananas, bicycles, and tin'; 'sunsets, passion, God, and Keats'; 'The septic East, a war, new flowers and new dresses'; 'A phonograph, a radio, a car and a frigidaire'; 'doubts, reproaches, boredom, the unknown'.

The list has large ambitions, but its means are small and additive, even addictive. It is as old as Homer's catalogue of ships, or older; that list was filched, internal evidence suggests, from an earlier poem. Auden could make and later disown a poem ('Spain 1937') from a sequence of lists, a catalogue of catalogues. The list, however, is subject to its inner limitations, its stutter. It can contribute to dramatic action, but it cannot normally be that action. By its nature it stalls, interrupts, prepares instead of provokes. The action and ambition must be elsewhere. The list serves as a locus of attention, and everywhere in his work Auden relied on technique or typography to supply similar loci, forces at work outside argument.

Our language was impoverished when typographical practice ceased to employ the capital as a common mark of emphasis, restricting it, like some *grande dame* of etiquette, largely to *proper* nouns, *proper* names. Auden's fondness for the Augustan Age may have suggested the force of capitalizing his notions, of moving, as he writes in an early poem, 'From the alone to the Alone'.[4] The capitals do not merely isolate and aggrandize; they have a personifying force, and therefore claim as their parent not Pope but Langland.

The character of Auden's abstractions only mirrors—in the way that a repressed don once through the Looking-Glass becomes a mad, triumphant logician—the abstraction of his characters. Wrath and Gluttony and Greed totter forth like Wonderland's pack of cards: 'Wrath who has learnt every trick of guerrilla warfare,/ The shamming dead, the night-raid, the feinted retreat'; then 'Gluttony living alone, austerer than us,/ Big simple Greed'.[5] They are neither so human that they can completely clothe themselves in allegory nor so inhuman that they lack a rudimentary psychology or anatomy. Theirs is a world of shadow actions; and if they often seem to partake only ironically of the world of being, it is because they are often occupied only ironically in that world. Their importance is exemplary, and they are introduced so their heads may decorate the gates of the palace, if we take meaning to be palatial and not circumstantial—that is, an action toward which actions are directed, not an accident of action (as Auden well knew, form calls forth its accidents, and we allow ourselves later to call inevitable what arrived by chance).

Most imaginations are habitual; they repeat their successes until they are failures. The implacable oddness that becomes a style (as a beauty may become an occasion, or a Beauty an Occasion), easily deteriorates into the tic of nervous affliction. When the capital letters have become a plague, noun infects noun until almost all are in danger of catching it. One may distinguish, however, between those nouns representing some political or social tendency (the Social Beast, Hobbesian Man, A Gadgeted Age, an Age of Care, the Daily Papers, My Personal City, The Unpolitical, The Hidden Law), psychological archetype (the Shadow, the Quest Perilous, the Not-Alone, The Higher Mind, the Naughty One), mere abstraction (Death, Success, Wrong, Duality, Goodness, Law, Dread), and various cartographic and historical entitlements (that Bridge of Dread, the Battle of Whispers, Cape Consumption, the Tosspot Seas, the Sneerers' Ball, the glum Reptilian Empire), though these categories, especially the last, bleed into one another.

Through the '30s Auden increased his tolerance for capitals until they had become an addiction, and finally a mannerism. It startles at first to come across 'gaga Falsehood' or 'Beauty scratching miserably for food', 'The Good Life' or 'Reality'. As with any addiction, however, the dose must be increased to maintain the level of satisfaction, and soon all of Auden's nouns are willy-nilly candidates for apotheosis, whether it is the 'Lost People' or merely 'Real Estate'. This is not to minimize the effects of Auden's capitals. There is a great difference between saying 'To go elsewhere' and 'To go Elsewhere'.[6] The first emphasizes the leaving, the second the arriving, and arriving at a place so firmly Other that it is not marked on any map. The first has a departure, the second a destination. *Another Time* (1940), Auden's first book after leaving England, marks the border where he exiled himself in the neutral country of literature, though from its safe estates he allowed himself to issue bulletins on the battles he had evaded. It is a book made up of capitals as well as literary capitalists: Auden's pre-Christian pantheon of Housman, Lear, Rimbaud, Melville, Pascal, Voltaire, Arnold, Yeats and Freud, with artistic nods toward Orpheus, The Novelist, Old Masters and The Composer.

The ennoblement of nouns had effect when practised discretely. If all common nouns are in danger of becoming lords, where will the commoners be to make the lords *feel* like lords? Like all kings, Auden played favourites, elevating one noun through revision only to lower another: 'Lords of limit' became 'Lords of Limit', the 'Lost People' the 'lost people'. An occasional countervailing tendency, in one who (like One) 'numbers each particle/ by its Proper Name',[7] reduced proper names to improper ones. Time and usage can rub away Plato to 'a platonic pash', Descartes to 'a cartesian doubt', but Auden's attempt to gain acceptance and accession for his terms (and the capitals assume an act of recognition by the reader) went further, to 'the raging herod of the will'; 'a kantian conscience'; 'De-narcissus-ized en-/ -during excrement'[8]; 'some mallarmesque/ syllabic fog'; and even 'How grahamgreeneish!' Capital letters can of course appear without escort, either masking an identity at an historical costume party ('N died (to be replaced by S)// And took T's job' where the figures are Napoleon, Stalin and Tamburlaine), or enforcing an anonymity ('Conductor X, that over-rated bore'; 'Director Y'; 'Z the Designer').[9]

The personifying tendency elsewhere supports the inhuman world's appropriation of the human, whether it is signalled by adjective ('the griping fern', 'the faithful roses') or, more usually, dramatized with Auden's insouciant air of inappropriateness: 'The stone is content/ With a formal anger'; 'The roads are so careless, the rivers so rude'; 'The prudent atom/ Simply insists upon its safety now'; 'snap/ Verdicts of sharks'; 'The disconsolate clocks are crying together'; 'cold's victorious wrestle/ With molten metal'. For Auden the pathetic fallacy never existed. Though many of these inventions are ambiguously light in intention and dangerously comic in effect, like those crying clocks, they create a world of social expression in which individual psychology projects its emotions outward upon the objects it cannot control, which seem in fact to possess perverse wills and desires. Auden's device admits what many poets have trouble denying—that the world acts as if rivers knew no etiquette and sharks sat in judgement (they are particularly suited for *snap* verdicts).

Abstractions own the landscape in Auden, and have private provinces and duchies in recognition of their status. Their ownership is guaranteed through the deed of *of*; the resulting metaphors create a panorama of incongruous and monumental geography: 'the valley of regret'; 'the dykes of our content'; 'The pool of silence'; 'Your map of desolation'; 'the haphazard alleys of the neighbours' pity'; 'The silent dumps of unemployed'; 'White shores of longing'; 'The green Bohemia of that myth'. More rarely, the house and grounds provide a domestic topography: 'the sudden mansion/ Of any joy'; 'the tower of a stammer'; 'the staircase of events'; 'the poky nursery of the brain'; 'the broken ladders of our lives'; 'All bolts of custom made secure'; 'the table of a father's rage'. Even the animal or human world may contribute its possessions: 'what worm of guilt'; 'the body of his happiness'; 'The hot rampageous horses of my will'; 'the beasts and cripples of resentment'; 'a coma of waiting'; 'the huge wild beast of the Unexpected'.

It may not seem, given Auden's generative capacity, to make much difference whether the stammer is a tower or a tor, desolation a map or a millrace; but their adventitious eccentricity must be bound the more firmly into the poem if they are not to seem mere ornament. The 'map of desolation' is something to be folded by a man under a tree, 'the tower of a stammer' not merely where someone is 'prisoned', but a feature mimicking the throat or neck. When events are a staircase they can be climbed (and they occur one at a time, and in order); the brain when a 'poky nursery' contains the dreads and desires of infancy. Such associations may be weak, as Auden may be weak; but the intention to anchor the metaphors, even or especially when they are employed for distraction, suggests how much Auden did not want his devices to *seem* merely devices, how much their presence was meant to support the order of the poem.

It may seem superfluous to say so, except that Auden was often by choice a frivolous and shallow poet. His devices, repeated with his easy negligence, came year by year to seem less the master's touch than the apprentice's ungainly mimicry.

His descent into light verse in the mid-'30s[10] produced some of the masterpieces of his canon, but the effect of such masterpieces seems to have been an inability ever to recover the unself-conscious and direct quality of his earlier poems, those which for many readers make Auden Auden. It could be argued that Auden was unable to sustain the manner of his early poems and had to cast about for compelling or comfortable alternatives; he was always a poet for comfort, and his late manner (or his late manner, then his later manner, then his last manner) behind the trappings and obstacles of form grew progressively cozy. Few would want to sacrifice the sharpest inventions of his light verse, early or late; they revivified a form much sneered at. However, the ponderous over-reaction of his poems of the late '30s and early '40s, and the frivolousness increasingly woven into serious poems, *could* be blamed on the discovery that one could be serious by being shallow (some of Auden's late poems discovered the reverse).

The tendency to dramatize abstraction is often a special if striking use of Auden's favourite device, the vignette. To a great extent, Auden used image as an archetype, divorced of the particulars that would specify or control it. His nouns, for example, are often features separated from landscape, existing more in the textbook than in any local topography ('Wind shakes the tree; the mountains darken'). Whatever realm the nouns derive from, they are isolated from actual circumstance, as if chosen from some Platonic catalogue, issued quarterly. Auden's images are essentially mental; it does not seem that his objects have been seen before they have been imagined. They have passed through the rectifying and distorting machinery of the imagination, if indeed they did not wholly originate there. Auden's world was essentially colourless, and distant scholarship may well quarrel over whether this was a social judgement or the result of colour blindness (it was mere distaste—'I've absolutely no use for colour', the young 'Hugh Weston' said to Christopher Isherwood).[11]

The vignette contrived the social life Auden found necessary but not sufficient. If Auden's poems were about life, they were about the life of mind; the vignettes exemplify life without over-representing it. Their small dramas reduced the compass of the world to the limits of one action. Existing mostly at the edge of the frame, they are mentioned only to be ignored, like Breughel's Icarus. In 'Musée des Beaux Arts', Auden's great poem on marginality, Icarus fatally plunges into the sea, ignored by the minor actors elsewhere in the painting, actors who under other circumstances might be similarly and fatally ignored (as, in another poem, 'The sinister tall-hatted botanist stoops at the spring/ With his insignificant phial, and looses/ The plague on the ignorant town').[12]

Such vignettes frequently have no effect on the course of the poem, and constitute dramas half-glimpsed, stories half-told.[13] The human condition exists in them, or through them, but it is the condition of that condition to be hurrying elsewhere. They offer a suggestiveness forever shorn of resolution: 'the blond boy/ Bites eagerly into the shining/ Apple'; 'A little crowd smash up a shop'; 'But the poor fat old banker in the sun-parlor car/ Has no one to love him except his cigar'; 'the frowning schoolgirl may/ Be dying to be asked to stay'; 'Altogether elsewhere, vast/ Herds of reindeer move across/ Miles and miles of golden moss,/ Silently and very fast'; 'A stranger's quiet collapse in a noisy street'; 'when elevators/ Raise blondes aloft to bachelor suites'; 'The mad gym-mistress, made to resign,/ Can pinch no more'.

Auden had a fondness for the double epithet or composite adjective, itself often a condensed or compressed vignette: 'The shepherd-killing thunderstorm'; 'the jaw-dropped/ Mildewed mob'; 'its skirt-and-bargain-chasing eye'; 'The honking bottom-pinching clown'; 'that eye-on-the-object look'; 'the bowel-loosening/ nasal war cry'; 'an Emperor's/ balda-chined and nightly-redamselled couch'. Elsewhere these adjectives are shards of simile, memories of metaphor: 'cloud-soft hand'; 'the dry-as-bone/ Night of the soul'; 'she joins girl's-ear lakes/ to bird's foot deltas'. Such hyphenated compression reads as desperation, an attempt to forge the new from material that, expanded, would seem commonplace or stale. Auden's devices frequently have a similar desperation at centre, an anxiety that the plain statement will prove too homely. The vocabulary of the *O.E.D.*, which in the final books became a menace, could not always hide the retailing of second-hand ideas.[14]

The vignette could deteriorate into delightful absurdity if

the landscape were allowed to caper or frolic: 'the river jumps over the mountain/ And the salmon sing in the street'; 'When the mountains swim away with slow calm strokes'; 'A burning village scampered down a lane'; or, in a less cartographic vein, 'The tables and chairs say suitable prayers'; 'In pelagic meadows/ The plankton open their parachutes'; 'dreams of cities where his cows are whores'. The majority of these moments were elected to represent the impossible or sublimely ridiculous, but Auden could easily become the lackey of his charms. It is not that tables and chairs play out their neuroses as atheists, but that such foolery could register as an anxious flight from seriousness.

The rhetorical device with which Auden is most associated is the simile. The particular ironic and idiosyncratic type he patented was, though present early in his poetry, largely confined to half a decade, 1936–41. Auden's most characteristic similes depend on utter incongruity, and proceed along a continuum from the apposite to the severely unlikely, from the apprehensible to the absurd. Unlike the similes of the Martian school, which are almost wholly a dislocation of the visual, Auden's similes work deeper and more indirect associations. There is rarely in his work that surprising exactness or rightness that attends the perfect simile elsewhere (and the Martian similes, which often confuse or mislead the reader the better to provide a subsequent Aha of surprise). Auden's similes exploit a suspicion that the comparison cannot possibly be apt; to make it so, the reader is forced to that leap of faith a *discordia concors* occasions.

In early poems, Auden's similes often let context inform their effects: 'Here a scrum breaks up like a bomb' depends on the previous line, 'War is declared there, here a treaty signed'; 'Do thoughts grow like feathers' on 'What's in your mind, my dove'. Others have an ominous visual aptitude, less exact than eerie: 'gradual ruin spreading like a stain'; 'fallen bicycles like huddled corpses'. As the gimmick propagates (like a farm, say, or a fire), its terms seem increasingly improbable: 'Who pursued understanding with patience like a sex'; 'Your breath's like luggage'; 'easy as a vow'.

Vows are not particularly easy, either to make or to keep, and context gives little comfort: 'Climbing with you was easy as a vow;/ We reached the top not hungry in the least'.[15] This may support 'Climbing with you was easy as a vow is easy', or 'as this particular vow was easy', or 'Climbing with you was as easy as making a vow to do so'. It may even suggest that as long as climbing was *considered* a vow, it was easy. Depending on his preference, the reader may have to posit a world where vows are made as effortlessly as broken, where the climb (and this particular climb has sexual significance) was no more morally or physically corrupting than a New Year's resolution forgotten on New Year's Day. The complicated reasoning such similes demand results from limiting the comparison to something not immediately apparent, or at least something that cannot immediately be assented to.

It is at times easier to acquiesce to the incongruity than attempt to untangle it. The similes of greatest compression, however, are often the most satisfying; they arrive like a small electric shock: 'remote as plants'; 'never nude and calm like a great door'; 'wears a stammer like a decoration'; *'casual as birds'*; 'the sea/ Calm as a clock'; 'Crooked to move as a moneybug or a cancer'; 'he frowned like thunder'; 'The winter holds them like the Opera'; 'Kept tears like dirty postcards in a drawer'; 'flinch from the horizon like a gun'; 'Anxiety/ Receives them like a grand hotel'; 'Our money sang like streams'. Because they distort an object to favour a resemblance, such similes are highly artificial, often dependent on suppressed metaphor; they emphasize rather than explain. Not simply subservient to appearance or other intrinsic qualities, they recast their objects: 'wears a stammer like a decoration', if a stammer is something to be worn; 'casual as birds', if birds are casual. The manner, as so often, easily became mannerism, and Auden's giddy ingenuity is equally responsible for 'the poets exploding like bombs'; 'hairless people/ Who like a cereal have inherited these valleys'; and 'As a trombone the clerk will bravely/ Go oompah-oompah to his minor grave'. The last is preceded by 'Metaphor bamboozles the most oppressed'.

The simile has often been considered a weak rhetorical device, whimperingly dependent on qualities that little need elaboration, tediously explicating what metaphor would pounce on. Auden's achievement was to transform the simile into a compressed vignette, an epic simile of dwarfish shape, dramatizing its objects without overwhelming them, unlike the similes of the Martian school. Auden's tropes were still mastered by their objects, but objects altered to accommodate the sense of the simile. By such displacement new meaning was smuggled in; the simile was for Auden a form of order, not ornament.

There is no space here to consider those rhetorical imageries Auden handled well, even magnificently, but not oddly or unusually. His metaphors, for instance: 'a hawk's vertical stooping from the sky'; 'Some possible dream, long coiled in the ammonite's slumber'[16]; 'empires stiff in their brocaded glory'; 'Truth is convertible to kilowatts'. Of them a chapter could be made, with perhaps a short note on unusual verbs ('that God or Nature will abrupt her earthly function', 'Shall we ever become adulted', 'dwellings/ vacancied long ago', 'I'll coffin you up'), and the compulsive use of certain adjectives, like 'crooked'.

Auden's rhetorics are a kind of exhaustion, as if an infinitely complex calculating machine programmed to certain toler- ances had churned out endless examples of a type. The repetition of means may explain why Auden so often changed his forms; his limitations were less evident when constantly employed for different ends. Yet these same limitations created an expectation they gradually fulfilled. They may be what we mean by style: not what one does but what one cannot help but do. It is not attractive to think of genius as a residue, as what the author is least responsible for, and may least value; but the images of Auden's poems order themselves into strategies that drive other strategies out. Auden's imagination found certain types of expression and certain subjects immensely congenial or immensely useful. His attach- ment to them reads less as possession than embrace.

2

Auden's imagery is a system, and a system coherent and controlled, though perhaps not at every level conscious. It gives a greater impression of unity, of the collaboration of many compulsions, than that of most poets—that is, it expresses an Ur-Story, a view of the world actual and ideal, yet one too idiosyncratic to command complete conviction from any reader. Auden's early poems are reports from a front that has not yet been opened, a border that exists only by some mental cartography. His images recur with such frequency that he does not seem to have to seek for them. In later poems the particular imagery of this world was diffused, an old myth whose elements lingered long after belief had vanished.

The key line in early Auden is perhaps 'For the game is in progress which tends to become like a war' (from a poem later dropped from the canon).[17] The poem is about love, but the game is played in earnest. Only through two qualifications is it allowed to become warlike—that it tends to become so (but need not), and that it tends to become *like* a war (not necessarily a war itself). Auden was not everywhere so hesitant to identify the combat around or within him. He could even joke about it:

> Lone scholars, sniping from the walls
> Of learned periodicals,
> > Our facts defend,
> Our intellectual marines,
> Landing in little magazines,
> > Capture a trend.[18]

Elsewhere, 'From morning to night, flowers duel incessantly,/ Color against color, in combats// Which they all win.'[19] Any sort of conflict (even the fight of the flowers) may be seen in terms of battle, but in Auden from the earliest poems the world is a battlefield where secret wars are being fought. These wars may be secret because they are fought within, or because others do not recognize that they are being fought without; in either case it is the poet's duty not merely to chronicle them but to enlist himself on the right side. Auden's twin gods of inner and outer are Freud and Marx; he appropriates the doctrines of both without fully converting to the religion of either.

Auden's early images were private and ingrown. They derived at times from the school world of his friends and acquaintances, and even their private languages and pet names; later, as Auden moved through Europe and taught in small schools in England, they incorporated fragments from private life. The Tower in one poem is not the destination of Childe Roland or any architecture of allegory, but a local cinema.[20] Context provides no clue, and the reader may assume the detail to be allegorical when it is merely personal. Early or late, Auden's images were forced from the personal toward the allegorical. The references may have been plain to Auden's circle, for the poems served as a public encoding of private thoughts, to be deciphered by those possessing the code (even if it were the property of Auden alone). It is not clear how much the world of the public school suggested or required these early fantasies of Us versus Them, but the fantasy soon matured into a lumpish *Weltanschauung*: 'the mouse we banished yesterday/ Is an enraged rhinoceros today.'[21]

Auden suggested in 'September 1, 1939' (the date of Hitler's invasion of Poland, and again a poem dropped from the canon) that 'I and the public know/ What all schoolchildren learn,/ Those to whom evil is done/ Do evil in return.'[22] It may not be unusual for children, especially male children, to acquit themselves in their fantasies of war; boys' magazines are as guilty of encouragement as newspapers. Auden's vision was weighted by the casual murders and strict codes of the Icelandic sagas, to which by birth and temperament he was early attracted (he was later to translate them). His particular home theatre crossed the betrayals and violence of the sagas with those of the schoolboy world, and from them forced a landscape where belief matched blood, where idea was an irritant.[23] Not many schoolboys are Auden, though more than a few have made lives from martial fantasies.

There is a war, then, or two sides engaged in an unnamed and unnameable conflict. The sides become countries, the countries share a border. The border is the mastering symbol of Auden's early poems. Psychological, political, or sexual, it suggests a demarcation between sides as well as an inter-section of them. It may appear variously as a frontier, a partition, a boundary, or merely a line: 'Before you reach the frontier you are caught'; 'Frontiers to cross'; 'frontier-conscious'; 'Love by ambition/ Of definition/ Suffers partition'; 'where two fears intersect'; 'not stopped at/ Borders by guards'; 'Where boundaries converge'; 'Upon this line between adventure'; 'The frontier of my Person'. The war may be imminent or declared: 'morning's levelled gun'; 'Are you aware what weapon you are loading'; 'Soldiers who swarm in the pubs in their pretty clothes'; 'The sharp crude patterns generals make'; 'Europe's frozen soldiery'; 'The violent howling of winter and war'. As the '30s progressed, the imaginary wars became actual ones, and it was either Auden's gift to have seen where the tensions tended or his fate to have his private system made public.

The landscape of these countries in tension may be strewn with barbed wire and guarded by sentries: 'The barbed wire runs through the abolished City'; 'Barbed wire enclosed an arbitrary spot'; 'Sentries against inner and outer'; 'Its sentinels yet keep their sleepless station'; 'The seasons stood like guards'; 'the guards at the front gate'; 'peasants with penthouse eyebrows/ Sullenly guard the sluices'. The world is a system of entrances, exits, passages, bridges, gates: 'Control of the passes was, he saw, the key'; 'We are the guardians of the gate in the rock'; 'through a low tunnel'; 'passports expire and ports are watched'; 'Through gates that will not relatch/ And doors marked *Private*'; 'On the bridge between your properties'; 'that narrow pass'. These are places of transition and danger, where to be safe one has to change identity. The lovers who stand on the bridge between the properties of the ambassador and the admiral *seem* safe in the power and glory of their love, unaffected by past wars and lost provinces. This is illusory:

> Nothing your strength, your skill, could do
>   Can alter their embrace
> Or dispersuade the Furies who
>   At the appointed place
> With claw and dreadful brow
>   Wait for them now.[24]

The war can be reduced to (or can destroy) love and lovers, and the frontier may be only the boundary of the self. There is always an enemy: 'Orders are given to the enemy for a time'; 'the visible enemy'; 'His enemies undone'; 'It is an enemy that sighs for you' (this last is followed by 'Love has one wish and that is, not to be'). The air is full of conspiracy and revolution:

'Waiting with bombs of conspiracy/ In arm-pit secrecy';
'Shooting and barricade in street'; 'what chances are of
revolution'; 'a loud/ And foreign language of revolt'; 'one
revolution/ Registers all things' (such imagery could again
become literal after the '60s—'young radicals plotting/ to
blow up a building'). The world is populated by strangers
('A stranger to strangers over undried sea'; 'Go home, now,
stranger'; 'Look, stranger, at this island now'); assassins
('Patrolling the gardens to keep assassins away'; 'It's like
some hidden assassin'; 'single assassins'; 'walked like an
assassin through the town'; 'scented assassins'), and spies
('the trained spy'; 'Our hopes were set still on the spies'
career'; 'As agents their importance quickly ceased'). There
is some personal identification with all these silent, secretive
actors, especially the spy, who because of his intellect, his
homosexuality, or his political beliefs, must always inhabit a
country whose intentions are hostile. Like the exile, he may
never be able to affect the decision of his false world or
communicate to a true one ('They ignored his wires./ The
bridges were unbuilt and trouble coming').[25] He must live
masked, his utterances safe in their species of code.

I need not linger on the talk of missions, groups (both good
and bad—'the belovèd group'; 'The gross behaviour of a
group'; 'the erudite committee'; 'vacant crowds'), secrets,
and escapes. The imagery is markedly juvenile, almost
embarrassing in its schoolyard vision, as what conflict is not?
Auden's 'charade' *Paid on Both Sides* and his 'English study'
*The Orators* (the country-house and public-school origins of
*charade* and *study* summon up only a little less quickly the
respective false and ironic associations) detail the psychology
of the group at war, a group that seems strikingly like, when
it is not in fact, a bunch of schoolboys variously afflicted with
cynicism and idealism. Soldiers are often not far removed
from the schoolyard; the playing fields of Eton, not Oxford,
determine the course of battle. The wars fought through such
imagery are distant from the Battle of the Marne or the
Bulge, from Ypres or St. Lô. The men who win these paper
battles are not later crippled veterans holding the Croix de
Guerre, the Victoria Cross, or the Silver Star; they are *heroes*:
'the would-be hero of the soul'; 'The mental hero who has

114

swooned'; 'The hero worship of the immature'; 'The hero was as daring as they thought him'; 'A hero owes a duty to his fame'; 'Where heroes roar and die'; 'the hero's/ Leap into love'.

Shorn of identifying characteristics, such nouns are already half-way to allegory. It is hard to know how much the mental landscape thereby impoverishes the physical one, yet the virtue of Auden's work is precisely its removal from the physical world and its substitution of a mental and moral discipline. Auden used the horrors of war, at least early in his career, to veer into his private imagery; and he tended to drop from his canon those poems, like 'Spain 1937' and 'September 1, 1939', which too overtly or too ambivalently practised politics. This first realm of his imagery, war and conflict, could stand under the stone figure of St. Freud (the old gods become the new religion's saints) for something as private and dangerous as love. Under the stone figure of St. Marx, it became a class war: 'the retired and rich/ From the french windows of their sheltered mansions'; 'where the rich are always waiting'; 'isolated like the very rich'; 'the monuments of an acquisitive society'; 'the great boots of the rich on our faces'; these against 'The ugly and the poor'; 'the poor in their fireless lodgings'; 'helpless as the poor have always been'; 'The low recessive houses of the poor'.

The second realm of Auden's imagery lies in nature, pastoral as counter-image to politics. The transitional image is that of the map, which may, depending on its use and its user, be benign or malignant: 'Conjectures on the maps'; 'With the finest of mapping pens'; 'a map of the country'; 'Gone from the map the shore where childhood played'; 'the map of his life'; 'like a lying map'; 'Look in the atlas and you'll find it there'; 'generals are already poring over maps'; 'might-be maps of might-have-been campaigns'; 'The maps at his disposal were out of date'.

Auden's topography is northern. Born in York of a family claiming Icelandic descent (later he equivocally notes, 'First I write *I was born in York*; then, *I was born in New York*'),[26] he could not shirk the northern temperament or the landscape that created it.[27] Except under the circumstance of travel (and Auden's first travel book was *Letters from Iceland*, as northern as one might wish to be), his maps illustrate a hard, glacial topography: 'From scars where kestrels hover'; 'Under the headlands in their windy dwelling'; 'the issue of steam from a cleft'; 'limestone heights'; 'Curlews on kettle moraines'; 'granite wastes'; 'up-thrust, crevasse-and-avalanche, troll country'; 'lonely on fell as chat,/ By pot-holed becks'; 'Rising in joy over wolds'; 'This fortress perched on the edge of the Atlantic scarp'; 'Tundras intense and irresponsive seas'.

The landscape is cold and forbidding, everywhere hemmed in by glaciers: 'glaciers calving'; 'far from the glacier'; 'The ice-sheet moving down'; 'the encroaching glaciers of despair'; 'the glitter/ Of glaciers'; 'The glacier knocks in the cupboard'; 'glaciers glitter in a chilly evening'; 'The horse-shoe glaciers curled up and died'; 'the glaciers guarding the Good Place'; 'Of gloom and glaciers'; 'between two glaciers'. Circumstances determine its employment, but it is an image ominously available, even as a chilling domestic feature ('The glacier knocks in the cupboard' has harsh associations of dearth and famine, though it might have proved an amusing description of a refrigerator).

Auden's landscapes are not otherwise exceptional, though their elements may be drawn into psychology or emotion: 'In strangled orchards'; 'our dreadful wood'; 'most desires end up in stinking ponds'; 'Saw in a fish-pool something horrid with a hay-rake'; 'orchards cling to the regime/ they know'; 'Trees are proud of their posture'; 'The mental mountains and the psychic creeks'; 'Our hill has made its submission'; 'the deathless minerals looked pleased'. They can have, on the other hand, a true pastoral air, free of mental fetters though at times mystical and strange: 'Hearing the frogs exhaling from the pond'; 'lush alluvial meadows'; 'down each dale'; 'from a wild to a formal vineyard'; 'Speak well of moonlight on a winding stair,/ Of light-boned children under great green oaks'; 'And the great plains are for ever where the cold fish is hunted'; 'To silent valleys on all sides'; 'By empty caves beneath an empty sky'.

Nature has its borders and battles too, and the border Auden most insistently recognized was the sea. The conjunction of these adjoining scapes finds balance in 'The eager

ridge, the steady sea',[28] where the human eagerness of 'eager'
infiltrates the suggestiveness of 'steady', not permitting it to
steady itself at the mere descriptiveness of 'fixed' or 'unvarying' but demanding the more personified 'reliable' or 'un-
wavering' (itself a suppressed pun) as a counter to the
aggressiveness of the ridge. The whole line is remarkably
*unsteady* in its reversal of rôles, the sea by erosion usually
claiming belligerence, the ridge by its firmness stability. In
Auden the sea may be 'ignorant', 'irresponsive', 'Corrosive',
'easy', 'untamed', or 'Calm as a clock'. Ships are everywhere
('into the undared ocean swung north their prow'; 'Luxury
liners laden with souls'; 'the expensive delicate ship'; 'the
stranded shipwrecks'; 'Our navy sailed away and sank';
'shadows of ships long-shattered'), as well as sailors ('learn the
sailors' words'; *'Doomed sailors'*; 'The sailors come ashore/ Out
of their hollow ships'), and piers and quays ('the ends of piers';
'Like a sea god the political orator lands at the pier';
'The effusive welcome of the pier'; 'a primitive, unsheltered
quay'; 'the watcher upon the quay'; 'the fashionable quays').

In landscape Auden discovered his psychological concomitant. The seas, caves, mountains and valleys of his disengaged
geography might have come from topographical glossaries, not
any individual observation. From the isolation of islands to the
mystery of caves, landscape plays out its dramas in psychological terms. Generalized until they form one generic domain,
the features could support any myth, generate any tale.
'Bucolics' is Auden's symbolic reading of some of them
(Winds, Woods, Mountains, Lakes, Islands, Plains, Streams),
though it omits the caves that were his personal emblem (in
'Thanksgiving for a Habitat' there are both a Cave of Making
and a Cave of Nakedness, and Isherwood recalled how 'Hugh
Weston' liked even in summer to sleep under a heavy pile of
blankets, coats, and rugs).[29] Auden's imagination worked from
the literature toward the world, rather than vice versa.

The flora and fauna of Auden's poems are ghostly presences.
In 'Posthumous Letter to Gilbert White' he asks, rhetorically,
'How many// birds and plants can I spot?' His answer: 'At
most two dozen'.[30] Would he have known a kestrel if he saw
one, or a scar? Was geography, like nature, just a series of
resonant syllables? His poems incorporate starlings, swallows,

117

sparrows, ravens, rooks, chaffinches, and even sedge-warblers, the common birds of English fields and hedgerows. His animals range further, but show a decided partiality for lions, tigers and bears, leaving the reader to wonder whether he visited them in a zoo or was merely recollecting Judy Garland's line from *The Wizard of Oz*. His odd animals and common birds, in their vague reality, might populate fairy tales. Auden's idea of nature may be said to begin with the harsh geography of northern maps and end with the chittering and growls of the Märchen.

The third realm of Auden's imagery is social life. The transition is performed by the Märchen; fairy-tales provide links to both the dreads of psychology and the heroism of the quest. The folk tales represent the past shorn of history, the static past replaced and repeated in each generation. They are the blood of the people, sometimes even the mind, and their settings are the haunted domains of nature: 'Lost in a haunted wood'; 'That calm enchanted wood'; 'the vague woods'; 'Wiltshire's witching countryside'. Their inhabitants are, in great number, ogres ('met the ogre and were turned to stone'; 'The cocky little ogre'; 'The Ogre does what ogres can'), dragons ('This is the dragon's day'; 'A sterile dragon lingered to a natural death'; 'Dragon and Knight set to with fang and sword'), witches ('A witch self-tortured as she spins'; 'The Witch gave a squawk'; 'the roaring oven/ Of a witch's heart'), giants ('The giantess shuffles nearer'; 'reasonable giants and remarkable fairies'; 'the giant who storms the sky'), dwarfs ('a sobbing dwarf/ Whom giants served only as they pleased'; 'a horror of dwarfs'), and elves and fairies ('the abolition of fairies and giants'; 'a fairy's kindness'; 'fair-haired Elves').

These are the figures the hero may meet on his quest. The quest for Auden is often the journey of spiritual discovery; it informs not only the sonnet sequence titled 'The Quest', but also *The Ascent of F6* and *The Age of Anxiety*. In later poems the hero has been tamed, become merely a traveller; in Auden the observer, whether he is the airman (and many poems exploit the overview) or the sightseer, accepts the necessary distance from events in order to judge them. The traveller mirrors the exile, who cannot choose his banishment, and cannot return;

and the spy, who journeys for others, and journeys in danger and disguise.

The fairy-tale characters symbolize for Auden the uncontrolled psychic possibility the modern age would cleanse itself of. In many examples they struggle for their lives; they are threatened as well as threatening. It is surprising even to find them in serious poetry, from which they were driven a century or two ago. There is no hope of restoring their position; in Auden they make no last stand. They are anachronisms the modern world has ground down to ghosts ('Where ghost has haunted'; 'Nor the ghost houseless'; 'any influential ghost'; 'the ghosts who haunt our lives'; 'their ghosts rise,/ Hanged or headless') or mere shadows ('chased by their shadows'; 'my ignorant shadow'; 'The shadow of his images'). The Märchen echo through other sorts of mystical or supernatural imagery, including cards ('All the dreaded cards foretell'; 'the assessment of insurance by cards,/ The divination of water'), mirrors ('a land of mirrors'; 'the room behind the mirror'; 'your echo and your mirror'), and even such ancient ceremonial occasions as marriage ('Bride and victim to a ghost'; 'deep in clear lake/ The lolling bridegroom, beautiful, there').

The mystical can easily be domesticated, appearing as an Agatha Christie mystery: 'Where the body of his happiness was first discovered'; 'Who left a hairpin in the room?'; 'The marked man of romantic thrillers'. The countryside in Auden is not even as up-to-date as in Christie. It seems to mediate between the primordial terrors of the woods and the modern contrivances of the city, and to exist in some post-medieval and pre-World War I limbo. There are knights and ladies ('chaste Milady awoke blushing'; 'The Knight at some lone cross-roads of his quest'; 'Milord chewed noisily, Milady talked'), nobility of various sorts ('A Grand Duke's glass coach'; 'Lord Lobcock'; 'evil Count ffoulkes'), and servants who might have groused in any century ('the servants' hall'; 'The stocky keepers of a wild estate'; 'he could send his servant to the wood'). Peasants lurk about: 'Tight-fisted as a peasant'; 'the pious peasant's only son'. The house and grounds, however, are the real landscape: 'One sold all his manors to fight'; 'country houses at the end of drives'; 'country houses long before the slump'; 'their secluded manors'; 'an ancient manor-house'. The home, if not the castle, was the centre of Auden's security; homes and apartments (and even the lowly bed-sitting room) have an importance only adumbrated by his sequence, 'Thanksgiving for a Habitat'.

Country life centres for Auden in manor and village: modern life in the city, a city chillingly indifferent to the human. The city models the disfigured social order, where police must always maintain a presence ('lights burn late at police stations'; 'in the policed unlucky city'). Auden's ideal may be the 'Just City', the 'Good Place', or the 'Just Society', but these are all versions of the 'Great Utopia' distant from the 'dark disordered city' (a metaphor, in fact, for Matthew Arnold; Randall Jarrell noted how often Auden turned people into landscape).[31] Auden's city is drearier and more depressing than Eliot's London, because he recognized more thoroughly the city's hopelessness. In Auden's city, his generic city (it was difficult, even when writing of, say, Macao, for him to do anything except make it a symbol), there are 'sallow oval faces', perhaps 'Faces in the subway', perhaps 'old men in hall-ways/ Tapping their barometers'. The lives are thwarted or pathetic: 'timid bar-flies boast aloud'; 'working in an office makes it worse'; 'Guilty intention still looks for a hotel'; 'behaving like an ass in front of the girls'. Even the city plan only accommodates 'Each great coercive avenue and square'.

The elements of modern life, absurd enough when singled out for praise ('Read *The New Yorker*, trust in God;/ And take short views'), categorize the absence of the spiritual, the soulless striving after material satisfactions: 'the wall/ Of public lavatories on which to scrawl'; 'I shall build myself a cathedral for home/ With a vacuum cleaner in every room'; 'the status of a broken-down/ Sofa or mutilated statue'; 'read the comic strips'; 'play Lacrosse or do the Modern Dance'; '*Pamina* may a *Time* researcher be/ To let *Tamino* take his Ph.D.' Even learning must be associated with commerce, even the characters from *The Magic Flute* end up short of funds.

The two urban institutions outside commerce and industry are science and the church. Science is forward-looking: 'In scrubbed laboratories research is hastened'; 'Nothing, says science, is impossible'; 'Science is happy to answer'. It is so forward-looking, in fact, that it may destroy us, whether with 'Honeyman's N.P.C.' or the hydrogen bomb ('unless at the nod/ of some jittery commander// I be translated in a nano-second/ to a c.c. of poisonous nothing/ in a giga-death'). Auden's hopes for science are tempered by its tendency toward amoral knowledge; it creates the circumstances where 'Quite soon computers may expel from the world/ all but the top intelligent few.' Science yearns toward the depths of space, but is anchored to 'the virile bacillus' and images of disease: 'the false journey really an illness'; 'Far from his illness'; 'germs besiege/ The walled towns'; 'When diseases waylay us'. The church, for later Auden a necessity, is earlier ridiculous, tied to outdated beliefs, offering (like the stone of Oxford) 'a bland hymn of comfort'. It can do nothing but abdicate: 'The Pope may quit to join the Oxford Groupers'; 'The Pope's turned protestant at last'. The Anglo-Catholic Auden might not have made such fun of Rome, but his faith tended to be personal and a little mystical even after his conversion, his respect reserved for Christian ideals, not idolatry.[32] The hierarchy of the church tended always to be stuffed with fools: 'my modern pieces shall be cheery/ Like English bishops on the Quantum Theory'; 'Law, says the priest with a priestly look,/ Expounding to an unpriestly people,/ Law is the words in my priestly book'; 'Clever cardinals with clammy hands'.

If neither science nor religion can offer comfort, it is the fault of the modern world's worship of industry. Everywhere in Auden men are seen by their occupations. Though some men survive outside the middle-class social order—beggars and thieves, hermits and hangmen (especially hangmen—there are a score of references to hangmen and gallows)—the world is the province of the clerk and the banker, the judge and the stockbroker, the diplomat and the doctor. The stock characters resemble the predictable gestures of the *commedia dell'arte*. Stock characters may be expected to have stock passions, and every poem must accommodate its passion before it can presume upon its intellect; or at least so the early Auden seems to have thought until he migrated to America and accepted a citizenship in prose (where intellect may presume on passion and finally drive it out altogether). In Auden's world of action, a man is only what he does.

Industry ruins, and industry is a ruin. Auden's images, despite his striving to be *au courant*, tended to derive from the

'20s and '30s, not the '60s. That he was fond of machines is well known. Though he recorded that as a child the moment came when he was forced to choose the brutal and efficient machines over the merely aesthetic ones,[33] still 'In my Eden we have a few beam-engines, saddle-tank locomotives, overshot waterwheels and other beautiful pieces of obsolete machinery to play with', and, elsewhere, 'Tramlines and slagheaps, pieces of machinery,/ That was, and still is, my ideal scenery', and even 'The enginry of which I dream/ Is moved by water or by steam.' That machinery has changed the world, Auden recognized: 'When kings were many and machines were few'; 'engines do better what biceps did'. It is difficult to find examples that suggest he thought it had changed for the better.

There is a beauty in the juxtaposition of mechanical and natural, where 'Smoke rises from factory in field', where 'The dripping mill-wheel is again turning.' But elsewhere, everywhere, the machinery is silent: 'An industry already comatose,/ Yet sparsely living'; 'The derelict lead-smelting mill'; 'the mill-wheels/ rust'; 'the shut gates of works'; 'Abandoned branch-lines'; 'decomposed machines'; and the stark list:

> Smokeless chimneys, damaged bridges, rotting wharves and
>   choked canals,
> Tramlines buckled, smashed trucks lying on their side
>   across the rails;
>
> Power-stations locked, deserted, since they drew the boiler
>   fires;
> Pylons fallen or subsiding, trailing dead high-tension wires;
>
> Head-gears gaunt on grass-grown pit-banks, seams
>   abandoned years ago. . . .[34]

This is a country abandoned to and then ruined by industry, where there is 'Equipment rusting in upweeded lanes', and in juxtaposition 'silted harbours, derelict works'. The collapsed economy produces images of general sterility and decay: 'Hearing of harvests rotting in the valleys,/ Seeing at end of street the barren mountains'; 'Through bankrupt countries where they mend the roads'; 'the sterile immature mountains'; 'some decaying orchard'; 'Conduits, ponds, canals,/ Distressed with weeds'. It is this economic dislocation, this overturn of the social order that extends through the natural one, which returns us to the first realm of confusion and contention.

The realms of Auden's images have further complications, and I have no space to explore the psychological divisions of doubles, lying, and dreams, which may be associated with both the secret wars and the world of mirrors; the telephone and post office, institutions of social connection allied to Auden's many references to gossip and rumour[35]; the ever-present and slightly terrifying symbol of the clock; the influence of the classical world, particularly Greek gods and Roman polity; or the references to Eden or Adam and Eve. The Grand Tour of Auden's imagery has yet to be taken.

Auden's early images seem, however distanced from the world, however thoroughly calculated, to derive from felt emotion, whether that experience be actual or not; the emotions may be cool, even chilly, but they are recognizably individual. The American Auden, unfortunately, used and re-used feeling that had hardened into prejudices. When his practices became habitual, they had nothing to feed on but themselves. The later career studies its exhaustions, a mere idea in one book laboured out to a sequence in the next (sometimes, indeed, a grand one). The expansive and devouring poems on literary figures are reduced or devoured to become the pathetic clerihews; the brief turns of wit that prefaced his books become the jottings or joggings (called 'Shorts') that infested them.[36] The late sequences are lovely; exhaustion can be a form of creation, but it is different from the dangerous possibilities of Auden's early work. The pulp was squeezed dry.

In his late poetry, Auden's techniques rarely created an entity sufficiently larger than his particular effects to blind the reader, however temporarily, *to* those effects. One must like the late poems *for* their devices, *for* their repetition of familiar imagery. Increasingly one must respond to his poems as a mind, not a creature of feeling. Auden may have been the minor poet he saw himself to be, even the minor poet he eventually made himself; but compared to this sort of minor poet most poets may be forgiven for feeling minuscule. Auden may secretly have preferred that his facility be admired before his faculties. His devices have proved a wicked temptation, and Auden knew enough about sinners to wish perhaps to be

123

sinned against in this manner. One cannot use a certain type of list or simile, cannot employ certain images of industry or folk tale, cannot capitalize an abstraction, without summoning up his name.

## NOTES

1. The two liveliest and intransigently witty articles on Auden's imagery are Randall Jarrell's 'Changes of Attitude and Rhetoric in Auden's Poetry' (1941) and 'Freud to Paul: The Stages of Auden's Ideology' (1945), reprinted posthumously in Jarrell, *The Third Book of Criticism* (New York: Farrar, Straus & Giroux, 1969). Some critics consider these essays hostile, but they are fond, even over-fond, of their subject. The form of my essay was largely suggested by Jarrell's essays, and the reader is urged to turn to them for a view that encompasses imagery, rhetoric and ideology, at least up until the early '40s. Very early there was a late Auden. I have also taken advantage of Monroe Spears, *The Poetry of W. H. Auden: The Disenchanted Island* (New York: Oxford, 1963), John Fuller, *A Reader's Guide to W. H. Auden* (London: Thames and Hudson, 1970), and Edward Mendelson, *Early Auden* (New York: Viking, 1981). In the notes below they are listed by the author's name only. With the exception of a remark on two revisions, all early texts have been taken from *The English Auden* (London: Faber and Faber, 1977) and later poems from *Collected Poems* (New York: Random House, 1976), both edited by Edward Mendelson (and abbreviated below as *EA* and *CP*).

2. Christopher Isherwood: 'If I didn't like a poem, he threw it away and wrote another. If I liked one line, he would keep it and work it into a new poem. In this way, whole poems were constructed which were simply anthologies of my favourite lines, entirely regardless of grammar or sense. This is the simple explanation of much of Auden's celebrated obscurity' (*New Verse*, November 1937, p. 6). Edward Mendelson disputes this recollection (Mendelson, 147n), arguing that there were no such poems. The account is important, however, not as an explanation of obscurity, but as evidence of Auden's wicked facility, noticed also by Richard Eberhart: '. . . [H]e'd show you a new poem and if you didn't like a line he'd strike it right out. "Why, yes, I see that exactly", and he'd take it right out and he'd actually mark through it.' Also, 'He was writing his early poems and would change a line on the instant if you suggested it and what you suggested seemed better' (Eberhart, *Of Poetry and Poets* (Urbana, Ill.: University of Illinois Press, 1979), 286, 203).

3. Auden loved to reduce his knowledge to order. A number of his lists, charts and formal organizations survive in *The Dyer's Hand* (New York: Random House, 1962), and others in Fuller (p. 56), Spears (p. 247) and Mendelson (pp. 41, 68, 76, 145–46).

4. *EA*, p. 122.
5. *EA*, p. 108.
6. *CP*, p. 542.
7. *CP*, p. 572.
8. Narcissus is de-narcissus-ized by the word itself—who can grow vain without his proper name?
9. *CP*, p. 458; *CP*, p. 442.
10. Auden edited *The Oxford Book of Light Verse*, which appeared in 1938. 'Letter to Lord Byron', a homage as reckless as delightful, laments that 'Light verse, poor girl, is under a sad weather' (*EA*, p. 172).
11. 'Hugh Weston' was Isherwood's pseudonym for Auden. The whole passage is symptomatic: ' "Man's got to assert himself against Nature, all the *time*. . . . Of course, I've absolutely no use for colour. Only form. The only really exciting things are volumes and *shapes*. . . . Poetry's got to be made up of images of form. I hate sunsets and flowers. And I loathe the *sea*. The sea is formless . . ." ' (*Lions and Shadows* (Norfolk, Ct.: New Directions, 1947), p. 189). One may be wary of taking Isherwood literally—his use of pseudonyms for his friends and his prefatory admonition that his characters are caricatures may argue for either the greater or lesser accuracy of the portraits.
12. *EA*, p. 165.
13. 'A waiter coupled sadly with a crow', Auden wrote in *For the Time Being* (*CP*, p. 277). The poem would have been different, but scarcely *affected*, if he had written, 'A banker coupled madly with a wren', 'A beggar coupled badly with a gull', or 'A doctor coupled gladly with a goose'.
14. 'Hugh Weston's' attraction to contrived vocabulary was present even at Oxford, as Isherwood notes: 'He peppered his work liberally with such terms as "eutectic", "sigmoid curve", "Arch-Monad", "ligature", "gastropod"; seeking thereby to produce what he himself described as a "clinical" effect' (*Lions and Shadows*, p. 191).
15. *EA*, p. 149.
16. Mendelson traces this metaphor to two phrases from Anthony Collett's *The Changing Face of England* (Mendelson, p. 336).
17. *EA*, p. 117.
18. *CP*, p. 262.
19. *CP*, p. 463.
20. Mendelson, p. 122.
21. *CP*, p. 256.
22. *EA*, p. 245.
23. Isherwood: 'The saga-world is a schoolboy world, with its feuds, its practical jokes, its dark threats conveyed in puns and riddles and understatements: "I think this day will end unluckily for some; but chiefly for those who least expect harm." I once remarked to Auden that the atmosphere of *Gisli the Outlaw* very much reminded me of our schooldays. He was pleased with the idea: and, soon after this, he produced his first play: *Paid on Both Sides*, in which the two worlds are so inextricably confused that it is impossible to say whether the characters are really epic heroes or only members of a school O.T.C.' (*New Verse*,

125

November 1937, pp. 5–6). This passage is quoted by Spears (p. 14), but confused with a similar passage from Isherwood's *Lions and Shadows*. Spears has a prescient observation: 'The persistent image of war is an obvious extension of [the fusion of the schoolboy world with that of the Icelandic sagas], suggesting both that the difference between adult and schoolboy society is less real than apparent and that social conflicts are disguised warfare' (p. 15).

24. *CP*, p. 438.
25. *EA*, p. 25.
26. *CP*, p. 492.
27. Isherwood again: 'The scenery of Auden's early poetry is, almost invariably, mountainous. As a boy, he visited Westmorland, the Peak District of Derbyshire, and Wales. For urban scenery, he preferred the industrial Midlands; particularly in districts where an industry is decaying. His romantic travel-wish was always towards the North. He could never understand how anybody could long for the sun, the blue sky, the palm-trees of the South. His favourite weather was autumnal; high wind and driving rain. He loved industrial ruins, a disused factory or an abandoned mill: a ruined abbey would leave him quite cold. He has always had a special feeling for caves and mines' (*New Verse*, November 1937, p. 8).
28. *CP*, p. 476.
29. *Lions and Shadows*, p. 194.
30. *CP*, p. 668.
31. *The Third Book of Criticism*, pp. 144–45.
32. 'What moves [the poet] to write are his encounters with the sacred in nature, in human beings, nothing else. By the sacred I do not, of course, mean only the good. The sacred can arouse horror and despair as well as awe, wonder, and gratitude. La belle Dame sans merci is no less a sacred figure than Beatrice. Nor is the sacred confined to the romantically mysterious, to "faery lands forlorn". Indeed, every set of verses, whatever their subject matter may be, are by their formal nature a hymn to Natural Law and a gesture of astonishment at the greatest of all mysteries, the order of the universe. Nothing and no one become sacred through their own efforts; it is rather the sacred that chooses them as vehicles through which to manifest itself' (Auden, 'Today's Poet', *Mademoiselle*, April 1962, quoted in Spears, p. 294).
33. Auden, *A Certain World* (New York: Random House, 1970), p. 424.
34. *EA*, p. 48.
35. In Auden's idea of Eden, *Sources of Public Information* are limited to 'Gossip. Technical and learned periodicals but no newspapers' (*The Dyer's Hand*, p. 7).
36. In *Collected Poems*, fifty-one are gathered from the forty-year period 1929–69, but seventy-seven from the last four years of Auden's life.

# Part Two: LANGUAGES AND NAMES

Yet maps and languages and names
Have meaning and their proper claims.

—Auden, *New Year Letter*

# 5

# Fortunate Fall:
# W. H. Auden at Michigan

by DONALD PEARCE

Five o'clock on a Thursday afternoon in Ann Arbor, in late October 1941, a small classroom on the street side of Angell Hall, fourteen or fifteen students in scattered seats, the large windows on the west side of the room beginning to admit long floods of yellow light. W. H. Auden, tall, youthful, blond is lecturing to his class on Fate and the Individual in European literature. He wears fairly shapeless dark trousers, and a coloured plaid work shirt buttoned at the neck. Strangely, no one in the room is taking any notes. ('I would like you, please, to take no notes in this class', he had announced at the first meeting. 'One only remembers what it is important for him to remember. . . . Note-taking interferes with this.') Strangely, too, the lecturer is not facing his class. He stands instead by the windows, half turned toward them, perhaps out of shyness, gravely addressing his remarks to the autumn sky, or to the mighty shades on the other side of the brimming panes of Kierkegaard, Shakespeare, Mozart who are the subjects of his talk, slant sunlight striking his serious face—almost a Cubist portrait with its shifting planes and angles—and the yellow hair that falls in two smooth folds over the temples, encasing them, so that he resembles one of those helmeted Vikings from whom, they say, he is descended, his speech solemn, measured, full of meditative halts and pauses, but continuous, insistent, moving from topic to topic as though from sentence to sentence, the diction slightly pedantic, and this seems somewhat at odds with the easy, rich baritone of the voice itself:

'. . . The Tragic Hero, then, is an inherently superior individual . . . Exceptional in some notable way . . . Someone of great strength . . . who is confronted by an external force greater than he is . . . which he goes forward to meet . . . which he decides to challenge . . . and by which he is crushed. But suppose he refuses to choose death . . . Suppose, instead, he makes an ethical compromise with his situation . . . Now what is his case? . . . He now ceases to be a Tragic Hero . . . that is to say, an Esthetic Hero . . . He becomes an Ethical Hero . . . We may distinguish between these two categories in the following way: When the universal principles . . . that make up the code of the community . . . are considered as being able to be changed by the individual . . . you have the Esthetic attitude. When the universal principles retain their authority over the wishes of the individual . . . so that he conforms his wishes to the principles . . . you have the Ethical attitude. You will find these categories fully treated by Kierkegaard . . . the last great ethical thinker of Europe . . . Esthetics, Kierkegaard says, has an ontology, but no teleology . . . Ethics, in contrast, has no ontology, but has a teleology . . . For Ethics, the preservation of the universal is the important consideration . . . For Esthetics, what is paramount is the intensity . . . the degree . . . of the individual's passion: the part *must be convinced* that it is more important than the whole . . . Now the meeting place of Ethics and Esthetics is Religion . . . Like Esthetics, Religion is concerned with the here, the now, the particular, the immediate . . . It has no relation to the past . . . It cannot operate in the future . . . Like Ethics, it is concerned with a vision of the larger whole . . . Let us take as an example the case of a man who wants to kiss another man's wife . . . This is his dilemma . . . What should be do about it? . . . Esthetics says to him: "Are you really and truly passionate about this . . . ? Can you make it interesting? . . . If so, then yes, you may kiss her." Ethics gives him a different answer: "No . . . You may not kiss her . . . You are categorically forbidden to do so . . . You must take a sedative." Religion says something wholly different from either: "No . . . You

may not kiss her . . . And you may not take the sedative." '
Here Auden went to the blackboard—he often used it for
diagrams, lists, and charts—and wrote out the following
schema:

> *Ethics: sacrifices individual to universal*
> *Esthetics: sacrifices universal to individual*
> *Religion: martyrs the individual*

'The exceptional, and only the exceptional', he went on, 'is
what interests Esthetics. A millionaire who steals a million
dollars is not interesting . . . A millionaire who steals eleven
cents . . . yes, of course, that is interesting . . . But it is the
common denominator alone that interests Ethics . . . Not who
steals . . . or how much is stolen . . . but the act of stealing itself
. . . *that* is what interests Ethics . . . Theft is approved by
Esthetics if the reason for it is interesting enough, exceptional
enough . . . But there is no *exceptional* for Ethics. . . .' A sudden
draught from a door's being opened here whisked several loose
pages from the table and strewed them over the floor. He
hurried from the window. I was in the first row, directly in
front of the table. I at once leaned forward to pick up some
that were within reach, and 'Fuck!' I heard him mutter as he
bent down to retrieve a couple of pages on the other side. It
was startling—appalling: I mean, the sudden and violent
juxtaposition of dictions, worlds.

Something similar had occurred at the first meeting of the
class. This time Mr. Auden was seated behind the table. He
was visibly uncomfortable, or rather undergoing something
like agony, for his forehead was wet with sweat and he
glanced nervously from left to right: 'I shall begin by reading
to you some definitions,' he said, over the top of a protective
sheaf of handwritten pages, 'so that we shall have some
ground in common . . . Know where we stand.' He proceeded
to read one difficult abstract proposition after another, in an
endless and at last virtually unintelligible stream that had
been intended to clarify the whole world for us. The reading
lasted five, maybe six minutes. I was able to take in every
third or fourth definition. Note-taking being forbidden, I
soon remembered even fewer. But here is a handful that
escaped oblivion:

(1) Every evil is a former good.

(2) The animal kingdom cannot be a model for the human: the only criterion among animals is physique, the only value survival.

(3) I believe in order that I may understand; never the reverse.

(4) Imagination is like breathing and hearing, independent of one's beliefs.

(5) A neurosis is a guardian angel: Dante had himself exiled in order to write *The Divine Comedy*, Milton went blind in order to write *Paradise Lost*, Beethoven went deaf in order to write the last quartets.

(6) The world is a psychic act in perpetual modification.

There were many more, most of them longer. A student here entered or left the room, the latter probably, and a sudden gust carried several loose pages to the floor. He rose quickly, stared down in dismay at the scattered leaves and said 'Oh dear!', with a look which I shall never forget of pure horror on his face. It was perfectly obvious that chaos, flux, the random element in the world simply appalled him. And it has often occurred to me since that all those categories, classifications, definitions, diagrams that one encounters in his published work, especially in the essays and shorter epigrammatic pieces, were really magical formulae, so to speak, or charms, by which he sought to stabilize the flux—organize it, make it stay in place.

But the net effect of his classes—the lost-in-thought dialogues by the windows with Paul Valéry, or St. Augustine, or Melville, the wonderful musical illustrations he imported, even the random minor accidents that befell him, like the ones just described—was somehow utterly spellbinding. Of course, I was only 23: though I do not think it was that, for others in the class experienced it, too. The special nicknames we invented for him tell something of the way he came across: 'The Everlasting Bonfire' was mine; to another he was 'The Dishevelled Star'; the T.A. next to me on my right (later well known as mystery writer Ross MacDonald) called him 'An old Ariel and a young Socrates rolled into one'.

But even before it had begun there had been something marvellous about the class. . . One afternoon, in September,

## Fortunate Fall: W. H. Auden at Michigan

just before the opening of Fall semester, I am walking down a dim corridor in Angell Hall, having just been told by my department chairman that I will be an assistant in a large class in American literature . . . But I can't possibly grade in American lit—I am ignorant of the subject . . . Still, I need the money . . . Even more, the prestige . . . I walk on . . . For some reason my eye falls on a small 3 × 5 white card tucked like a secret in the lower right hand corner of the frosted glass panel of an office door. I stoop and peer at it. It reads 'W. H. Auden', in a small, neat hand. Astounding! I stare again. For three years or more this name, appearing above such poems as 'Musée des Beaux Arts', 'Sir, no man's enemy', 'In Memory of W. B. Yeats', 'Letter to Lord Byron', has been that of the most dazzling poet in the world, my world anyway, even if whole passages have sometimes proved unintelligible—that has not seemed to matter in the least. I raise my hand, rap. A quick shadow passes over the glass and the door part way opens. He is tall, slender, in shirt sleeves, smiling vaguely, scrutinizing me with rather close-set eyes.

'Mr. Auden?' Fatuous . . . I know exactly who he is from a dozen photographs. 'I see by your card . . . By this card here . . . I am wondering if, from your card, you are contemplating a course . . . And if I might attend it, if . . .' I stopped.

'Ah yes! Please come in.' The door opens the rest of the way. 'But first we must have a conference to determine if you have the right preparation.'

His voice is rich and musical, and fuller than I had imagined. Beautifully cultivated. The office is narrow, almost barren— metal desk and table, two chairs. He draws up a chair quickly for me, sits at once on the other one to my right, folds his hands on the desk top, turns in my direction and peers at me. It is becoming unnerving. I identify myself. He identifies the course: 'Fate and the Individual in European literature'. He names a few of the authors that will be covered: Horace, Dante, Shakespeare, Goethe, Melville, Kafka, Rimbaud, Valéry. 'There will also be some opera scores and libretti: *Carmen, Don Giovanni, Tristan and Isolde.*' What languages do I read? . . . Which do I speak? . . . Where have I come from? . . . What is my schooling? . . . Have I travelled much? . . . Have I read many Fairy Tales? . . . What music do I like? . . .

I hesitate. 'Beethoven and Mozart,' I offer at last.

'Good,' he replies, pleased. 'One should listen to Mozart when one is feeling ill, or out of sorts, and to Beethoven when one is feeling too happy. That is one of the uses of music—to harmonize the psyche.' A few more comments, where the class will meet, at what times, and—incredible!—I am in. He returns me to the hallway—I may or may not have made a sort of parting bow—and the door clicks to behind me.

The class met twice a week, Tuesday and Thursday afternoons, from 3.30 to 5.30. The first few meetings are now almost a total blank. Like most students I had been trained to remember only what I had committed to a notebook. Before long I began to disobey the no-notes-injunction and would slip into a nearby classroom after a lecture and get down a desperate page or two before most of what he had said—his special phrasing, I mean, for I had no trouble remembering the main ideas—had vanished into air. Gradually my memory improved, soon complete sentences would remain, then whole passages. And it is those hectic fragments—relics, I should say—only an hour or so cold, miraculously preserved in the pages of a 1940 'Spiral' notebook, which I am reproducing here—unaltered, except for occasional narrative bridges—as fleeting vestiges, mere fragments really, of his wonderful talks.

The earliest of these jottings with any continuity are from a lecture on the idea of the Ego in St. Augustine and Franz Kafka. He is standing as usual by the windows speaking to the late afternoon sky, winding up his remarks just before our short break: '. . . No . . . For while the conflict of self and ego . . . as we have it in St. Augustine . . . the subtlest introspectionist between Aristotle and Freud . . . is a classic of self-analysis . . . and the earliest such text . . . still, in a post-Freudian world, we are aware of inner states of complexity . . . multiplicity . . . undreamed of by Augustine—of an ego, for instance, that is no longer the static, continuous, and unified fictional entity it had been for him . . . but a psychological complex . . . or congeries . . . of competitive elements and impulses . . . reminiscent of the modern model of the atom . . . so that Augustine's discussion interests us now not primarily as a document in psychology . . . but rather in Ethics . . . where, of course, it must always be a primary . . . an archetypal text. The same must be said of

Descartes.' (He turns from the window and pads—I think in bedroom slippers—toward the other side of the classroom, pausing at the table to touch, or ruffle, without glancing down at them, some handwritten pages lying there, and passes on.) "*I think*", Descartes says, "*therefore I am*" . . . How very comfortable . . . How very simple . . . But who, in fact, is this "I" who "thinks"? . . . Which of my several self-interested egos . . . each superbly gifted in the arts of personal and interpersonal deception . . . is the one who can arrogate to itself . . . the authority to say that it . . . rather than any of my other "I"s . . . is the "I" that does the thinking? . . . In Descartes' case, was it the "I" that was the military captain? . . . Or the lover? . . . The philosopher? . . . The mathematician . . . The equestrian? . . . The Latin scholar? . . . And which is the "I" that can now . . . in consequence . . . be said *to be*? . . . Not the "I" that does the thinking . . . for plainly it must be another "I" entirely . . . one which is objective to the "I" that says "I think" . . . And as for the thinking itself: what thinking does he mean? . . . That of the doubting process? . . . That in virtue of which another "I" is said to exist? . . . That of the scientific, the rational Descartes? . . . The thinking of memory? . . . That of the fantasy, or dreams? . . . Each element of the celebrated formulation, in light of modern psychology appears unstable. Appears to break down . . . Of all modern writers, it is Franz Kafka . . . especially in *The Castle* . . . who best expresses these contemporary psychological and metaphysical predicaments . . . I want you to read *The Castle* for Tuesday . . . Disguised as a satire of modern European bureaucracy . . . it is actually a theological and psychological parable . . . and holds, we may say . . . the same relation to the culture of our century as Dante's poem did to that of the fourteenth . . . Please keep *The Divine Comedy* in mind as you read *The Castle* . . . In what points are their interests similar? . . . In what points the same? . . . In what points do they differ? . . . Why? . . . Would Virgil be a useful guide and counsellor for the land surveyor? . . . Keep in mind, too, your Melville . . . Do Ahab and the land surveyor have any traits or problems in common? . . . In what ways does K's quest resemble Ahab's? . . . If the whale is the object of Ahab's quest, who or what is the object of K's? . . . Of Dante's?'

There was a small brown portable phonograph—he often

brought it to class—on the table. He went over to it at this point and proceeded to carry out what turned out to be the most beautiful demonstration of the way music and literature speak to each other I had ever witnessed in a classroom. With concentration he worked a record onto the turntable—this was often a very trying process—commenting intermittently, rather mutteringly, as he did so: 'The relationship . . . between an individual . . . and his fate . . . between Ahab and the White Whale . . . or, if you prefer, between K and the Castle . . . is . . . as far as this kind of thing can be expressed in music . . . best reflected . . . I would say . . . in this passage . . . by Beethoven . . . Now . . . this is the second movement . . . of the Fourth Piano Concerto . . . of Beethoven . . . Notice how when the piano departs . . . I mean, defies . . . so to speak . . . the orchestra . . . defies its fate . . . let us say . . . and goes off, egotistically, on its own . . . it soon becomes lost . . . hysterical . . . and only when it rediscovers . . . re-accepts . . . the orchestra does it return to something like normalcy . . . sanity . . . But does the rediscovery come too late?' He started the recording—Artur Schnabel performing with the London Philharmonic—which I now heard for the first time. The famous dialogue began to fill the room: the egotism of the piano versus—whatever it was the orchestra was, some huge, lurching presence, force, or menace even, it was hard to say what—their gradual alienation and separation, then the frenzied vertigo, or hubris, of the piano, leading at last to the exhausted return, the subdued and poignant close. The entire experience was enormously impressive, even portentous. And yet it had all been done so simply; two or three things had been brought together, set side by side in our minds, that was all: these fictions are like this music. But I am perfectly certain that it is only through such fortunate juxtapositions that any real understanding of anything ever manages to come about.

'And now', he was saying, his back to the class, and bent low above the phonograph, attending to wires, or switches, or something, 'we will have a ten minute recess . . . So that you may rest your behinds.'

We would disperse, or stretch and remain in the classroom. During a recess he was, when present, always very approachable by any students who had questions. Often, though, the time was taken up coping with the phonograph, its various wires, plugs, switches, or—desperate task—trying to find the exact place on a record where the part that would be needed next hour began. Somehow we all seemed to get drawn into it and turn by degrees into a sort of huddled committee, the questions anyone had saved to ask him soon for the most part lost in a compulsive act of attention that was, I remember, almost physical as we studied the problem of finding the correct record, withdrawing it from its slip case, transporting it to the waiting turntable, then, worst of all, locating the exact groove—excruciating moment—on the spinning disc where the desired passage began. . . . If he did not stay but went outside between sessions, it was for a quick smoke or to walk about a little and think. Though the space between South Hall and the General Library was actually quite open, with few trees, hedges, or other means of concealment, he would unless you were very alert—yet somehow as if not in the least intending to do so—simply vanish from sight. He walked very quickly, with frequent, sudden divagations. Turn your heard and he could be gone.

That semester, possibly because he was at work on *The Sea and the Mirror*, Auden lectured fairly frequently on the theme of love. We were assigned the libretti of *Tristan und Isolde* and *Carmen*, *Romeo and Juliet*, and a new book which he was enthusiastic about by Denis de Rougemont called *Love in the Western World*; if we would also read C. S. Lewis's *The Allegory of Love* ('a right good book', he informed us: Lewis had been his teacher at Oxford—'terribly severe', Auden confided, and made a quick face), so much the better. When we returned from the short break, the topic was indeed the Psychology of Romantic Love.

On this theme, Auden made two main points, pretty much along the lines of de Rougemont. Romantic love involves 'mirroring'. The Romantic Lover, 'like most other people, is narcissist . . . but to an unusual degree . . . He nurtures in fantasy an heroic image of his own uniqueness . . . and it is the unwelcome rôle of others . . . "the world" . . . to disenchant and revise this image . . . so that he may become a useful member of society . . . Now if two such persons meet . . . and fall in love . . . which is very likely . . . each proceeds to

137

validate the other's heroic self-image . . . which has routinely been denied by the rest of the world: "You are every bit as exceptional as you have always held yourself to be!" Each in this way finds in the other the heavenly verifier of his or her own uniqueness . . . The flood of mutual gratitude produced by these revelations is overwhelming . . . It is this powerful intoxicant that serves both as the fuel and the immediate goal of the relationship . . . Now stage two commences: "the Barrier". For the intoxicant to remain effective . . . it is essential that the relationship not change into something else . . . dwindle, for instance, into friendship . . . or into domestic love, married love, with its ties to the community . . . No, something must come between the lovers . . . preventing their union . . . One of them is already married . . . Or an inter-family feud has erected a wall between them . . . Or he has professional (e.g. military) obligations that supervene . . . Etcetera . . . Or there is a barrier of religion, or of race . . . Should no objective barrier be present, the lovers *must* supply it . . . Hence the unsheathed sword which Tristan and Iseult place between their sleeping bodies after they have run away together . . . The purpose of the obstacle is clear: it is to intensify desire by impeding its fulfilment . . . till desire at last becomes intense enough to surmount the obstacle that impedes it . . . Now the right obstacle . . . the one the lovers ideally require . . . must be insurmountable. That is to say, their union must be possible only through their deaths . . . This is the secret, the religious mystery, of Romantic Love . . . And it is the reason why it must be classed among the illnesses. Its *telos* is the death of the lovers . . . Romantic lovers are in love with death . . . Which is not to say that falling in love is only a kind of death-wish . . . Falling in love with love, however, is a step in that direction . . . I would like now to illustrate some of these things for you by a passage from one of Wagner's operas . . . Here is the love duet . . . from Wagner's *Tristan und Isolde* . . . Wagner perfectly understood . . . the psychology of Romantic Love . . . Notice how . . . with the greatest deliberateness . . . he keeps the voices of the lovers . . . phrase after phrase . . . from meeting in unison . . . until the end of the duet . . . Which is, of course, also how it is to be with their lives.' He lowered the tone arm slowly to the spinning surface, raised it again, bent down more steeply, inspected the needle with care, lowered the arm gently once more, shifted his position gingerly, hovered above the turning disc . . . There was a sudden *yelp* as the needle jumped and bit into a groove. It didn't seem to matter: the marvellous tortured voices at once took over, floating, circling, twining, calling to each other, pursuing and eluding each other, beckoning, it seemed, over immense gulfs, repeating their protestations, complaints, rising by degrees to their final union, and the record stopped. Nobody stirred for a while, as I recall. I left the classroom feeling that I knew everything in the world.

The next few meetings were on Shakespeare—*Othello*, *Henry IV*, *The Tempest*. Auden lectured mainly on the psychology of the characters and the social and historical circumstances affecting action in the plays. He rarely, even in an aside, commented on matters of technique, the music of the verses, rhetorical effects, style, ambiguity, the physical and sensuous features of poetry—all the things so dear at the time to American New Critics, nothing seemed farther from his thoughts, which might perhaps strike one as strange in the case of so medium-conscious a poet as Auden—though he did ask us to read Wilson Knight, who regularly concerns himself with such things; no, the plays were classic case-histories in psychology, and Shakespeare was a profound and original psycho-historian. My notes begin to get more detailed now, partly because he would often put diagrams and charts on the blackboard that neatly mapped the tensions and conflicts in a play, such as the following which I took directly from the lecture on *Othello*:

I. *Stratified Society*

| Gentles: | Duke, Brabantio Roderigo, Cassio Lodovico | Desdemona |
|---|---|---|
| ——————————————Othello—————————————— | | |
| Non-Gentles: | Iago | Emilia |
| ———————————————————————————————— | | |
| | Clown | Bianca |

II. *Self-confident vs. Self-distrusting*

| Self-conf: | Lodovico | Iago | Desdemona |
|---|---|---|---|
| —————————————Othello——————————————— | | | |
| Un-conf: | Roderigo | · | Cassio |

III. *Sex-Appeal*

| Have: | Cassio<br>Lodovico | | Desdemona<br>Emilia |
|---|---|---|---|
| —————————————Iago——————————————— | | | |
| Lack: | Roderigo<br>(Sex is low to R.) | | Othello |

IV. *Passionate vs. Cold*

| Pass: | Othello<br>Cassio | Bianca |
|---|---|---|
| | | |
| Cold: | Desdemona<br>Roderigo<br>Iago | Emilia |

V. *Sophisticated vs. Naïve*

| Soph: | Cassio<br>Roderigo | Iago<br>Emilia |
|---|---|---|
| | | |
| Naïve: | Othello<br>(delib.) | Desdemona<br>(by nat.) |

VI. *Intelligent vs. Stupid*

| Intell: | Iago |
|---|---|
| | |
| Stu: | The rest |

As he put these schemata on the board he lectured to us, haltingly: 'Othello . . . first of all . . . concerns a stratified society . . . This fact is of the utmost importance for the play . . . It is productive of all manner of strained relations . . . frustrations . . . among the dramatis personae . . . of conscious versus sub-conscious wishes . . . hidden versus open motives . . . All of which, of course, become manifest, in various ways . . . in the actions of the characters . . . in increased susceptibility to misunderstandings . . . obsessions . . . even paranoia . . . The Duke, Brabantio, Roderigo, Cassio, Lodovico, Desdemona . . . as you can see . . . are all from the upper crust . . . Iago and Emilia are clearly from a class lower than these . . . Bianca and the Clown are from a still lower class . . . Notice Othello's anomalous position . . . While he is indispensable to the nobility . . . owing to his military competence . . . he is, at the same time, regarded as a social inferior . . . even as an intruder . . . In part, because he is black . . . So his situation is very difficult: politically he is necessary to the state, but only tolerated socially . . . This subjects him to great private strain . . . continuous private strain . . . But this external situation only exacerbates an internal problem of Othello's personal psychology . . . which is . . . that he tends to vacillate between feelings of self-confidence and feelings of self-distrust. For he is a very sensitive . . . a very proud person . . . but he isn't very intelligent . . . He's warm, passionate. This is, in fact, the mainspring of his character . . . He is exactly Pascal's *homme d'esprit de coeur* . . . one who tries to solve the problems of life by his feelings alone . . . and by the help of few moral maxims . . . Othello is a self-made man . . . and very impressive in the sphere of his own expertise . . . which is that of physical action . . . Here he possesses great confidence . . . Yet in other ways he is a prey to uncertainties . . . misgivings . . . which spring largely from his having only limited sex-appeal . . . But they spring also from the limitations of his self-made character . . . These factors, taken together, put him at a serious disadvantage in a sophisticated social environment . . . such as the one in which he actually finds himself . . . We often see him ill at ease . . . awkward. He therefore parades his physical prowess . . . his military accomplishments . . .

141

depends upon them almost childishly . . . They are his instinctive defences. He tries at times to be genial, egalitarian, festive . . . and is, of course, quite sincere whenever he does so . . . But you can see that he is under strain at these times. Othello is naïve . . . But *deliberately* naïve . . . He is naïve in order to escape the knowledge of his inferiority . . . He is very trusting . . . but also very credulous: men, he thinks, should be what they seem . . . He is a babe-in-arms, philosophically—which is clear from the great emphasis he places on simple virtues like honesty, fidelity, trustfulness . . . Iago, of course, unerringly spots in this trait the key to Othello's character.

'Desdemona . . . his Venetian lady . . . is likewise naïve . . . She is a simple school girl, with no view whatsoever of the world of action . . . the rougher side of life. She has no idea of sex . . . and is totally without guile . . . She is a complete romantic . . . Pervertedly romantic . . . All romantics are. Her imagination is entirely plastic—she sees, almost at once, everything through Othello's eyes . . . She is without a philosophy of life . . . except one of gentle trust . . . This is Othello's philosophy, too . . . Like him, she isn't very intelligent . . . Her love for him is really a kind of mother love: she needs and adores his feats and proofs of manhood . . . and reciprocally he needs her adoration, gentleness, and innocence. Each makes a sheet anchor out of the other's naïveté . . . Again, this situation doesn't escape Iago's notice.

'Now, Cassio . . . In contrast to Othello, has great confidence with women . . . He is a lady killer . . . But he is very ill at ease with men. He's definitely not a fraternity boy . . . While he has lots of sex-appeal, his consciousness of inadequacy in a masculine world . . . puts him under severe strain in the army: the fact that he can't hold his liquor is an indication of this . . . an indication of his femininity. The friendship of Cassio and Othello is, in this way, based on complementary strengths and weaknesses . . . Othello is confident with men, and in a world of action, Cassio not . . . Cassio is confident in a world of women, and in the world of Venice, Othello is not. They see each other wholly esthetically . . . as ideal figures, that complement and support each other.

'Iago . . . Well, Iago, manifestly . . . first of all . . . is lacking in passion. He is cold . . . This is a primary fact of his

142

nature . . . He is not ruled . . . not troubled . . . by emotion, by
sentiment . . . His prime deficiency—which by now, of course,
he has learned to convert into a source of strength—is that he
can't love other people . . . This gives him a great advantage
over everyone else in the play . . . The advantage of detachment . . . Other people are merely objects to him . . . Human
objects . . . in a setting. His most striking characteristic . . . the
thing that distinguishes him from all the other persons in the
play . . . is his brilliance. Iago is the only brilliant character in
the play . . . He has, to a marked degree, what Pascal calls the
"geometrical mind", *l'esprit géométrique*. He solves the problems of life by reason alone, by intellect alone . . . He doesn't
see, doesn't care about the principles, but he can reason
without a flaw . . . Geometricity is what characterizes his mind
. . . He is by no means just a malcontent . . . Something else, at
once more remarkable, and more tragic, makes him tick . . .
makes him the villain he is . . . able to manipulate the lives of
others as if they were simply pieces on a gaming board . . .
Now there must be some significance in the fact that Iago is
the only person in the play who exhibits any knowledge of
Holy Writ: "I am not what I am", he says . . . He can lecture
. . . and catechize . . . on virtue like a theologian . . . His lines,
in fact, have frequent theological overtones and allusions . . .
In Iago we have, I think, a very remarkable portrait by
Shakespeare of the villain as inverted saint . . . That is to say,
Iago's real passion was to be a saint . . . He is a saint manqué
. . . On the surface, nothing might seem less probable . . . Yet
Shakespeare was surely right about this . . . The saint and the
villain have very similar psychologies . . . In both, Ethics and
Esthetics have become almost the same thing . . . There is a
similar detachment . . . similar freedom . . . in both, where
human relations are concerned . . . an absence of the usual
scruples, motivations, that trouble or govern most living. I
would like you to think about the psychology of the saint and
of the villain, or criminal, for next day . . . List the points of
similarity which you find . . . And also . . . as you read *Henry
IV* for next Tuesday . . . look for similarities between the
psychologies of Iago and Falstaff. Why was Shakespeare so
obsessed with this mentality? . . . What is his attitude toward
it in *The Tempest*?'

He was gathering up loose pages and books while talking, and the class was starting to break up noisily: 'Read lots of fairy stories over the weekend!', he shouted to us above the mounting clatter, 'as you study *The Tempest!*' . . . and loaded with armfuls of books, papers, phonograph records and the record player itself, he steered for the doorway, and down the hall, and out into the early night.

Auden must have talked about other things than the psychology of Falstaff and Prince Hal next time, but my notes seem confined to that. 'Falstaff', he began, 'is a comic edition of Iago.' I felt a little startled. 'He delights in the varieties . . . the types and modes . . . of human behaviour . . . and in playing with them. He's really a very shrewd student of human nature . . . Quite as much so as Iago . . . But his approach is, of course, very different . . . For one thing, Falstaff is basically a Feeling-Intuitive type . . . His thinking processes are essentially non-rational . . . a very rapid affair of the feelings . . . a kind of short-circuited thinking via the feelings: hence his sudden wit . . . and his characteristic unpredictability in word and action. Falstaff is not governed by reason . . . or logic. He differs sharply in this respect from Iago . . . What Falstaff and Iago have in common is a fundamental detachment from the ethical in human relations . . . Both keep themselves at a distance from life, though without seeming to do so . . . Iago's detachment is that of the scientist—analytic, cold. Falstaff's is that of the playwright— he is a superb actor and amateur . . . or instinctive . . . playwright. He generates dramatic occasions around him spontaneously . . . the way some people generate trouble . . . or others orderliness, or calm . . . Wherever he happens to be, a little dramatic scene . . . a little play . . . is before long in progress. This is his method for dealing with problems of human relationship—you turn everything into a play . . . into a game . . . Here he is a real virtuoso.

'Iago is, of course, a virtuoso, too . . . and a playwright . . . only a calculative, a deliberative one. Essentially, both are manipulators of other people. They have this trait in common, however differently they manifest it. Something else they have in common is a Machiavellian cruel streak . . . This is often overlooked in the case of Falstaff . . . yet notice his behaviour

144

toward the dead Hotspur: that little scene is a solus, after all. His pranks . . . his improvisations . . . often have more than a spirit of fun about them.

'But the real Machiavel of the play is, of course, Prince Hal . . . For all his apparent bonhomie and boyish charm, Hal is a real schemer underneath . . . cruel, self-oriented, cunning . . . one of the most odious characters in Shakespeare. He eavesdrops, lies, wins hearts when and where he wants to . . . and only when he wants to . . . He pretends to be hale-fellow-well-met, but he's nothing of the kind . . . On the contrary, he's obsessively curious about crafty and unprincipled human conduct . . . He seeks it out for study . . . practises it . . . wants to learn about it . . . for the obvious political reason that when he becomes king he will have to understand this kind of behaviour and employ it . . . In this respect, Hal is clearly Falstaff's pupil . . . There is studiousness in his attitude toward Falstaff . . . the studiousness of the devoted pupil. And he learns his lessons remarkably well . . . His courtship of Catherine in *Henry V*, for instance, is as Falstaffian as it can be.

'Hal's father, King Henry, like all English rulers before him, has failed . . . or hasn't found it necessary . . . to pay much attention to the lower classes of the realm . . . But now history has begun to change . . . begun to move toward the formation of the modern nation state . . . Commoners are beginning to come into their own . . . to possess new power . . . new significance. Hal, always astute about power, has his ear and eye on this change, which he can see occurring everywhere around him in England . . . He wants to understand it from the inside . . . so as to be able to use it . . . control it . . . Hal's objectivity, like Iago's, springs from an inner coldness. At the end of Part II of the play he rejects his former companions . . . simply and without regret . . . not because he is a great man who sees they aren't fitting companions for a king . . . but because he has no further use for them . . . In this he is very much like his father . . . Consider Henry's identical treatment of his country cousins, the Percies, who had championed his cause initially . . . had even succeeded in setting him on the throne.

'In sociological terms, the Percies . . . the factious nobles . . . represent an agrarian-based feudal England which is already

historically on the wane . . . and that is due to be superseded
by a new city-oriented, finance-oriented ethos . . . the world of
London, and the other rising English cities . . . the world of the
modern nation state. The Percies aren't unaware of the change
that is taking place . . . but they have repressed the knowledge
. . . evaded it . . . with the usual results psychologically:
intensification of attitudes, paranoia, fanaticism . . . especially
in the case of the young Hotspur: fanaticism, as Jung has
pointed out, is exactly that, "overcompensated doubt".
Falstaff has his roots in the waning Feudal order . . . so that by
rights one might expect to find him on the Feudal side. But he
is, of course, an absolutely conscienceless opportunist . . . And
it is typical of his opportunism that he has moved—intuitively,
one feels—to London, to Eastcheap . . . in order, simply, to be
on the side of the future . . . He and his tavern companions are
quite indifferent, politically, as to which side they're on in the
coming conflict . . . as long as it's the winning side . . . But
here again there are ironic consequences. For Falstaff's strong
points . . . his wit, intuition, sensitive feelings, geniality . . . are
precisely the qualities which render him vulnerable . . . prone
to failure, to disappointment . . . in a business-oriented milieu
. . . where calculation and logic rather than intuition and
feelings are paramount . . . are essential to success. Not that
Falstaff has no worldly ambitions—for obviously he has . . .
He would like, for instance, to hold an important post in Hal's
new administration . . . But he hasn't the brains needed to
realize such hopes . . . not in the kind of milieu, at least, in
which he finds himself. Privately, Falstaff is a deeply dis-
appointed man. His heavy drinking is a classic case of
compensation—a swallowing of disappointments. His great
belly derives . . . as he himself astutely points out . . . from
"sighing and grief" which "swells a man up like a bladder"—
the psychosomatic index not of a happy but of a very unhappy
life.

'He is, moreover, a displaced person . . . a country boy in
the big city. His way of protecting himself against painful
situations and relationships . . . against shrewdness, hardness,
hard people, unfeeling people . . . is literally to pad himself
with fat . . . And also to play at being a child—a common and
familiar neurotic tactic—in order, precisely, not to be hurt . . .

But then, of course, Falstaff really *is* a child. He is his own unborn child . . . or unborn self, if you prefer . . . His great belly . . . of which so much is made in the play . . . is in fact a mock-pregnancy . . . This is a well known medical phenomenon . . . I mean, even among males . . . It has been studied, in recent times by, for example, Georg Groddeck, the pioneer pre-Freudian German analyst . . . Falstaff reverts to childishness . . . to pranks, word-play, triviality, sensuality . . . as a deliberate strategy for making people like him . . . be nice to him . . . treat him affectionately, rather than coldly, or cruelly. His only effective social resources are his feelings . . . He winds himself into other people's feelings and affections in order to gain their indulgence . . . their protection. He is of course, a great coward . . . Which is why be brags so much, puffs himself up so much . . . His belly is, in fact, the corporeal symbolization of this spiritual disorder . . . Falstaff is capable of personal and sentimental relations only . . . He is without any idea of external or philosophic relations . . . Hal, on the other hand, has no sentimental or personal ties or relations whatsoever. Hence their inevitable break-up . . . Falstaff cannot understand why he is rejected by Hal, for he doesn't understand political and abstract relations. And Hal doesn't understand . . . sets no store by . . . personal relations. Essentially, Hal is an unfeeling Machiavel . . . Like Iago, he is thought honest and sociable; but like Iago, he is expert in deception. In cruelty, too.

'More generally, the Falstaff of *Henry IV* . . . is a psycho-political symbol . . . of the body politic of an England that is idle, irrational, bloated, appetitive, diseased, full of woes . . . Scholars have called attention to all the body imagery . . . and the allusions to disease, in the play. Falstaff represents what is wrong, spiritually, with contemporary England . . . In King Henry's view, what the country needs is discipline, exercise, purging by a foreign war . . . He is planning one when the play opens.

'As for Henry himself, he is, like his son, a skilled opportunist . . . but a hollow man. Notice the hollowness of his rhetoric throughout the play . . . which comes from his having all his life turned a deaf ear to his feelings . . . He has come, as a result, to feel that there is something the matter with himself

... with his life, the world ... that he has missed something
... and he has grown, as such people almost always do,
melancholic in his later years ... He pleads for feeling from his
son and gets only hollow rhetoric in return ... Hal's relations
with his own father are much less complex than his relations
with his mentor and surrogate father, Falstaff. Hal sees
Falstaff in a variety of rôles: as father, sage, fool, child ... A
hard man will often have a love of the childlike, the tender ...
crave his own opposite, his "lame shadow"—that part of
himself which he has maimed, or repressed, or insufficiently
developed ... Reciprocally, Falstaff sees Hal as a child ... *His*
child ... Notice the strength of the feeling-bond that exists
between them ... And also the disparity in their ages. Of
course, Falstaff sees in Hal the symbol par excellence of
success ... And of his own chance for success ... No one
would dispute that. But that is really only a secondary aspect
of the relationship.

'The Elizabethans were ... in many ways ... an extrava-
gant and childish people. There is a good deal of this reflected
in this play ... In many of the plays. Every culture, every
civilization, has something exaggerated ... aggravated ...
about it. A city civilization will have an aggravation of the
calculative, the manipulative faculties ... and a corresponding underdevelopment of the feelings, the intuitive side ...
Worldly success in the city is dependent upon brain-power,
detachment, planning, skill in manoeuvring, and the like—all
Hal's strengths ... Now Falstaff, or Merrie England, cannot
survive in that kind of atmosphere ...' It was dark outside
when I had got this far with these notes. I had stopped, I
remember, out of exhaustion. There had been more, on Rilke's
*Elegies*, I believe, which I had intended to write down later
that night. But it got away.

The last lecture I have any record of was in December 1941.
The part I made notes on was Auden's discussion of *The
Tempest*. He was propped against a table at the front of the
room, facing us, having by that time overcome his fear of the
class. He still addressed, or appeared to address, some
invisible auditor who was, on that occasion, located fairly high
up the back wall of the room. 'All literature is allegory', he was
saying. 'You only know yourself, your own reactions ... When

you read, what you see is yourself in different situations . . . yourself as different persons . . . Your knowledge of the world is wholly within yourself . . . Poems, fictions, merely tap it and let it out. One's knowledge of Shakespeare is strictly commensurate with one's experience of life.'

'. . . In Shakespeare', he continued, looking toward the windows, and squinting, as if at some bright light source, 'you have the human mind at its fullest degree of integration . . .' I remember I found the remark thrilling, almost bulging with meaning. I longed to explore it, but he was pressing on, in his best prophetic vein: 'Everything he knew . . . or had experienced . . . or had imagined . . . was always available to his poetic faculty . . . This is why the unitary . . . or organic study of his plays is valid . . . The late, early and middle plays all relate to each other . . . They are like the movements of one large many-faceted musical composition. His last play, *The Tempest* . . . which I want us to consider today . . . should be read as one segment of a suite of closely connected late plays . . . The sea, in particular, is present in all of them . . . Now the sea to Shakespeare . . . The sea is always the place from which new life comes . . . where the old is deposited . . . where rich treasures are found. There are numerous instances of this in the mature plays . . . Scene two of *Twelfth Night* is an example . . . The scene in *Pericles*—it is in Act III—is another . . . in which a baby is born at sea, with the apparent death of the mother . . . The entire sea-frame . . . sea-theme . . . of *The Tempest* is still another instance . . . All of these late plays should be read and experienced together . . . as a single long poem in several parts . . . Thus, the sea-scene in *Pericles* anticipates . . . sets the tone for . . . the sea scene of *The Tempest* . . . The central theme in both is "sea-change, into something rich and strange". What Shakespeare is dealing with here is transformation . . . Well, it is almost *transmutation*, in the alchemical sense . . . And it affects not only material things in *The Tempest*, but the minds and lives of the people as well . . . This gives a meditative . . . a spiritual dimension to the play . . . saves it from being only a succession of physical marvels, like any of numerous other Elizabethan Romances. But the people in this play really undergo change . . . They are transformed . . . Notably, of course, Prospero . . . But

149

Shakespeare, too, is transformed . . . I want to return to that presently.

'The narrative form of *The Tempest* is Romance. . . . Better still, Fairy Tale: a unique but erring hero . . . after a long sojourn in a land of marvels . . . returns home, enriched . . . to resume and renew his kingdom. How has Prospero erred? He has erred in failing to attend to the immediate tasks of administering his Dukedom . . . Why does he fail to do so? Because of an egotistical determination to perfect himself in esoteric arts and sciences . . . to enter, in other words, the fairyland of the subjective life . . . which he finds much more alluring, much more exciting, than the dutiful life of public service . . . Because of his dereliction, he is ousted . . . quite properly . . . by his brother . . . his "other self". After several years of isolation on a private island, he decides to renounce his laborious wisdom . . . his magical skills . . . and return to the ordinary world of Milan . . . the world of real appearances, of humdrum human problems and people. He gives himself back to that world . . . Arranges to go back to it.

'Shakespeare is, of course, here dealing with an age-old literary theme: renunciation of supernormal powers, or abilities, for the blessings of the commonplace. It is a theme which has interested the occident for centuries . . . Faust, you will recall, makes a similar renunciation. Faust gives up the possibilities of elaborate knowledge . . . elaborate power . . . for the privilege . . . as he finally comes to view it . . . of being of immediate service to his fellow man . . . In his case building, or helping to build, dykes—the allurements of a life of egotistical baroque intellect renounced in favour of a life of simple public service.

'Prospero's magic island . . . his ivory tower . . . far from all human intrusions . . . is ideal as a place in which to carry out his private studies. What he eventually learns there, however, is not the secret art of magic . . . which, yes, he does learn . . . but the secret of the art of life . . . which consists in honouring and discharging the immediate requisitions of ordinary living . . . honouring the sweetness and simplicity of human life above its complexities . . . Shakespeare is insisting on this . . . he is affirming basic priorities in this play . . . The recognition of these priorities constitutes the fairy-tale wealth . . . the

Philosopher's Stone . . . which Prospero in the end brings back with him to Milan. We see the theme repeated . . . reinforced . . . in his depiction of Miranda and Ferdinand. In this uncomplicated relationship . . . its only complexity is an affectionate squabble during a chess game . . . we have Shakespeare's final word on love. Love is no longer the exhausting, dangerous rapture it is in *Romeo and Juliet* . . . nor the rhetorical, sweaty passion we have in the case of that middle-aged and fat pair Antony and Cleopatra . . . No, love is now pictured as a very simple . . . very unheroic . . . un-rhetorical thing, the true prelude to marriage and children.

'Prospero, as has often been said, is Shakespeare's complete man . . . of balanced humours, balanced faculties . . . But Prospero is also Shakespeare . . . and the play conveys his mind . . . his conclusions . . . on a number of basic things— basic, I mean, to satisfactory human living . . . It is a play, but it is also a testament . . . Shakespeare is summing up certain themes that have preoccupied him in various ways over the years . . . Thus, Caliban is clearly the vegetable beastliness in human nature which he had studied . . . and pictured . . . in a dozen plays . . . and which, while it must be kept in its place, cannot be eliminated, or ignored . . . Notice that Prospero makes Miranda go with him and confront Caliban, makes her look at him . . . One has to face it . . . As Blake said, each man lives in his spectre's power, till he sees it reflected in the lake . . . sees his ghost . . . knows his apparent self from his real self.

'Gonzalo is the character in this play most easily overlooked . . . his very ordinariness tends, in fact, to render him more or less invisible : . . . But he is certainly an important character . . . an iconic character. He is a re-handling of Polonius . . . But with this difference, that Shakespeare now finds something in the Gonzalo/Polonius type to respect . . . In *Wilhelm Meister*, there is a passage in which Goethe distinguishes three sorts, or modes, of reverence which are, I think, compatible with Shakespeare's late vision . . . his philosophic vision . . . as we have it in this play.' He went to the blackboard and inscribed a characteristic suite of propositions:

(1) *Reverence for what is above you*: ignorant and inferior fear; superior avoid.

(2) *Reverence for one's equals*: philosophers seek to attain . . . "humanitas".

(3) *Reverence for what is beneath you*: necessary part of life; need to see as form of beauty.

He did not discuss them—one could see their application easily enough—but came back from the board and continued: 'Gonzalo . . . though at times blundering, and a bore . . . is now seen by Shakespeare as essentially good . . . essentially trustworthy . . . The brilliant scintillators . . . Antonio's court-hangers-on are all that remains of them in *The Tempest* . . . and the intellectual "heavy" . . . people like Iago, and Richard the Third . . . are seen to be hollow and untrustworthy after all . . . of little interest to Shakespeare anymore . . . Gonzalo is now given full respect . . . True, the intelligentsia are made to gull and bait him . . . Shakespeare isn't blind to the limitations of the type . . . But he isn't out any longer to glorify intellect—intellectual ingeniousness. It is now definitely linked by him to treacherousness . . . to possibilities of treacherousness . . . For the purposes of normal human life, the gentle, honest soul is best.'

He dropped the theme briefly in order to talk about Paul Valéry, of which I kept no record, but my notes show him returning to it in his closing comments: 'One can never judge the work of a living author with any finality . . . because an artist's work . . . to be judged . . . must be seen as a complete whole . . . in all its interrelations . . . which are as unknown to him as to anyone else . . . But we *can* see the work of Shakespeare as a whole . . . As a unit . . . We *can* see, for example, the last four plays, *Pericles, Cymbeline, The Winter's Tale, The Tempest* forming a unit . . . We can also see a progressive sweetening of his attitude to life in these plays . . . as well as a corresponding, unmistakable dimming of . . . fading out of interest in the subtle Machiavellian type which had fascinated him for so many years . . . in *The Tempest*, we see the type shrunk merely to a petty villain who would attempt to stab a sleeping person . . . Does Shakespeare's fascination with Machiavellianism throughout most of his mature life as a playwright mean that he was personally tempted by it . . . by just such a spectre . . . or alter ego . . . which for him would have been Baconianism . . . and had finally mastered its temptation by the time he came to write the late plays . . . in which there is so marked an increase of reverence for the blessings of the commonplace . . . ?'

Auden returned at this point to the blackboard where, starting at the far left, he proceeded to copy out a double-decker chart, or schematization, which he had made for us—it extended, when he had finished writing it out, all the way across the board to the right hand edge at the other side of the room. It was, he said, a summary of certain themes and relationships we had been concerned with during the semester. The two-ply synoptic scroll, which I copied down as he wrote it, ran as follows (broken here into three segments):

| Health | Bourgeois social stability | Gaiety | Voluntarism |
| --- | --- | --- | --- |
| Sickness | Revolution | Sadness | Determinism |

| Faith in personal integrity | Pragmatic specialized science |
| --- | --- |
| Doubts about personal integrity | Synthetic heroic ironism |

| Classical values | Catholicism | Pragmatic and practical morality |
| --- | --- | --- |
| Romantic values | Protestantism | Uncoded morality |

When he finished this, he explained what we should expect in the way of a final exam, four or five weeks down the road, after Christmas vacation. Pens, pencils, papers for the first time in the semester suddenly materialized and flashed into view. It would be a three hour written exam. We would write from memory seven cantos of *The Divine Comedy*, in the Carlyle/Wicksteed prose version—'the one used by Eliot in *The Waste Land*', he confided—beginning with *Inferno* III, and V, then certain *Purgatorio* cantos (e.g. XXVIII) and finishing with *Paradiso* XXXIII. The consternation of the class on hearing this was what one might expect: frozen silence. In a few minutes grumblings began to be heard, mutterings. A group of students, forming themselves into a 'committee', declared the exam impossible and inhumane. Auden, surprised, replied that he did not think it was either, but offered to reduce the number of cantos from seven to five. Resistance, nevertheless, continued, 'Very well. I am going to be driving to California over the Christmas vacation. If I find I can't memorize these five cantos by the time I reach Los Angeles, I'll phone your representative and cancel the assignment.' It was a deal—rather a reluctant one, on both sides.

The 'phone call never came, so the Dante exam was on. I threw myself at *Inferno* III, devoting each afternoon to it for days. I tried every mnemonic trick I had ever heard of, tried colour schemes, acronyms, numbers—it seemed hopeless. But then, after a concentrated week of effort, amazingly, I could repeat Canto III of *The Divine Comedy*. I began to take heart. A couple more weeks and I needed only three afternoons to memorize a canto. The last one, the dazzling close of the *Paradiso*, I learned entire in a single afternoon. At the exam, I wrote for three hours without stopping, and filled five blue-books without, I think, any errors. This was possibly the most valuable thing I learned from W. H. Auden, and I have never ceased to be grateful to him for it. Sometimes I have asked classes of my own to attempt similar feats—with the same initial resistance and, eventually, similar gratitude.

Conflict with a 'required course' kept me from taking the next semester of Auden's class. I felt as if a life support system had been shut off. I showed up one afternoon, out of sheer curiosity, after hearing that the topic was to be Wordsworth. I found a place at the back of the room, and sure enough, the poem under consideration was 'The Solitary Reaper'. Before turning to it, Auden gave the class its research project for the semester, which was to compile a list, drawn from the *O.E.D.*, of all the variant meanings, including the etymologies, of each word in Milton's 'Lycidas', from the earliest recorded usages down to those that were current in the year Milton wrote it. No one complained, no one blenched. That was 1942. In 1985, I doubt that I could get away with asking an undergraduate class to do this. Not being enrolled in the class, I never did the assignment; but one of the students who did once said to me that 'Lycidas' was the only poem in the English language he really felt he knew very much about. Anyway, fifteen or twenty minutes into the hour, in a lull in the discussion, Auden looked quizzically in my direction and said: 'And now let's ask our visitor what he thinks of the image of the girl in the poem.' I had never given much thought to the poem. The lines about the cuckoo 'breaking the silence of the seas' had always seemed wonderful, but about the girl herself I had no special thoughts. In an essay I had written for him in the other class on Kafka's *The Castle*, I had found almost everything in the story—characters, action, circumstances, even the houses and the furnishings of the rooms—to be somehow symbolic of great psychological and spiritual truths, so obviously he had me typed as his symbol person . . . I replied: 'I think she is a symbol', and immediately regretted it.

'Good!' he said . . . 'And what kind of symbol is she? . . . What is she a symbol of?'

I hesitated. 'Well, this is a peasant girl. Peasants were very important to Wordsworth. She could be an idealization of the peasantry. Or perhaps of peasant England . . . I mean, rural England . . . Which he was afraid was passing away.' He thought a bit, said nothing, left the corner of the table, walked slowly toward the windows, and I knew we were in for something. He turned about, leaned his back against the window sill, fixed his gaze on a patch of ceiling above the doorway on the opposite side of the room perhaps thirty feet away. 'A poem is a marriage of a poet's conscious mind and his daemon', he began. 'Making contact with his daemon— his genius—of whose existence, even at the beginning of his career . . . when he has as yet very little to show . . . he has no doubt . . . is never simply a matter of will or determination for a poet . . . Nor is it simply a matter of chance, either . . . It's more like an act of faith . . . like wanting to make a phone call to a friend whose number you can't for the moment remember but which you refuse to look up in the Directory: "Is it 91435? . . . No . . . 95134? . . . No . . . 91354? . . . No . . . Ah! I have it! It's 91534!" . . . In *The Castle*, as some of you will recall, Kafka describes the connection between the village . . . the conscious mind . . . and the Castle . . . or the unconscious . . . in exactly these terms . . . in terms of a telephone exchange which sometimes works beautifully but which often fails . . . Or it functions irrationally . . . with misplaced calls and responses, and half-decipherable messages, and so on . . . I do not know a better analogy than that for the act . . . the initial stages, at least . . . or even the ongoing stages . . . of poetic composition

. . . of getting in touch with one's daemon: "Will no one tell me what she sings?", asks Wordsworth. This is a question every poet finds himself asking at some point . . . at many points . . . during the composition of a poem: "Can you speak a little louder?" . . . "I can't quite make out what you are saying!" . . . "There! I can hear you better now."

'The maiden in this poem is Wordsworth's poetic genius— his "daemon" . . . in Jung's terminology, his "anima", or "soul-image" . . . The anima of the male, in dreams, in poems, appears in the form of a woman . . . Now if we substitute first-person pronouns for the third person pronouns of the poem—"I" for "she", "me" for "her" throughout—we have an unconscious . . . that is to say, unintentional . . . self-portrait of Wordsworth at the very height of his early career, questioning and affirming through the figure of the peasant girl the power and nature of his poetic genius . . . and its importance in the literary landscape of his time . . . You have, after all, in Wordsworth . . . a very great pioneer of modern poetry in English . . . You have the possessor of an enormous lyric talent . . . In the case of this poem one imagines him saying: *Behold me single in the field* (of late eighteenth-century English poetry), *Yon solitary highland boy* (Cumberland and the Lake District were Wordsworth's native "highlands"), *Reaping and singing by myself* (his sense of his singularity in the "field" of contemporary English poetry), in a *melancholy strain* (the very tone of many of his finest lyrics), *the vale profound/Is overflowing with the sound* (literary England seems to be overflowing with my voice).

'Stanza two continues the affirmation: 'My poetry is more surprising than the song of a nightingale suddenly heard in a desert . . . or a cuckoo's far out at sea" . . . These are not immodest, wild boasts by Wordsworth. Not only did they happen to be literally true of him . . . they are also universally true: every poet, at one time or another, must feel this way about his own work, however dissatisfied he may be with it at other times . . . The next stanza puts into a mere eight lines all those tortured questions in Book I of *The Prelude*: "What shall I sing about?"—"Will no one tell me?" . . . "What kind of poet am I?" . . . "How can I discover my real subject?" . . . And he ends by declaring the inexhaustibility of his poetic genius—a

memorable irony, when he was already on the verge . . . it is
now 1805 . . . of the decay of his lyric gift . . . Did the whole
poem perhaps spring from troubled depths of unacknowledged
self-doubt concerning this very point?:

> I listened motionless and still;
> And as I mounted up the hill
> The music in my heart I bore
> Long after it was heard no more.'

I was, I remember, completely enchanted by his remarks—
which I am sure I have given verbatim, for I went over them
carefully immediately after the class, and I have had several
occasions to think about them since. For whatever reason,
they seemed to open up to me whole worlds of possibilities in
literary criticism and analysis—what more can a teacher do
for a student?—and all trace of whatever else transpired that
afternoon has utterly vanished from my memory . . . All this,
of course, was forty years ago. The assumptions of Anglo-
American literary theory and criticism have changed a good
deal in the interval. The psycho-biographical approach which
he favoured, and handled so brilliantly, has yielded to the
methods of other schools; but the sense of a verbal text as
interdisciplinary conflux, or event, is if anything more alive
now than ever. It was this sense, of convergent-and-explosive
text, that Auden unfailingly communicated, more memorably
than any teacher I had ever listened to—though once I heard
him say, in evident despair, that he had no talent for teaching.
There have been times, teaching my own students, when I
have been a little startled, after so many years, to hear his
voice, almost as if in the room, and like some shameless
spirit-medium have heard myself speaking his words, as
though they were my own, and for an instant have seemed to
see him there, half-turned toward the windows, addressing the
late afternoon sky. There must have been some of my students
who wondered, on those occasions, what it was I was smiling
at.

# 6

# Significant Situations: Auden and the Idea of Opera

by ROBERT GIDDINGS

> No good opera can be sensible, for people do not sing when they
> are feeling sensible.
> —W. H. Auden, in *Time, 29 December 1961*

### *1*

As English men of letters go, Auden is unusual in his active
interest in opera. Few of our leading writers have had much
time for opera. They seem unthinkingly to have adopted
Samuel Johnson's much quoted dictum to the effect that opera
was a foreign importation seriously deficient in good sense.
Not only is Auden's work full of references to opera, but he
elaborated some very interesting theories on the nature and
conventions of opera. He also contributed significantly as
librettist to opera in the twentieth century. The last sixty or so
pages of *The Dyer's Hand* (1948)—which includes 'Notes on
Music and Opera', 'Cav and Pag', 'Translating Opera
Libretti' (written in collaboration with Chester Kallman) and
'Music in Shakespeare'—are full of interesting ideas about
opera and lyric theatre.

Chester Kallman introduced Auden to opera in New York
in the early 1940s. This is important. It would suggest that

Auden's initial operatic experience was through the Italian repertory. He escaped the unfortunate (and in most respects infantile) domination of the Glyndebourne-Mozart-*haute bourgeois* axis. This heavily affected other intellectual members of the British middle class of Auden's generation. In British cultural experience the rediscovery and revaluation of Italian opera—the recognition of the true stature of Verdi, Bellini, Donizetti and Rossini—is recent. It dates from some years after the end of World War II.

Verdi's *Macbeth* was produced at Glyndebourne in 1938 and four times in later years. Rossini's *Il Barbiere di Siviglia* was produced in 1954, as was *Le Comte Ory* and *L'Italiana in Algeri* in 1957. There have been productions of Bellini's *I Puritani* and Donizetti's *Don Pasquale* and *L'Elisir d'Amore*. These productions were few in number and quite late in the post-war Glyndebourne period.[1] The arrogant neglect of *bel canto* opera and the exclusive admiration for Mozart opera which amounted to uncritical idolatry were characteristic of British operatic taste at the time Auden intellectually matured.

The most influential operatic pundit of the day was Edward J. Dent, an old Etonian friend of John Christie, the founder of the Glyndebourne Festivals. Dent's *Mozart's Operas: A Critical Study* was first published in 1913 and made an unfortunately immense impact on the development of British operatic taste in the first half of the century. Dent's ever popular *Opera*, put into wide circulation by Penguin Books, was full of superior, snobbish, sneering and jeering about Italian nineteenth-century opera, and provided several generations of the smart set with off-the-peg assertions which originated from the intellect of an opinionated but articulate bigot. There is an unmistakable sub-text in most of the books and journals devoted to the cultivation of musical taste in Britain from the early '30s, until very recent years—many of them written by Oxbridge educated musicologists, born into affluent families (often with double-barrelled names) and educated at public schools. I am referring to such publications as *Gramophone*, the *Record Guide* and its succeeding volumes and the *Penguin Stereo Record Guide*. The sociology of all this is very interesting. It tells one a great deal about the production, distribution and consumption of high culture in our society. It is as if one particular class has gained hegemony over the commodities of culture and shaped, textured and conditioned the cultural taste of the rest. The monopoly of the B.B.C. in this respect is vitally important.[2] The hidden curriculum effectively implied that nineteenth-century Italian opera was mostly junk anyway, far more suitable to the barrel organ than the serious opera house, and that the few honourable exceptions to this were to be found in *opera buffa*. Italians had some gift for this (but even this was pretty limited) and none at all for the pathetic or the tragic. Thus the *Record Guide* 1950 on Donizetti: 'To modern taste . . . the best of Donizetti is contained in his buffo comedies.' In praising John McCormack's 1910 recording of 'Una furtiva lagrima', the book went out of its way to push what's on the other side: 'the only one of his operatic records to survive, and is especially valuable for its fine coupling'. What is this coupling?—why 'Il mio tesoro' from Mozart's *Don Giovanni*, of course.[3] Italian music and Italian musicians and singers tended to the crude; the *Penguin Stereo Record Guide* finds itself quite ready and willing to say of the Guilini recording of Verdi's *Requiem*, for example, 'What Guilini proves is that refinement added to power can provide an even more intense experience than the traditional Italian approach.'[4] And of Karajan's *Aïda*: 'Karajan is of course helped by having a Viennese orchestra rather than an Italian one determined to do things in the "traditional" manner.'[5] This is simply outrageous. Fully to appreciate how outrageous and arrogant it is only necessary to transpose the argument to another sphere and imagine how the British would feel, say, if they were to read in an Australian textbook that it was refreshing to have an American production of *Hamlet* or *King Lear* rather than a British company 'determined to do things in the traditional British manner'. The *Record Guide* asserted that although it was a long time since Bellini's *Norma* had been heard in England, and a complete recording had vanished from the catalogue, 'This is not so regrettable as it might seem.'[6] There is even a widely believed myth which accounts for the disappearance of the *bel canto* repertory from British operatic experience until its rediscovery in the 1950s under the influence of Maria Callas and Joan Sutherland. It used to be claimed that the art of *bel canto* was lost, that there were simply not the singers around who could sing the notes written by Rossini, Donizetti, Bellini and Verdi before *Il Trovatore*. This monumental fabrication is easily deconstructed by scanning the Cetra catalogue of operatic recordings made of the Italian repertory since the 1940s. Here you will find the golden voices who kept alive the masterpieces of the Italian tradition: Rossini's *Mosé, William Tell, Tancredi, La Cenerentola, La Gazza Ladra*; Bellini's *Norma, I Puritani, La Sonnambula*; Donizetti's *Don Pasquale, La Favorita, Lucia di Lammermoor, L'Elisir d'Amore, La Fille du Régiment* and the early works of Verdi. Hard though it is for the British, apparently, to believe, these works *were sung*, and beautifully sung, by fine singers in Italian and American opera houses, and broadcast and recorded, long before the 'discovery' of early nineteenth-century Italian opera by the British in the late 1950s. The smug insularity of British taste in all its morbidity and self-satisfaction is only the cultural counterpart of the famous joke about the fog in the English Channel, which earned the newspaper headline: CONTINENT CUT-OFF BY FOG.

In New York, under the tutelage of Chester Kallman, Auden was introduced to opera at a time and place where the Italian experience of opera was still vigorously espoused by such masters as Arturo Toscanini, Fausto Cleva, Tullio Serafin, Renato Cellini and Jonel Perlea. As Humphrey Carpenter records:

> Auden had been brought up, despite his enthusiasm for music, to be almost totally ignorant of opera—'to think', as he put it, 'that opera was impossible.' This attitude was typical of his parents' generation in England, which believed, as he said, that 'the great Mozart operas might just do because Mozart was Mozart,' but regarded Wagner and Verdi as vulgar and considered Rossini, Bellini and Donizetti to be 'simply beyond the pale'. Auden had scarcely encountered opera before he came to New York.[7]

Auden took to Wagner in a big way, describing Wagner in an article as 'the greatest and most typical modern artist'. He also praised Mozart and Verdi, terming them 'the top composers'. But—as Carpenter points out—he also admired Donizetti and Bellini. He is on record as saying 'No gentleman can fail to admire Bellini.'

Although Auden's comments and analytic insights on opera are randomly distributed amongst the several essays which (significantly) are collected under the title 'Homage to Igor Stravinsky' in *The Dyer's Hand* (1948), it is possible to discern a fairly thoroughly worked out and coherent set of theories about the nature of opera, to recognize the qualities which Auden admired in opera and to apply these standards to the several operas to which he contributed. 'Notes on Music and Opera' is approvingly prefaced by a quotation from Goethe: 'Opera consists of significant situations in artificially arranged sequence.' This is a recognition of the essential ingredient in Auden's conception of opera: the combination of music with striking dramatic situations. In effect it is only a high-fallutin' version of Alfred Hitchcock's joke to the effect that drama is only life with the dull bits cut out, *plus* music.

In discussing the nature of music, Auden is noticeably taken with its physical qualities, its ability to excite, soothe, move or stimulate:

> Man's musical imagination seems to be derived almost exclusively from his primary experiences—his direct experience of his own body, its tensions and rhythms, and his direct experience of desiring and choosing—and to have very little to do with the experience of the outside world brought to him through his senses.[8]

When he considers the nature of operatic experience he seems to concentrate considerably on those examples which feature demoniac, frenzied, larger-than-life characters, placed in life-and-death situations in which their very being is pushed to the extremes of endurance. He writes that opera is 'an imitation of human wilfulness; it is rooted in the fact that we not only have feelings but insist on having them at whatever cost to ourselves'. He seems, then, to emphasize the passionate nature of opera.[9] In discussing the things which, in his view, opera does well, and in outlining its severe limitations, he writes that opera 'cannot present character in the novelist's sense of the word, namely, people who are potentially good *and* bad, active *and* passive, for music is immediate actuality and neither potentiality nor passivity can live in its presence'.[10] He then goes so far as to suggest that complex characters cannot be created operatically, and the richness of personality is a hindrance to its direct expression in music. The example he uses to argue this case is that of Figaro. Mozart's Figaro is too subtle and reflective to succeed operatically, but Rossini's, who is 'not a person but a musical busybody' goes into song exactly 'with nothing left over'.[11] I would strongly argue against Auden's case, but accept his example. Rossini's Figaro *is*, on the whole, a vastly more fully achieved operatic character than Mozart's Figaro. But I think complex and reflective personalities can be presented operatically. In some ways the very nature of opera—which is drama plus music— makes this possible. Music can fill out all sorts of gaps and subtleties not possible solely in words. It can move the senses more immediately and, I think, more deeply than words alone. As Schopenhauer so rightly observed in *The World as Will and Idea* (1819): 'Music does not . . . express this or that particular and definite joy, this or that sorrow, pain, or horror, or delight . . . but joy, sorrow, pain, delight *themselves*.' Music can contradict what words say. It can reveal what a character thinks and feels even when she or he proclaims the opposite. In the hands of the masters, this is what happens in opera— one thinks of Cherubini's Medea, for example, or of Verdi's Falstaff or of Wagner's Wotan and Mime. But, nevertheless, if we are to see what Auden sought to achieve in opera, we must grasp the fact that he saw opera as a rather one-dimensional art. This may help us understand his attraction to particular subjects and the way in which he treated them.

Consequently he assumed that opera best presented characters who were the embodiment of one dominating idea or emotion: 'The quality common to all the great operatic rôles, e.g. Don Giovanni, Norma, Lucia, Tristan, Isolde, Brünnhilde, is that each of them is a passionate and wilful state of being. In real life they would all be bores, even Don Giovanni.'[12] Putting aside the sad fact that this kind of thinking shows the woeful influence of such as A. C. Bradley—the very idea that 'characters' can be abstracted from the dramatic/literary/ operatic context in which they have been put into existence by their creators and considered as personalities, e.g. you might even bump into them in the street, is very Bradleyan—even taking Auden's own evidence we may see that it is demonstrably

untrue, as Norma, Lucia, Tristan, Isolde, Brünnhilde are all
characters who are riven by complexities of motivation and
who present a very wide range of behaviour and emotion.
They are not dominated by one emotional drive, but by
considerable and subtle pressures and conflicts. He is correct
about Don Giovanni, who would be a bore in real life. He is a
bore on stage too.

A compensation for music's inability to present psychological complexity, Auden believed, was its ability to do what
words could not do, that is 'present the immediate and
simultaneous relation of these states to each other. The
crowning glory of opera is the big ensemble.' This too is a
baseless theory. It is nonsensical to award the palm to the
ensemble, and to underrate the extraordinary revelation of
character possible in aria, to neglect the possibilities of duet,
trio and quartet and (as we should all have learned from
Wagner by now) the astonishing things which are possible in
recitative. However, once again, the point of the exercise is to
take note of Auden's ideas about the texture and quality of
opera as an aesthetic experience, to assess what he thought
opera could and could not do.

The chorus, he believed, had severe limitations in its
contribution to opera. It had only two rôles, either that of the
mob or of the faithful, sorrowing or rejoicing community. A
little of this went a long way, he thought: 'Opera is not
oratorio.' To which one might be tempted to add, yes, and
oratorio is not opera.

The basis of drama, he believed, was the mistake: 'I think
someone is my friend when he is really my enemy, that I am
free to marry a woman when in fact she is my mother.' Opera
has to subscribe to the same principle, but is more limited: 'in
comparison to the dramatist . . . in the kinds of mistake he can
use.' Dramatists can show how people deceive themselves, but
'self-deception is impossible in opera because music is
immediate, not reflective'.[13] The only possibility in presenting
self-deception operatically, he believed, lay in having an
orchestral accompaniment which is at variance with the
singer, so that we in the audience know things that the singer
does not know. But this device, he says, causes confusion
rather than insight. Part of the quality of great drama is that it

164

can show the revelation of the 'mistake' as a gradual process. This is denied opera: 'for music cannot exist in an atmosphere of uncertainty: song cannot walk, it can only jump.' A few pages of the last Act of *Tristan* would dispose of this argument, but again, the point is to note the theory, and pass on.

Opera does not have to bother about being *credible*, as opera is by definition melodrama:

> in both the strict and the conventional sense . . . it offers as many opportunities as possible for the characters to be swept off their feet by placing them in situations which are too tragic or too fantastic for 'words'. No good opera plot can be sensible, for people do not sing when they are feeling sensible.[14]

He develops this point in a splendid anti-Wagnerian joke:

> The theory of 'music-drama' presupposes a libretto in which there is not one sensible moment or one sensible remark: this is not only very difficult to manage, though Wagner managed it, but also extremely exhausting on both singers and audience.[15]

Sensible passages, he asserts, have to be set as recitative.

The orchestra is there for the singers, not for the audience. It has no function apart from that it performs for the vocal part. Long orchestral parts are boring. Again, his evidence is valid (the 'Leonora' Overture in Beethoven's *Fidelio*, which *is* boring) but his case is ridiculous—we need only think of Siegfried's *Rheinfahrt* or *Trauermusik* in *Götterdämmerung*.

A libretto cannot be poetry. Poetry, he argues, is reflective, but music is immediate, and it follows from this that the words of a song cannot be poetry. (I sometimes wonder what Schumann or Schubert Lieder Auden ever listened to?) Words are only important insofar as they inspire the composer. They are not addressed to the public, but are 'really a private letter to the composer. They have their moment of glory, the moment in which they suggest to him a certain melody; once that is over, they are as expendable as infantry to a Chinese general.'[16] People do not listen to words. They only hear sung syllables.

There has been an important shift of perspective in modern literature, Auden believes, which has affected opera. As modern man feels incapable of intervening in collective history, so writers since Poe have become interested in timeless passionate moments in a life, rather than seeing a life as a total narrative experience, with a beginning, a middle and an end. Auden detects the same trend in music:

> a static kind of music in which there is no marked difference between its beginning, its middle and its end, a music which sounds remarkably like primitive proto-music. It is not for me to criticise a composer who writes such music. One can say, however, that he will never be able to write an opera. But, probably, he won't want to.[17]

It is Auden's belief that opera was inescapably the result of man's belief in liberal humanism, of unquestioning belief in freedom and progress. Modern opera is a rarity because these fundamental beliefs have been dismantled. Opera is essentially the expression of free will and the personality: 'Every high C accurately struck demolishes the theory that we are the irresponsible puppets of fate or chance.'[18]

It is obvious that these theories are firmly based on the experience of nineteenth-century Italian opera, from Rossini, through Bellini, Donizetti and on to Verdi—but the Verdi of *Rigoletto*, *La Traviata* and the operas up to *I Vespri Siciliani* (1853), rather than the grander and more majestic Verdi of *Simon Boccanegra*, *Un Ballo in Maschera*, *La Forza del Destino* and *Aïda*. In much the same way as we assume Aristotle to have drawn up his basic assumptions about the nature of tragic drama by exploring the fundamentals of the Greek tragedies that he knew, Auden's theoretical apparatus on the nature of opera is based on the Italian operas to which he had been exposed. The friendship with Chester Kallman is crucial, as it was with him that he went regularly to the Metropolitan Opera House during the period when the general manager was Edward Johnson (1878–1979) whose stewardship during the years 1935–50 saw the encouragement of American artists; among the stars were Leonard Warren (a leading Verdi baritone), Dorothy Kirsten (who specialized in the major Italian rôles), Jan Peerce and Richard Tucker, who were both celebrated in Italian tenor rôles—the latter chosen by Toscanini for his N.B.C. radio production of *Aïda* in 1949. Jan Peerce starred in Toscanini broadcasts of *La Bohème*, *La Traviata* and *Un Ballo in Maschera*.

It is also important evidence that the most complete and sustained analysis of opera that Auden wrote is his discussion of Mascagni's *Cavalleria Rusticana* (1884) and Leoncavallo's *I Pagliacci* (1892).[19] To put no finer point on it, Auden's conception of the nature of opera was formed almost entirely from his knowledge of nineteenth-century Italian lyric or *bel canto* operas, immediately prior to the emergence of Puccini. It is true that he refers several times to *Don Giovanni* and other operas by Mozart (not many times) and occasionally to Wagner, but nevertheless his views are founded on the Italian repertory up to middle-period Verdi:

> About the music of these two operas (*Cavalleria Rusticana* and *I Pagliacci*) I can, of course, only speak as a layman. The first thing that strikes me on hearing them is the extraordinary strength and vitality of the Italian operatic tradition. Since 1800 the Italian opera had already produced four fertile geniuses, Bellini, Rossini, Donizetti and Verdi, yet there was still enough left to allow, not only the lesser but still formidable figure of Puccini, but also the talents of Ponchielli, Giordana and Leoncavallo to create original and successful works. Today, indeed—it may have seemed different in the nineties—we are more conscious in the works of these later composers of the continuity of the tradition than of any revolutionary novelty. We do not emerge from the house after hearing *Cavalleria* or *Pagliacci* for the first time, saying to ourselves, 'What a strange new kind of opera!' No, before the first ten bars are over, we are thinking: 'Ah, another Italian opera. How jolly!'[20]

## 2

Given this evidence it is difficult to account for the nature and kind of operas to which Auden himself so significantly contributed as librettist: *Paul Bunyan* (1941), with music by Benjamin Britten: *The Rake's Progress* (1951), with music by Igor Stravinsky; *Elegy for Young Lovers* (1960) and *The Bassarids* (1966), both with music by Hans Werner Henze. But there is another vital influence which Auden accommodated, albeit not uncritically—that of Bertolt Brecht.

When Auden arrived in Berlin in 1928 he could not have timed his visit better had his intention been to absorb the influence of Brecht and the tradition in which he worked and which he was to fashion into his own idiom. As Charles Osborne writes:

> Berlin, in the last days of the Weimar Republic before the advent of the Nazis, was an exhilarating place. It was a time when social and artistic life had a great variety of excitement to offer; when there was, for instance, as much experimental music to be heard in the concert halls and opera houses as there was experimental sex to be had in the streets leading off the Kurfürstendamm. Something in the much lauded Berlin air seemed to be conducive to both a mental alertness and a moral laxity. Music, theatre, cinema and the visual arts all flourished. The collaboration of Bertolt Brecht and Kurt Weill had produced *Der Dreigroschenoper* . . . which opened at the Theater am Schiffbauerdamm, with Weill's wife Lotte Lenya as Jenny, some weeks before Auden's arrival in Berlin and which he saw soon afterwards. The political cabaret was still very active and influential, though, as later events were to prove, not quite influential enough. Auden revelled in his newly found freedom. . . .[21]

Auden's famous off-the-cuff remarks about Brecht are often bandied about, and indeed the poet himself made rather a party-piece out of them. They are quoted in full by John Willett:

> Now what were Auden's real feelings about Brecht? Why, after admiring his writings and collaborating apparently painlessly with him, did he switch to an attitude of evident distaste for Brecht after the Second World War? In 1975 I got a letter from Charles Monteith of Faber's saying, among other things: 'Auden said to me—not once but many times as it was one of his favourite conversation-stoppers—that of the literary men he had known only three struck him as positively evil: Robert Frost, Yeats and Brecht! When I asked him to expand a little he said, about Brecht, 'He was simply a crook. Never gave up either his Austrian nationality or his Swiss bank account.'[22]

There are several reasons for Auden's apparent dislike of Brecht, apart from the poet's tendency to overstate and to come forward with outrageous opinions. John Willett suggests that Auden was aware that it was dangerous in the McCarthy era too openly to associate with the Left, and he also quotes a

very interesting comment by Edward Mendelson to the effect
that at bottom Auden and Brecht were in fact very much alike:
'Both started as romantic anarchists, then converted to an
orthodoxy around the age of thirty.' It may have been Auden's
view that he had converted to the true orthodoxy and that
Brecht had converted to the false one. Hannah Arendt
believed that the pair had more in common than Auden was
ever ready to admit. It is not so much their beliefs which are
similar, but the kinds of works they created which they
believed would propagate those beliefs:

> They liked hymns, the Bible, the poems of Kipling, old and new
> popular ballads, scientific thought and technical gadgets. They
> had wonderful imaginations, which, like Kipling, they could
> harness to simple colloquial language and quite rigid and
> traditional verse forms. They wrote clearly. They had a
> subversive, plebian angle on things. They didn't try to bullshit
> you.

This admirable summing up is by John Willett.[23]

It is only correct that a discussion of Brecht must sooner or
later find itself located in definitions of *modernism*, but nevertheless there is a very strong case to be made to demonstrate
that far from being a new departure, Brecht's work was really
the apotheosis of a tradition long maturing through Shakespeare, ballad opera, Lenz, the early works of Schiller, Goethe
(*Faust* I and *Faust* II, no less than *Götz von Berlichingen*),
Grabbe, Büchner, Wedekind and Kipling.[24] It is difficult to
see whether Auden was drawn to what we now take to be
characteristic of Brecht's work because he himself was
sympathetic to it, or whether the Brechtian qualities in Auden
are the result of the British writer's attempts to imitate, to
learn from and to assimilate the format and style of Brechtian
theatre. But the clear fact is that Auden's contributions to the
Group Theatre[25] clearly evidence Brechtian qualities—a
seemingly radical commitment, the use of popular and
vernacular language, cabaret and ballad forms—which
produced a mixture of university revue, light verse, popular
song, powerful and moving verse. The result was an equal mix
of cabaret and serious political purpose. Auden's acquaintance
with Brecht/Weill opera was absolutely first hand, as Chester

Kallman and Auden translated *Das Sieben Todsunden*. And he had some interesting things to say about the nature of Brechtian ballad-opera which would indicate an understanding of the use of Brecht's theories in the practical business of constructing an opera:

> *Die sieben Todsünden* is not a traditional opera in which, as Mozart said, 'poetry absolutely has to be the obedient daughter of music', but, like all the Brecht/Weill collaborations, a work in which the words are at least as important as the music, and its language is that of contemporary speech and full of popular idiom.[26]

It becomes quite clear when examining the evidence of *Paul Bunyan*, *The Rake's Progress*, *Elegy for Young Lovers* and *The Bassarids* that Auden took several Brechtian lessons to heart. The texts Auden provided show his reaction against the traditional Aristotelian theatre which purports to present something resembling 'real life' and the use of several of Brecht's *Verfremdungseffekte* which distance the spectator from the sense of theatrical illusion and reminds him or her continually and continuously that they are watching a performance, not observing 'life'. Although Auden seems on the face of it to be attracted to the lyrical and emotional qualities of Italian opera, it was the artificiality of opera which truly fascinated him. He seems to strive to create an operatic text (libretto) which is obviously artificial, but is at the same time idiomatic, and which will make its impact on spectators not through their feelings, emotions, passions or whatever, but *intellectually*.

### 3

The earliest opportunity Auden had of putting some of these ideas practically to the test was in the operetta *Paul Bunyan*, which dates from 1939. Auden's old friend, the composer Benjamin Britten, had arrived in New York. He had recently toured Canada with Peter Pears, intending to return to Europe in August. When the German invasion of Poland precipitated World War II they decided to stay in America a little longer. Britten actually considered staying in America.

The Auden-Britten friendship[27] was renewed. It was at the suggestion of the New York office of Britten's publishers, Boosey and Hawkes, that the two of them worked together on a composition which could be performed by high school students. They selected the American folk-hero, Paul Bunyan, as a suitable subject. The character had several obvious qualities which seemed to make him a sensible subject. Paul Bunyan was a widely known figure. He was a giant lumberjack with superhuman powers who seemed to personify the spirit of the nation. Auden found these archetypal qualities interesting and attractive.

As he wrote in the *New York Times* the day before the premier on 5 May 1941: 'At first sight it may seem presumptuous for a foreigner to take an American folk-tale as his subject, but in fact the implications of the Bunyan legend are not only American but universal.' It is very interesting that Auden was always attracted to write operas about figures whose activities bodied forth the great mythic truths of human experience, and that he used such subject matter didactically. These are very Brechtian qualities. The programme of the first performance at the Brander Matthews Hall of Columbia University contained an interesting description of *Paul Bunyan*, suggesting that Auden and Britten had conceived Paul Bunyan, the lumberjacks' giant hero, as

> a projection of the collective state of mind of a people whose tasks were primarily the physical mastery of nature. This operetta presents in a compressed fairy-story form the development of the continent from a virgin forest before the birth of Paul Bunyan to settlement and cultivation when Paul Bunyan says goodbye because he is no longer needed, i.e. the human task is now a different one, of how to live well in a country that the pioneers have made it possible to live in.

Auden, an ex-patriot Englishman who had resolved to remain in the U.S.A. (he took American nationality in 1946), had pounced on one of the most dearly held of American myths, the pioneer who tames the virgin land as the initial process to the founding of the new nation—the Great Society.

One effect was rather forced upon them, and that was in the presentation of Paul Bunyan himself. It was considered

impossible to show him on stage because he was a giant.
Auden and Britten resolved the problem by having the hero
presented by means of an off-stage voice, speaking rather than
singing. Although not personally visible, the hope was that the
personality of Paul Bunyan would preside over the whole
action. This is an interesting solution to what was a technical
problem, as in fact it projects Bunyan as a spirit, as an isolated
and detached voice—the soul of his people.

The story of the opera is told by a ballad-singer. The birth
and early life of Bunyan is narrated in simple couplets. The
clearing in the virgin forest is described as 'America, but not
yet'. Bunyan asks that all the energetic madmen and disturbers
of the public order from everywhere should join him in his
efforts to create the new society. This is a fundamental
American myth, a representation of the 'huddled masses' and
the 'new found land' so all-pervasive in American ideology,
taken in with American mothers' milk and worked up into a
high quality mass media confection in Alistair Cooke's B.B.C./
Time-Life *America: A Personal History*—the thinking man's
Disneyland.[28] One of the new arrivals is Slim, who falls in love
with Bunyan's daughter, Tiny, who—as her name implies—is
of normal size. The matter of size is very interesting and
curiously transatlantic. We are constantly being reminded that
Abe Lincoln was tall for his period—as in Aaron Copland's *A
Lincoln Portrait*[29]—and Alistair Cooke gratuitously informs us
that Columbus was 'a giant of a redhead, six feet tall'.[30] We live
in times devoted to Ronald Reagan's lauded attempts to make
America stand tall in the saddle. It is interesting that Auden
homed on this transatlantic fetish for the perpendicular.

Another American element Auden attempts to absorb is the
musical show, and he found himself obliged to write 'lyrics'.
There are frequent moments in *Paul Bunyan* when proceedings
come to a stop because he felt he had to embark on a display of
verbal pyrotechnics. This complexity suited Britten, but in his
later collaborations with Stravinsky and Henze, Auden found
his tendency to verbal intoxication held rather beneficially in
check. In Act 1 scene 2 we find this dialogue:

*Johnny*: You must sing her a love song.
*Chorus*: That's too hard and takes too long.

*Johnny*: Nonsense. It's quite easy, and the longer it is, the more she'll like it. Use the longest words you can think of. Like this:

> In this emergency
> Of so much urgency
>   What can I
> Except wax lyrical?
> Don't look satirical;
> I have empirical
>   Proof I love you.
> Speaking with deference,
> I have a preference
>   For a nice view:
> Your look of spaciousness,
> Your manner's graciousness,
> Your mind's herbaceousness
> Your whole palatiousness
>   Makes me love you.[31]

And it goes on and on. As Johnny actually says, 'Got the idea? . . . When I think of a word, you think of another word to rhyme with it.' This principle, rhyming for the sake of rhyming, is far too often Auden's guiding inspiration in *Paul Bunyan*, though some of the rhymes are funny—'All nouns are dedicate/ To this one predicate/ Adjective too:/ Appendectomy/'s a pain in the neck to me.' The effect is of a W. S. Gilbert with pretensions to high art. Britten loved it.[32]

The second act shows that unrest has developed among the pioneers; the moment for the change from the primitive stage of the nation's development from a woodland and farming economy to that of business, trade, commerce and all that goes with it, has arrived. The opera ends with the marriage of Slim and Tiny. He has now become the manager of a large hotel in Manhattan; other characters are slotted in appropriate job-rôles. Johnny, a clerk, goes to Hollywood to be a technical adviser, and Hel Helson goes to Washington to an administrative task in the 'Federal Plan of Public Works for the Nation'. U.S.A. is seen as the ultimate home for the self-made man:

> The pattern is already clear
> That machinery imposes
> On you as the frontier closes,
> Gone the natural disciplines

173

And the life of choice begins . . .
America's destroyed and created, America is what you do,
America is you and I, America is what you choose to make it.

In *Paul Bunyan* some of the various parts are more impressive than the sum of the whole. The theme of the play is interesting and well presented in words and music, but often it gets lost in its own smart-aleckery. The reviews were not good.[33] The *New Yorker*'s columnist said the work did not jell. This is well put; the ingredients had not been well mixed and the dish did not set.

In October 1947 Auden received a letter from Igor Stravinsky in Los Angeles. He had visited the Chicago Art Institute, where he had examined the engravings of William Hogarth's *Rake's Progress*. He had wanted to compose a full length opera in English for some time. The engravings impressed him and suggested a possible subject.[34] In effect Stravinsky had chosen the subject of the opera. On the advice of Aldous Huxley he wrote to Auden to ask if he would be interested in writing the libretto. Auden saw it as his task to satisfy the composer. To some considerable extent the subject of the opera dictated the form. As the composer himself wrote: 'Rather than seek musical forms symbolically expressive of the dramatic content . . . I chose to cast *The Rake* in the mould of an eighteenth-century "number" opera, one in which the dramatic progress depends on the succession of separate pieces—recitatives and arias, duets, trios, choruses, instrumental interludes.'[35]

Having resolved on a period piece the composer decided also to assume the conventions of the period. The writers of the libretto (Auden enlisted the aid of Chester Kallman) therefore had a double task; they had to provide a narrative structure based on those elements of Hogarth's paintings which seemed useful for the construction of an opera—in other words Stravinsky was taken with the theme of *The Rake*, and Auden and Kallman had to provide the fable—and they had to lay out this narrative in terms of the conventions of eighteenth-century opera, with recitatives, duets, arias, concerted numbers, choruses and finales. On both counts the basic anatomical requirements were good for Auden's imagination. He and

Kallman got together to flesh out the bare bones.

The story they created is extremely effective, given that we understand the basic assumptions of the composers and his librettists. Stravinsky was quite conscious that he was re-using the past, and accepted fully the fact that opera was both exotic and irrational—these are the words used by the composer. We are not to see the work as realistic or naturalistic. It is not a chunk of life as it is lived. But it is a slice of the very essence of life. It concerns itself with matters of life and death. It is a morality, as *Everyman*, Goethe's *Faust* dramas, as Wagner's *Der Ring* are all moralities. It is as unreasonable as the stuff of dreams, but like dreams it is fully convincing. Also, like dream-stuff, it is charged with meanings and messages if we only know how to read them. It is no accident that Auden admired Freud so much, the man who tried to teach the century to learn from dreams not because they told us the future but because they told us about ourselves.

The impression gained from looking at the Auden/Kallman libretto is very eighteenth-century. The work is made up from the basic operatic 'Lego' of Mozart—recitatives, duets, concerted numbers, etc. And no doubt in production, what with the Hogarthian influence being very hard to ignore, the visual impression would be Georgian too. But these are really surface qualities. The core of *The Rake*'s moral conflict is presented in terms of the *humanus genus* figure of Tom Rakewell. He stands for humanity and all its temptations, in the best morality tradition.

The opening is idyllic. The garden of Trulove's house in the country. It is spring. Tom is in love with Trulove's daughter, Anne. Her father hopes to gain Tom a sound job in the city. This is not welcome news for Tom, who prefers to rely on fortune rather than hard work:

> Since it is not by merit
> We rise or fall,
> But the favour of Fortune
> That governs us all,
> Why should I labour
> For what in the end
> She will give me for nothing
> If she be my friend?

175

And he ends by saying, 'I wish I had money.' As if called by inner mythic necessity, Nick Shadow appears, with the news that Tom has been left a fortune by his uncle. Nick explains that certain arrangements will need his attention in London and after fond farewells to Anne and her father the two set off, with Nick in the rôle of Tom's servant in the picaresque traditional manner, Tom having agreed to reckon up what Nick's services are worth in a year and a day.

The echoes of the relationship between Faust and Mephistopheles are obvious, as Nick attempts to entertain Tom with all the indulgences of London. The pleasures of the flesh begin to pall, and Tom is persuaded to marry Baba the Turk, the bearded lady, and to buy a phoney invention which it is claimed will turn stones into bread. Tom goes bankrupt and all his things are sold. When the stipulated year and a day are up, Nick reveals to his master that he is the Devil, and claim's Tom's soul. This scene is set in a graveyard heavy with symbolic overtones. As the clock strikes midnight Nick suggests they gamble for Tom's soul. Tom wins, and Shadow sinks into the ground. His departing act is to turn Tom insane:

> I burn! I freeze! In shame I hear
> My famished legions roar:
> My own delay lost me my prey
> And damns myself the more.
> Defeated, mocked, again I sink
> In ice and flame to lie,
> But Heaven's will I'll hate and till
> Eternity defy.
> Your sins, my foe, before I go
> Give me some power to pain:
> To reason blind shall be your mind.
> Henceforth be you insane!

The opera ends with Tom in Bedlam, believing himself Adonis. He tells his insane companions to prepare for his wedding to Venus. They say no Venus shall come to him. Anne comes to wish him farewell, and she rocks him to sleep on his straw bed. She calls him Adonis to humour him. Tom is delighted to be vindicated before his peers. He sinks back and dies. In a very Mozartian finale Tom, Anne, Baba, Nick and

Trulove point up the moral that the Devil makes work for idle hands.

The collaboration between the composer and his librettists was in the main a harmonious one and the result is a cohesive work which nevertheless reveals several major ingredients. The most obvious is the Mozartian-Italian opera[37] and the links with Mozart are very strong. At the time of its composition Auden and Stravinsky were very taken up with *Così fan Tutte*[38] and Auden was to translate *Don Giovanni* and *Die Zauberflöte*. Several scenes are obvious in their derivation—the churchyard and the epilogue immediately remind one of parallel moments in *Don Giovanni*. There are other Italianate qualities which owe much to Stravinsky's profound and beneficial knowledge of Verdi's operas and to Donizetti and Rossini; he uses *cavatina* and *cabaletta* in such a way as to cause Eric Walter White to assert: 'There is nothing to show that Stravinsky has been affected by any operatic developments subsequent to Donizetti and middle-period Verdi.' But also the construction and style of *The Rake's Progress* owes much to *The Beggar's Opera*, the original prototype of *Der Dreigroschenoper*. The relationship between the opera being performed and the audience on stage as well as the audience in the auditorium in *The Beggar's Opera* places it firmly in the great tradition which was to lead to Bertolt Brecht. There is throughout *The Rake's Progress* a self-conscious and artificial quality which constantly reminds us we are watching a play-with-music-and-singing and not observing 'real' life.

## 4

Auden's next operatic venture paradoxically was to be less successful but more fruitful. In 1954 he met the young German composer Hans Werner Henze, then 28 years old. Henze had considerable experience as an operatic composer. *Das Wundertheater* (after Cervantes) was produced in 1948. This was followed by the radio opera *Ein Landarzt* (1951) and *Boulevarde Solitude* (1952), based on the play by Walter Jokisch, which in turn is a modern version of *Manon Lescaut*. It is worth noting that as well as having considerable experience as a conductor of ballet and orchestral music, as well as opera, Henze was a composer who was not hidebound by the German *Kapellmeister* tradition. In fact, politically, temperamentally and musically it would not be an exaggeration to say Henze is more Italianate than Germanic.

This shows strongly in his approach to opera. *Boulevarde Solitude* is constructed in separate numbers and features a significant ballet—nothing could be more un-Wagnerian! This was followed in 1953 by a further radio opera *Das Ende einer Welt*, a satire of cultural snobbery. It contains interesting evidence of Henze's concern for the place of the artist in society and his relationship with his fellows. This theme was further to be explored in the opera Auden and Kallman were to write for him—*Elegy for Young Lovers*. When he met Auden on Ischia he was writing his second full-length opera, *König Hirsch*, which was produced in 1956. Auden was impressed with this work.[39] In 1958 Henze was commissioned by the South German Radio to write an opera and he asked Auden and Kallman to collaborate with him. The venture was to be a chamber opera, with a small cast and no chorus. Auden has left on record the comment: 'Our original idea was that we should have four or five characters, each of whom was mad in a different way.' As Humphrey Carpenter says, this follows naturally from Auden's belief that in order to sing, all characters must be a little mad.[40] There are various forms of insanity presented in the work which was to become *Elegy for Young Lovers*, produced at Schwitzingen in 1961.

The drama is set at a mountain inn, the Schwarze Adler, in the Austrian Alps. The great poet Gregor Mittenhofer (who was based on W. B. Yeats, one of Auden's most unfavourite persons) stays here each year. He arrives in the company of Carolina von Kirchstetten, his patroness, Elizabeth Zimmer, his mistress, Dr. Reischmann, his physician, and his son Toni. The subject of the drama, according to the composer, is the gestation and creation of a poem that is in the process throughout the three acts, from its first idea to its final public reading. There was a deliberate attempt to mix the hilarious, the wicked, the vulgar, the murderous and the banal in order to question the nineteenth-century romantic construction of the artist-as-hero. Mittenhofer has always relied on gaining inspiration from the deranged visions of the widow, Hilda

Mack, who has lived at the Schwarze Adler for four decades. She is an amalgam of Miss Havisham and Mrs. Clennam, believing that she still lives at the time when her husband was killed in a mountaineering accident on the first day of their honeymoon.

When the late Herr Mack's body is found, preserved in a glacier, Hilda's madness is cured, to be replaced by insights into the motives of her neighbours' behaviour. Elizabeth Zimmer falls in love with Toni Reischmann, but they are doomed to die in the same conditions which killed Herr Mack. Mittenhofer has lost the inspiration he always had from Hilda Mack, but he now draws on the terrible tragedy of the young lovers. The end of the opera finds Mittenhofer reading his poem to a fashionable audience.

Henze constructed the work not so much in terms of its themes as in terms of instrumental colours which are associated with the various characters: Mittenhofer/brass, Carolina/cor anglais, the lovers/violin and viola, Reischmann/bassoon and saxophone, and Hilda/flute. The point of the drama is that in order to create his poem Mittenhofer has destroyed two young people, whom he could have saved. His poem is represented wordlessly by the interwoven themes and instruments of the various characters. His vanity, and the vanity of the world of which he is a lionized product, is brilliantly rendered in the finale; just before he goes on stage in Vienna we find him tying his white tie and going through a cheer sequence: 'One. Two. Three. Whom do we adore?' And then dedicating his poem to 'the memory of a brave and beautiful young couple'.

Most of the text is by Kallman. Auden admitted to writing only about 25 per cent. Significantly it was dedicated to Hugo von Hofmannsthal, who wrote so many operas for Richard Strauss. Indeed *Elegy for Young Lovers* has much of the Viennese decadence which is at the core of the Strauss/ Hofmannsthal operas. There is also much of Thomas Mann; one is reminded strongly of the *fin-de-siècle* morbidity of *Der Tod in Venedig*. It was successful in Germany. Chester wrote to friends after its premier: 'Our opera went well in Germany, I think. Fischer-Dieskau (as Mittenhofer) was fabulous, the sets were God-awful left-over faggot chic by a German heterosexual, and absolutely unpractical for the action. Oh well.' (Letter dated 21 May 1961 in Carpenter, p. 401.)

Like *Paul Bunyan*, this opera failed to hold itself together properly, though full of good ideas. German audiences liked it but it struck its first English audiences as phoney, arty-crafty and decidedly lacking musical interest. At Glyndebourne the orchestral sounds were not admired in 1961, and it was booed at its conclusion: 'Unfortunately, booing *Elegy for Young Lovers* didn't make it a *Pelléas*; or a *Traviata*; or a *Barber of Seville*; or even a *Wozzeck*', wrote Spike Hughes,

> It was just booed and failed to convince even the ordinary non-booing Glyndebourne listener that it was of any world-shattering consequence. The personal columns of *The Times* reflected this apathy almost immediately in the number of advertisers who had tickets for Henze's opera that they wanted to exchange for something, anything, else at Glyndebourne that season.[42]

It was said that when John Christie met Auden and Kallman in the grounds at Glyndebourne and was told they had written *Elegy for Young Lovers*, he said: 'Oh dear, you shouldn't have, really you shouldn't.'[43]

Henze hoped that Auden would write another opera and suggested they work on a tragedy together.[44] Auden put forward *The Bachhae* of Euripides, and during the autumn and winter of 1962–63 Kallman and Auden composed a libretto. (Interestingly enough, Auden was also attracted at the same time to another project, a Broadway musical based on *Don Quixote*. In the event his lyrics were not used in the show which was to become *The Man of la Mancha*, but his attraction to archetypal figures is always striking.) *The Bachhae* was a subject charged with magnetism for Auden, who had been deeply imbued with Freudian ideas, which were part of the intellectual furniture of his generation.

*The Bassarids*, as Henze's opera was called, received its premier at the Salzburg Festival in a German translation in 1966. The English libretto was not staged until the Sante Fé production in August 1968.[45] At this stage Auden was seriously considering translating the whole of Wagner's *Der Ring der Nibelungen*. This again demonstrates his characteristic inclination towards the mythopoetical subjects which seem to act out the primal nature of human kind. Euripides's *The Bacchae* is concerned with the mother/son theme, which is placed against a background of a religious power struggle. Dionysus travels to Thebes, where King Cadmus, father of the god's mother, Semele, has abdicated in favour of his son, Pentheus, who represents the New Order. Pentheus finds Dionysus and his followers a socially disturbing force and commands their imprisonment. The god escapes and takes his revenge by striking Pentheus's mother, as well as other women of Thebes, with insanity. They are changed into Maenads, the Bacchantes, raving votaries of Dionysus. They rush to Mount Cithareon to take part in Dionysus's orgies. Pentheus follows them and climbs into a pine tree better to observe their activities. His mother, Argave, in a frenzy, tears him to pieces and returns in triumph with his head.

In an interview published in the *Opern-Journal der Deutschen Oper Berlin* in 1966 on the occasion of its German premier, Henze quoted with approval the comments of Eric Neumann in *The Origins and History of Consciousness*, which discuss the conflict between the old and the new order so centrally thematic in *The Bacchae*:

> Pentheus belongs to those who resist, but are not yet capable of a liberatory heroic deed. It is Bacchus Dionysus whom he resists, but as his fate and his sin show, here too the real enemy is the terrible figure of the Great Mother. It is well known that Dionysus belongs to the orgiastic realm of the Great Mother and her son-lover Osiris, Adonis, Tamuz ... At Delphi Dionysus is worshipped as an infant or a *putto* in the corn-hopper. It is an earth cult, with the Moon goddess Semele (Dionysus's mother) as earth mother. Since he originates from Thebes and settles in Asia Minor, fusing with the Magna Mater cult there, he probably perpetuates a universal early cult of the original pre-Greek religion.
>
> The heroic King Pentheus, proud of his reason, and with his mother the closest relative of Dionysus, advances towards the orgies and is overwhelmed by the orgiastic power of Dionysus. Pentheus suffers the fate of all victims of the Great Mother; he goes mad, and comes to the orgies in woman's clothing, where he is torn to pieces by his own mother, who in a fit of madness takes him for a lion. The fact that she triumphantly carries his

181

head home with her is a residue of the castration that originally
occurs, in addition to the mutilation of the body.[46]

The subject matter is clearly latent with meaning for those
who go armed with the insights of Freud, Jung and Adler. In
this respect Auden was a field officer with many years' front
line experience. Also it was a subject which he felt would
respond to some of the techniques he had learned from Brecht.
Henze does not think that these archetypal figures are
'alienated' by the librettists 'in the Brechtian sense'[47] but that
by placing them in various and changing period settings—
between antiquity and *la belle epoque*—they are clarified and
explained:

> What has occurred is an interpretation—resting moreover on a
> Christian world view—of Euripides's play, by laying bare the
> primal mythical motifs it contains. Of course, in the process all
> elements come into the integument of contemporary problems:
> the discoveries of Freud, Adler and especially Jung play a part,
> not only in the diversely elaborated mother-son theme, but also
> in tension between Dionysus and Pentheus themselves. The
> timelessness of the themes requires no alienation but, at most,
> to be brought up to conscious and decisive part in a music
> drama of mine.[48]

As Henze rightly perceived, the basic conflict in the drama
is that between social repression and sexual liberation—a
theme to which Auden would feel a deep pull, as it leads to the
liberation of the individual. It explores the nature of the revolt
made by personalities who go against powerful social conventions. Self-realization is seen as a kind of intoxication as the
Dionysus within the personality is released. Auden is aware
that often those who seek to repress this self-realization are not
necessarily evil people. Pentheus is no Nazi. He is a notable
King of Thebes, educated by the best minds in Greece. But
nevertheless the social context ensures that he becomes the
victim of his own repressed sexuality. The danger really comes
when his inner conflicts and stresses are projected onto a wider
social canvas. The Auden/Kallman libretto is Euripides
rewritten in the light of modern experience. One bold stroke is
the inclusion of Christian experience which is deployed to
balance the archaic Euripides, and the other is psychoanalysis.

The ending is courageous in its originality. Euripides's drama ended with Dionysus exiling the Theban royal family, but Auden ends with the apotheosis of Dionysus, who commands Persephone, the goddess of the underworld, to surrender his mother, Semele, to him. He rises into the sky with her, unmistakable ruler of the world. The parallels with Christ and the Virgin Mary are obvious enough.[49]

Auden's contribution to modern opera was true to his theoretic assumptions about the nature of opera, and he was profoundly influenced by Italian models of lyric theatre. As Tonio says in the rôle of chorus at the opening of *I Pagliacci*: 'our author has attempted to draw you a piece of real life. His sole maxim is that the artist is a man, writing for men. Our author took his inspiration from the truth.' Auden's libretti, though they may be cast in an artificial and highly stylized form, and though his characters may be larger than life, use the opportunities of opera to explore aspects of real life by presenting 'significant situations in artificially arranged sequences'. He found the very artificial nature of opera enabled him to realize some basic Brechtian qualities. The audiences of *Paul Bunyan*, *The Rake's Progress*, *Elegy for Young Lovers* and *The Bassarids* will be constantly aware that they are watching music drama, in which the most highly charged sections are sung not spoken, and they will therefore—as Brecht believed—not become emotionally involved as in naturalistic/realistic theatre, but remain outside the action as observers and judges of character and event. In this respect Auden was more Brechtian than he might have thought. And Brecht more traditional than he believed.[50]

## NOTES

1. Spike Hughes, *Glyndebourne: A History of the Festival Opera* (David and Charles, 1981), pp. 279 and following.
2. See Arthur Marwick, *Class: Image and Reality in Britain, France and the USA Since 1930* (Collins, 1980), pp. 157 and following.
3. Edward Sackville-West and Desmond Shawe-Taylor, *The Record Guide* (Collins, 1951), pp. 203–5.

4. Edward Greenfield, Robert Layton and Ivan March, *The Penguin Stereo Record Guide*, second edition (Penguin Books, 1979), p. 1083.
5. Ibid., p. 1084.
6. *The Record Guide*, op. cit., p. 96.
7. Humphrey Carpenter, *W. H. Auden: A Biography* (George Allen and Unwin, 1981), pp. 261–62.
8. 'Notes on Music and Opera' in *The Dyer's Hand* (1962), p. 467.
9. Ibid., p. 470.
10. Ibid.
11. Ibid.
12. Ibid.
13. Ibid., p. 471.
14. Ibid., p. 471–72.
15. Ibid., p. 472.
16. Ibid., p. 473.
17. Ibid., pp. 473–74.
18. Ibid., p. 474.
19. See *The Dyer's Hand*, op. cit., pp. 475–82.
20. 'Cav & Pag' in *The Dyer's Hand*, op. cit., p. 481.
21. Charles Osborne, *W. H. Auden: The Life of a Poet* (Eyre Methuen, 1979), pp. 58–9, cf. Carpenter, op. cit., pp. 85 and following.
22. John Willett, *Brecht in Context: Comparative Approaches* (Methuen, 1984), p. 71, cf. Ronald Hayman, *Brecht: A Biography* (Weidenfeld and Nicolson, 1984), pp. 300 and following.
23. Willett, op. cit., p. 72.
24. See Malcolm Bradbury and James McFarlane, *Modernism 1890–1930* (Penguin Books, 1976), pp. 556 and following; Willett, op. cit., pp. 74 and following; and Edward Callan, *Auden: A Carnival of Intellect* (Oxford University Press, New York, 1983), pp. 62 and following. Cf. Donald Mitchell, *Britten and Auden in the Thirties: The Year 1936* (Faber and Faber, 1981), pp. 71, 109 and 120.
25. See pp. 186–200.
26. *The Dyer's Hand*, op. cit., p. 484 and cf. ibid., pp. 492–93.
27. See Carpenter, op. cit., pp. 178, 181–84, 187–89, 205, 208, 216, 222, 229, 232–33, 246 and Osborne, op. cit., pp. 108–12, 127–28, 138, 139, 148–49, 174, 176, 178, 179, 193, 195, 196 and Mitchell, op. cit., passim.
28. Robert Giddings, 'Cooking the Books' in *New Society* 14 June 1979, pp. 652–53.
29. There is a self-indulgent performance of this work, somewhat inevitably narrated by Henry Fonda, on CBS 72872.
30. Alistair Cooke, *America* (Alfred Knopf, New York, 1974), p. 30.
31. For an interesting discussion of this see Mitchell, op. cit., pp. 136–37.
32. Carpenter, op. cit., p. 278.
33. Osborne, op. cit., pp. 208–9.
34. Osborne, op. cit., p. 225 and see Eric Walter White, *Stravinsky: The Composer and his Works* (Faber and Faber, 1979), pp. 450–68.
35. Igor Stravinsky, *A Programme Note* (Paris, 1964), quoted in Paul A.

Griffiths, *Igor Stravinsky: The Rake's Progress* (Cambridge University Press, 1982), p. 2.

36. Ibid., p. 3.
37. Francis Routh, *Stravinsky* (J. M. Dent, 1975), pp. 88–9; Roman Vlad, *Stravinsky*, translated from the Italian by Frederick and Ann Fuller (Oxford University Press, 1967), pp. 168 and following and White, op. cit., pp. 458 and following.
38. White, op. cit., p. 458.
39. Carpenter, op. cit., p. 398.
40. Ibid.
41. Carpenter, op. cit., p. 401.
42. Spike Hughes, op. cit., p. 222. This is not a great deal to go on, of course, for the taste of the *haute bourgeoisie* is notoriously timid.
43. Ibid.
44. Osborne, op. cit., p. 273.
45. Osborne, op. cit., p. 286.
46. Hans Werner Henze, *Music and Politics: Collected Writings 1953–1981*, translated by Peter Labanyi (Faber and Faber, 1982), pp. 147–48.
47. Henze, op. cit., p. 148.
48. Ibid.
49. *The Bassarids* did not receive its British premier until the English National Opera production at the London Coliseum on 10 October 1974.
50. In 1969 Auden and Kallman wrote a libretto based on Shakespeare's *Love's Labour's Lost*, for the Russian born composer Nicolas Nabokov, who lived in the U.S.A. See Carpenter, op. cit., pp. 428–29 and 447. It was premiered at Brussels in 1973 and scored a mild success but has not since been revived.

# 7

# Engaging an Audience: Auden as Playwright

## by MARGARET MOAN ROWE

### *1*

In his 'Introduction' to *The Oxford Book of Light Verse*, W. H. Auden provides a most concise description of the creative imperative:

> Behind the work of any creative artist there are three principal wishes: the wish to make something; the wish to perceive something, either in the external world of sense or the internal world of feeling; and the wish to communicate these perceptions to others.[1]

It is one thing, however, to describe one's wishes and quite another to realize them, particularly in so conflict-ridden a decade as the '30s in England. Like other artists of his generation, Auden faced the task of realizing his wishes in an 'external world' described by Louis MacNeice as a place 'more and more on the slant so that no mere abstract geometry or lyrical uplift could cure it'.[2]

Yet the idea of writers being called on to help prescribe a 'cure' for society's ills was a particularly appealing one in the '30s. For unlike the writers of the '20s, those who came to maturity in the '30s felt compelled to dovetail aesthetic and social obligations; as W. W. Robson has observed:

> The new writers of the 1930's shared a definite sense of reaction against the temper of the previous decade. Novelists

186

like Lawrence, Huxley, or the Powys brothers were stigmatized as morbid, socially irresponsible, navel-staring. The brittle gaiety of the twenties seemed as alien as its despair and hysteria. The new writers had in common a sense of urgency, a crispness, a shedding of affectations and frills. Where the twenties had been indifferent to political or religious commitments, the thirties were obsessed with them. The day of the cultured *rentier* was over. The harsh, bracing facts of modern society had to be understood, the growing menace of the international scene confronted.[3]

Even so formidable a critic as Virginia Woolf could not ignore the sense of urgency that dominated Auden's generation: 'in 1930 it was impossible—if you were young, sensitive, imaginative—not to be interested in politics; not to find public causes of much more pressing interest than philosophy.'[4] And Auden, in his work throughout the decade, demonstrated his own interest in and reflected his generation's preoccupation with politics. But despite all the pressures to do otherwise, Auden, for the most part, avoided the temptation to allow the pressure of 'public causes' to dominate his 'wish to perceive something'. Thus, in the shaping of his poetic vision he sought to reconcile the demands of private and of public worlds without obliterating the former.

Indeed, given Auden's description of the creative impulse, it is difficult to consider the nature of his poetic vision without referring to its relationship to technique and to audience. In fact one can argue, as John Blair has, that the make-up of his audience had much influence in the selection of those techniques that Auden used to present his vision in his '30s' poetry.[5] For the question of audience was and is a central problem for artists working in a century in which not one but many audiences exist. 'For whom should we write?' asks Virginia Woolf, and she goes on to speak of

> the present supply of patrons . . . of unexampled and bewildering variety. There is the daily Press, the weekly Press, the monthly Press; and the English public and the American public; the best-seller public and the worst-seller public; the high-brow public and the red-blood public; all now organised self-conscious entities capable through their various mouthpieces of making their needs known and their approval or displeasure felt.[6]

Like Woolf, Auden, throughout his career, displays great concern with the diversity of audiences but nowhere is that concern more obvious than in his work in the '30s. In that period, Auden's idea of an audience takes on added importance when one realizes that he so often links the artist's 'wish to communicate' with the idea of community, for, as he notes in *The Poet's Tongue* (1935), 'a universal art can only be the product of a community united in sympathy, a sense of worth, and aspiration; and it is improbable that the artist can do his best except in such a society.'[7] Auden's notion of community clearly springs from social as well as aesthetic demands; on the one hand, the community functions as a source of 'universal art', but more than that it is the place where the poet can be a man as well as an artist, because according to Auden, 'The problem of the modern poet, as for every one else today, is how to find or form a genuine community, in which each has his valued place and can feel at home.'[8]

Theoretically, Auden's community is made up of every level of society, and, as a result, his prospective readers could be drawn from varied groups. In actuality, however, Auden's initial attempts to communicate with an audience belie the egalitarian idea of community in the preceding quotations. What one sees in the imagerial and syntactical obscurity, the preparatory school motif, and the private jokes in the works written between 1928 and 1934 are efforts to communicate with a very definite audience—a community of peers. In his early works, Auden self-consciously relies on a readership of friends who shared his sense of rebellion against the old ways and who, to some extent, suffered from the same ambivalence about the very nature of that rebellion.[9] It is not until the middle of the decade and particularly in his work for the Group Theatre, that one sees Auden working toward greater clarity and trying to reach a larger audience.

## 2

In Auden's early poems the revolution which would release the young from repression was primarily moral and psychological in nature—any suggestion of political change, even in 'It was Easter as I walked in the public gardens' (*Poems*

(1930)), was at best vague. But the opposition to 'the old gang' that permeates the first poems and *The Orators* (1932) becomes more focused in the four plays[10] written by Auden, three in collaboration with Christopher Isherwood. For in the plays, Auden, influenced by historical Marxism, unites his call for a revolution within with limited support for a revolution without as he politicizes his call for a change.

The small band led by 'The tall unwounded leader' who people the early poems and battle the forces of internal repression are merged in the plays with the revolutionary forces of history. The transformation itself is not difficult to understand because as Justin Replogle has noted: 'Obviously psychological allegory could easily be converted to Marxist allegory. Both have common philosophical roots, and both psychological and political traditions provide, in their dialectical structure, a built-in drama of opposing groups.'[11] And just as one sees Auden modifying the schoolboy mythology of his early works in the plays, so too one sees Auden the playwright attempting to reach beyond the private audience. There are private jokes and symbols still, particularly in *The Dog Beneath the Skin*, but the plays are far more accessible to the wider public than most of the works that preceded them.

Auden sought not just to address a larger audience through his plays, but, more importantly, he tried to forge that 'genuine community' of which he speaks in *The Oxford Book of Light Verse*. Thus, he attempted to involve his audience in the dramatic action itself, because as he noted in the programme for *The Dance of Death*: 'Drama began as the act of a whole community. Ideally there would be no spectators. In practice every member of the audience should feel like an understudy.'[12] That involvement, obviously, was not to end with the dramatic production itself. Like Brecht, Auden shaped drama designed to turn his audience from the ways of illness to the ways of health. Caught by the spirit of his decade, Auden sought to use the drama, and the productions of the Group Theatre in particular,[13] to educate the public so that they might be roused to necessary political action.

It was such an intent that caused Auden to write *The Dance of Death*, staged by the Group Theatre in 1933. In this drama the Announcer, acting as an intermediary between the action on the stage and the audience, expounds the theme at the outset:

> We present to you this evening a picture of the decline of a class, of how its members dream of a new life, but secretly desire the old, for there is death inside them. We show you that death as a dancer. (p. 185)[14]

And the overtly didactic intent of the play is obvious in the dramatic manner as well. In depicting the decline and final collapse of capitalistic society, Auden uses types, a device familiar to readers of *Poems* (1930), and basically static scenes, rather than emphasizing character development or the interaction of characters. Moving from summer camps where mankind is invited to 'Come out into the sun' and forget 'Europe's in a hole/ Millions on the dole' (p. 187) through emerging militarism and rabid nationalism, the play presents a society informed by its own drive to destruction. The *coup de grâce* is delivered by the latecomer Karl Marx who portentously announces: 'The instruments of production have been too much for him [the Dancer]. He is liquidated' (p. 218).

In delineating the inevitability of capitalistic decline, Auden relies heavily on the popular song model for suitably parodic purposes. This very reliance is obviously part of Auden's teaching technique; for these parodies are more easily remembered because of the popularity of the original forms. The most effective example of this technique appears at the end of the play when to the tune of 'Casey Jones' the Dancer, embodying capitalism's death wish, makes his final will:

> He leaves you his engines and his machines
> The sum of all his productive means.
> He leaves you his railways, his liners and
> his banks
> And he leaves you his money to spend with
> thanks.

(p. 214)

Along with the Dancer's last wishes, Auden intersperses a choral synopsis of history:

> Luther and Calvin put in a word
> The god of your priests, they said, is
> absurd.

190

His laws are inscrutable and depend upon
    grace
So laissez-faire please for the chosen
    race.

The bourgeois thought this splendid advice
They cut off the head of their king in a
    trice.
They enclosed the common lands and laid
    them for sheep
And the peasants were told they could play
    bo-peep.

(p. 214)

The song model allows Auden to exploit the familiar as a vehicle for a Marxist reading of history, now popularized for the theatre audience. In the above stanzas, the fragmented syntax with extensive ellipsis that one finds so often in Auden's first volumes is avoided in favour of a clearer syntactical pattern. Simple sentences with an almost unvarying subject/verb/object structure are linked paratactically making no terrible demands on the audience's comprehension. The technique itself is quite rudimentary: clarity is the syntactical hallmark, and both tune and stanza form are already known. As a result, concentration can be focused on content, and, again, the passion for simplicity is obvious as historical complexities are reduced to basics; capitalism is nothing more than the sum of its 'productive means' and the creeds of Luther and Calvin are reduced to the catalysts of capitalism's excesses.

In this example and in others, particularly the presentation of the hedonistic sun-worshippers at the beginning of the play and the nationalists in the 'Alma Mater' sequence, Auden uses effective parody to battle the enemy because he knows what he is against. Yet for all its success in cleverly satirizing the enemy, Auden's attempt as a whole is not successful, for the parody all too often seems to have become an end in itself. The enemy is attacked, but who, asks the onlooker, are 'We' in the drama? One questions the overall effect of parody that is so diffuse as to cause the reader to wonder which side he is supposed to be on. In general, Auden is against the old forms and for the

coming new order, but so much is ridiculed that one cannot be
sure what is really intended. So many alternatives are
parodied that one cannot be sure when, if ever, Auden is
acting as advocate.[15]

Nothing stands against Auden's indictment; among the
many positions presented, then discarded, in the drama is one
not unlike an earlier attitude of Auden himself—'But what
you're needing/ 'S a revolution within.' And when attacking
the hedonistic sun-worshippers, Auden includes aims which
might be Marxian as well as nationalistic as they seek to 'build
to-morrow/ A new clean town'. For that matter, the Marxist
position itself is presented ambivalently as workers chant:

> One, two, three, four
> The last war was a bosses' war.
> Five, six, seven, eight
> Rise and make a worker's state.
> Nine, ten, eleven, twelve
> Seize the factories and run them
>       yourself.

(p. 195)

Again regular syntax, with simple and compound sentences
linked paratactically, dominates so that the message is quickly
conveyed to the audience. There is nice irony, too, in using the
model of a child's chant—the means used to introduce the
child to numbers and, perhaps, to a capitalist economy—as
bearer of the Marxist message.

But again there is a basic problem of intent here: is the
chant to be treated as a serious statement or is the form of a
child's song to be interpreted as criticism of the content? If one
looks at the other parodies in the play, one sees form under-
cutting content; for example, in the 'Casey Jones' section the
content which describes the rise and fall of capitalism can be
attacked by being reduced to the lyric of a parody. How then is
one to respond to the imperative sentences in the workers'
chant; are they to be accepted as serious injunctions or is the
form acting as a criticism of those very commands? Not even
Marx, whose appearance Herbert Greenberg has called 'more
appropriate to Groucho than Karl',[16] is free from Auden's
humour as he enters with the play's summation to the

'Wedding March' and leaves to a Dead March. Thus, despite the cleverness of much of the satire and the impressiveness of the dance motif, the play does not really work because of an ambiguous point of view; it is clear that 'They' are opposed in *The Dance of Death*, but how 'We' are viewed remains the big question in the play.

The problem of attitude toward 'They' and 'We' is not so obvious in the three plays Auden wrote in collaboration with Christopher Isherwood[17] between 1935 and 1939. In *The Dog Beneath the Skin*, *The Ascent of F6*, and *On the Frontier*, the forces of the established order array themselves against the small number of the select who will bring the new day. And in all the plays, the end, even when bringing the deaths of those who might be termed 'We' (Michael Ransom in *The Ascent of F6* and Eric and Anna in *On the Frontier*), brings also the sentimental, and often baseless, assurance that 'they to dissolution go'.

In *The Dog Beneath the Skin* (1935), their first collaboration, Auden and Isherwood employ the fairy-tale quest as the basis of the drama in which Alan Norman travels through Europe seeking Sir Francis Crewe, the missing heir of Pressan Ambo. In the course of the search,[18] Alan, accompanied by a dog who in the end reveals himself as Sir Francis, witnesses, and to some extent becomes involved in, decadence and corruption on all levels of society. But after their return to Pressan Ambo, Alan, Francis, and several others who join them elect to leave and enlist 'in the army of the other side' to battle groups like the fascist Lads of Pressan who stand: 'outside all of political parties and factions, for Church, King and State, against communism, terrorism, pacifism, and all other forms of international anarchy, to protect Religion and succour England in times of national crisis' (p. 100).[19] Thus, they begin what appears to be the right quest for a new moral and social order: for 'another country/ Where grace may grow outward and be given praise' (p. 112). And as in *The Dance of Death* that new order is associated with Marxism, typified by the final promise of the play: 'To each his need: from each his power' (p. 112).

Using Alan's somewhat disjointed search, which takes him to a variety of places—court, red light district, asylum, and luxury hotel among others—the authors work within the frame of the musical comedy, appealing to a larger audience, even as they score some satirical points against the enemy. Particularly effective is the lyrical exchange between chorus and journalists in Act I, Scene II. Employing the example of John Gay, Auden implicates everyone from the Queen of Poland to Oxbridge dons in the corruption of society. And effective too is the Destructive Desmond episode (Act II, Scene II) which Auden attributes to Isherwood.[20] That scene captures all the vulgarity of the bored bourgeoisie and the destructiveness of excessive egoism as Desmond entertains a suitably coarse audience at the Nineveh Hotel by slashing a Rembrandt canvas.

At the same time, however, one finds a deep stylistic division in *The Dog Beneath the Skin* where the focus in what might be termed the 'inner play' is on the fairy-tale quest and the decision made by Alan and Francis, while the focus in the choral poems is on reality. In his choruses, the most impressive poetry in any of his dramatic works, Auden attempts to deal with the problems of emotion and intellect, the divisions in man. And as a result of what Julian Symons has termed 'choruses which seem part of the parable-art that is to teach us to unlearn hatred and learn love',[21] the choral poems tend to be pronouncements directed toward the audience. The public tone of the choruses is established at the beginning of the play when the chorus as orator, as in the earlier poem 'Who stands, the crux left of the watershed' (*Poems* (1928)), invites the onlookers to an overview:

> The Summer holds: upon its glittering lake
> Lie Europe and the islands; many rivers
> Wrinkling its surface like a ploughman's
>     palm.
>
> .    .    .    .    .
>
> We would show you at first an English
>     village: You shall choose its
>     location
> Wherever your heart directs you most
>     longingly to look; you are
>     loving towards it:
> Whether north to Scots Gap and Bellingham
>     where the black rams defy the
>     panting engine:

Or west to the Welsh Marches; to the
    lilting speech and the magicians'
    faces;
Wherever you were a child or had your
    first affair
There it stands amidst your darling
    scenery:
A parish bounded by the wreckers' cliff; or
    meadows where browse the shorthorn
    and the maplike Frisian.

(p. 5)

The chorus, typically, is directed toward 'you' the audience, to some extent involving that body in the action itself—'You shall choose its location'. And reflecting the greater heterogeneity of Auden's theatre audience, any location in England is possible; the backdrop of the play is not limited to the country of mountains and weirs populated by small bands of outsiders that appealed to the more homogeneous, myth-oriented audience addressed in the 1928 and 1930 volumes. But at the same time, even as there is an attempt in the choruses to involve the audience in the play, the choruses are also used to keep the audience from viewing the play as an end in itself. Auden employs the choruses to distinguish between the play which is the creature of the imagination and the reality which lies beyond the aesthetic creation. The nature of the choral poems is to expand the play so that the central concerns, psychological as well as political, will be remembered long after the experience of viewing the dramatic action is over.

The emphasis in the first choral poem and elsewhere in the play is on the mind attempting to contain many elements: 'the black rams who defy the panting engine' as well as 'the lilting speech and the magicians' faces'. The brevity of the music hall skits in the inner play disappears, and the emphasis in the choruses is constantly on the speaker's attempt to present as many details as possible, as seen in the choral poem at the end of Scene IV, Act III:

Visit from house to house, from country to
    country: consider the populations
Beneath the communions and the coiffures:
    discover your image.

195

Man divided always and restless always:
    afraid and unable to forgive:
Unable to forgive his parents, or his first
    voluptuous rectal sins,
Afraid of the clock, afraid of catching his
    neighbour's cold, afraid of his own
    body,
Desperately anxious about his health and his
    position: calling upon the Universe
    to justify his existence,
Slovenly in posture and thinking: the greater
    part of the will devoted
To warding off pain from the water-logged
    areas.

(pp. 97–8)

The repetition of the colon here is typical of Auden's use of that punctuation mark in the choruses of *The Dog Beneath the Skin*. In lines 1 and 2 the colon is used to balance independent clauses while in lines 3 through 8 the colon shows progression and accumulation, underscoring the emphasis on a continuous flow of observations in the choral poems in general. The chain of evidence could have been linked by other marks of punctuation, but the use of periods might have produced too great a division. And the semicolons which could have been substituted in lines 1 and 2 and the commas which might have served in place of the second colon in line 3 and the colon at the end of line 8 are omitted in favour of a punctuation mark with more historical and practical use in the drama.

The colon serves as a strong breathing mark in the choruses as well as the mechanism for syntactical progression. As Eric Partridge has noted:

> Etymologically, *colon* (Greek *kólon*) was originally a person's limb; hence, portion of a strophe in choral dancing, hence a division in prosody; hence, also, a clause—notably a principal clause—in a sentence; hence, finally, the sign . . . marking the breathing-space at the end of such a clause.[22]

Thus, Auden's marked preference for the colon in *The Dog Beneath the Skin* would seem to spring from two sources: the necessity to make the choral poems effective as spoken poetry and the necessity to stress the semantic connections between the sections of his many catalogues.

The latter need arises from Auden's frequent omission of syntactical connections in his basically paratactical syntax. Many paratactical constructions appear in the play perhaps as a result of Auden's employment of catalogues. In his saga *Paid on Both Sides* (1930) parataxis and a fragmented syntax suggested the rudimentary apprehension of reality by people in the saga world where 'Shot answered shot/ Bullets screamed/ Guns shook Hot in Hand.' But in *The Dog Beneath the Skin*, parataxis and basically regular sentence patterns form accretive catalogues which suggest the mind's attempt to comprehend the very complexity of reality:

> A man and a dog are entering a city: They
>       are approaching a centre of culture:
> First the suburban dormitories spreading over
>       fields,
> Villas on vegetation like saxifrage on stone,
> Isolated from each other like cases of fever
> And uniform in design, uniform as nurses.
> To each a lean-to shed, containing a well-
>       oiled engine of escape.
> Section these dwellings: expose the life of
>       a people
> Living by law and the length of a reference.
>
> (p. 74)

Here in Act III and elsewhere in the play, the chorus conveys the sense of an experienced viewer telling what he has seen in 'a centre of culture', but there is no overt attempt to order that scene by subordinating some images to others. It is the camera eye moving across the landscape leaving judgement to others—in this case the members of the audience who are asked to participate ('Section these dwellings: expose the life of a people'). Ironically perhaps, the very absence of subordinating conjunctions and the ordering suggested by them underscores the futility of any attempt to order experience until man has overcome the many problems which the choruses present.

Throughout the choruses there is that undertone of futility, as the internal and external complexity of man whose

197

'impulses are unseasonal and image-ridden' is contrasted to the world of 'the black rams, the Shorthorn, and the mating of lions'. The choruses in the play depict the conflict in man, caught as he is between conscious and subconscious demands; and the simpler existence of non-human life serves as a dramatic backdrop for that conflict, as in Act II:

> Happy the hare at morning, for she cannot read
> The Hunter's waking thoughts. Lucky the leaf
> Unable to predict the fall. Lucky indeed
> The rampant suffering suffocating jelly
> Burgeoning in pools, lapping the grits
>     of the desert,
> The elementary sensual cures,
> The hibernations and the growth of hair
>     assuage:
> Or best of all the mineral stars disintegrating
>     quietly into light.

(p. 57)

Here the contrast, working from animate to inanimate objects, points indirectly to the complexity of man's problem—he is 'divided always and restless always'—and the intensity of his desire to escape. This choral speech is very like an earlier creation of Auden's in *Paid on Both Sides*; in the speech beginning with the line 'Could I have been some simpleton that lived', John Nower, the hero, demonstrates his yearning for release from the saga world and from his own consciousness. In both works, however, there is the ultimate recognition that escape to a simpler existence is impossible for 'Man caught in the trap of his terror'.

Thus, it is difficult to reconcile the choral speculation about the splendour and the misery of the human condition with the rather sentimental victory 'We', represented by Francis and Alan, achieve at the end of the inner play. For the quest which they undertake is the authors' creation and, therefore, subject to whatever ending they choose. But the choruses, concerned as they are with the very shapelessness and complexity of man's experience, can offer no solutions. Of course, the authors attempt some sort of reconciliation: the chorus is called on to sanctify the final departure from Pressan Ambo, and that is done in the name of love, an often invoked but never defined term in Auden's '30s' poetry. The chorus exhorts the audience to 'Choose therefore that you may recover: both your charity and your place' (p. 112).

Doubleness of vision plagues *The Ascent of F6*, too; in their 1936 collaboration Auden and Isherwood once more attack the establishment represented by Sir James Ransom, General Dellaby-Couch, and their cohorts who ask for sacrifice for 'the future of England, of the Empire' (p. 135).[23] On another level, in the character of Michael Ransom the mountaineer, the play tentatively explores the complexity of the human being caught between the demands of the will and the ego. In the play, the characters Mr. and Mrs. A act as a chorus and comment on the limitations of ordinary existence: 'Evening. A slick and unctuous Time/ Has sold us yet another shop-soiled day' (p. 119). For them and the common people they represent, the government prepares its 'gaudy box': a public sharing in the Ransom expedition to climb F6.

The poetry in the second collaboration is limited, for the most part, to the commentary of Mr. and Mrs. A (much of it in couplets to reflect the tedious sameness of everyday life) and to the encounters between Michael Ransom and his domineering mother. There is little of the complexity of the choruses or the cleverness of the songs found in *The Dog Beneath the Skin*, but the central problem in both plays is the same; for all the commitment to political regeneration, both Isherwood and Auden show greater interest in the intricacy of the human personality. In both plays the stated focus is political, but in both the complexity of human nature eludes the rather simple solutions that the political theory seems to offer.

So it would seem that for all the satirical humour directed against his own belief in the need for 'a revolution within' in *The Dance of Death*, for all the certainty in *The Dance of Death, On the Frontier*,[24] and even in parts of *The Dog Beneath the Skin* and *The Ascent of F6*, that change of government will be a magic wand for human progress, there remains in the work of Auden the playwright an even stronger, albeit often unfocused, conviction that change must really begin within man before it is truly effective without. For all the Brechtian ingredients in the plays, Auden seems less than convinced that the complex problem of being human will become simpler in a more politically compatible climate. The psychological almost always overpowers the political in Auden's plays.

While political commitment proves to be only part of the cure for a sick world in the plays, a sense of commitment—a desire to change his society—compelled Auden to seek a larger audience, a wider sphere of influence. And through his work in the theatre, he learned that a less esoteric style was necessary to secure that audience. *Paid on Both Sides* and *The Orators* may certainly be termed dramatic, but they are often obscure and incomprehensible. By wedding his talent for the dramatic with a desire to teach the ways of health, Auden the playwright began to develop a style that, according to M. K. Spears, 'makes possible for him to work out a mode of discourse in which the public (including the political) and the private can meet',[25] a style that led to a surer poetic voice in the middle and late '30s, in volumes like *On This Island* (1936), *Letters from Iceland* (1937), and *Journey to a War* (1939).

## NOTES

1. W. H. Auden, *The Oxford Book of Light Verse* (Oxford, 1938), vii.
2. Louis MacNeice, 'The Tower that Once', *Folios of New Writing* (London, 1941), p. 38. MacNeice was replying to Virginia Woolf's criticism of '30s' writers in her essay 'The Leaning Tower' (see note 4).
3. W. W. Robson, *Modern English Literature* (London, 1970), p. 125.
4. Virginia Woolf, 'The Leaning Tower', *Folios of New Writing* (London, 1940), p. 22.
5. In *The Poetic Art of W. H. Auden* (Princeton, 1965), John Blair contends that Auden 'is aware and perhaps even hyperconscious of his audience. So much so that many of his changes in style and manner have been stimulated by the attempt to isolate and engage different sorts of audiences', p. 21.
6. Virginia Woolf, 'The Patron and the Crocus', *The Common Reader* (New York, 1925), p. 212.
7. W. H. Auden, 'Introduction', *The Poet's Tongue* (London, 1935), viii.
8. Auden, *The Oxford Book of Light Verse*, xix.
9. Although often extreme in her criticism of '30s' writers, Virginia Woolf pinpoints the dilemma of many of her younger colleagues when she notes that no matter how revolutionary their stance 'They cannot throw

away their education; they cannot throw away their upbringing. Eleven years at school and college have been stamped upon them indelibly', ('The Leaning Tower', p. 22).

10. For the purposes of this essay only two of these plays will be examined closely as examples of the influence on his poetry of Auden's attempt to reach a larger audience: *The Dance of Death*, Auden's first performed play, and *The Dog Beneath the Skin*, Auden's first collaboration with Isherwood.
11. Justin Replogle, *Auden's Poetry* (Seattle and London, 1969), pp. 30–1.
12. As quoted by Julian Symons in *The Thirties: A Dream Revolved* (London, 1960), p. 79.
13. Julian Symons maintains that 'The Group Theatre had aesthetic ideas, and it had a social attitude; the first springing largely from Doone [Rupert Doone, director], the second from Auden', *The Thirties*, p. 79. See also 'Parables of Action: I' in Edward Mendelson's *Early Auden* (New York, 1981), pp. 264–68.
14. Quotations from *The Dance of Death* are from the text in *Poems* (New York, 1934).
15. In *The Making of the Auden Canon* (Minneapolis, 1957), J. W. Beach notes that 'the style of presentation in *The Dance of Death* is such that we cannot resist laughing at every position as it is stated', p. 154. Justin Replogle maintains: 'If we must decide finally whether *The Dance of Death* is a statement of or a parody of Auden's familiar evolutionary death wish theme, surely we must choose parody (with a parody of Marx added)', *Auden's Poetry*, p. 112.
16. Herbert Greenberg, *Quest for the Necessary* (Cambridge, Massachusetts, 1968) p. 65.
17. There is the problem of identifying individual contributions in the collaborative works, although several critics have made attempts: J. W. Beach, *The Making of the Auden Canon*, p. 155; B. H. Bloomfield, *W. H. Auden: A Bibliography* (Charlottesville, Va., 1964), pp. 13–14; and Mardi Valgemae, 'Auden's Collaboration with Isherwood on *The Dog Beneath the Skin*', *H.L.Q.*, 31 (August 1968), 373–83. Thus, only the poetry, all of which except for one lyric in *The Dog Beneath the Skin* has been attributed to Auden, will be discussed.
18. Alan Wilde refers to Alan Norman's initial quest as 'one of the false journeys that recur in Auden's poetry', *Christopher Isherwood* (New York, 1971), p. 79.
19. Quotations from *The Dog Beneath the Skin* are from the text in *Two Great Plays* by W. H. Auden and Christopher Isherwood (New York, 1962).
20. Bloomfield, *Bibliography*, p. 14.
21. Symons, *The Thirties*, p. 83.
22. Eric Partridge, *You Have a Point There* (London, 1953), p. 52.
23. Quotations from *The Ascent of F6* are from the text in *Two Great Plays*.
24. Like *The Dance of Death*, *On the Frontier*, the final Auden-Isherwood dramatic collaboration, uses a Marxist interpretation of history to depict the plight of the warring states of Ostnia and Westland, caught as they are in the manipulations of the military-industrial complex represented

by the capitalist Valerian. Auden uses songs, none of them noteworthy, by workers, soldiers, and students as choruses, but these songs have none of the cleverness or satirical bite of the productions in *The Dance of Death*. *On the Frontier* is much more focused than *The Dance of Death* but is much less imaginatively appealing than the early play. It is also the most politically dogmatic and least interesting Auden-Isherwood collaboration.

25. M. K. Spears, *The Poetry of W. H. Auden: The Disenchanted Island* (New York, 1963), p. 89.

# 8

# Auden's Prose

## by STEWART CREHAN

As a writer of prose Auden was a craftsman, but often as the master of somebody else's prose style. Ransom's opening soliloquy in *The Ascent of F6*, for example, is a pastiche, just as 'Caliban to the Audience', the long prose section of 'The Sea and the Mirror', is a parody (yet more than 'just' a parody) of Henry James:

> Into that world of freedom without anxiety, sincerity without loss of vigour, feeling that loosens rather than ties the tongue, we are not, we reiterate, so blinded by presumption to our proper status and interest as to expect or even wish at any time to enter, far less to dwell there.

The four oratorical voices of *The Orators*, identified as the hectoring headmaster, the meditating priest, the objective assessor, and the voice of tender love—the last 'exploded with far the greatest subtlety, sinister force, and razor's edge poise'[1]—exemplify Auden's exhibitionist and chameleon-like powers; the catalogue of 'Statement' has an Elizabethan inventiveness, where words are used like coloured counters in a game whose aim seems to be to produce the most varied and surprising patterns within a certain set of rules, these being defined by the limits of the catalogue itself. Auden wrote highly polished and baroque prose, declamatory prose, figurative and imaginative prose, discursive and autobiographical prose, a 'Commonplace Book', and travelogues. Faced with such quantity and variety, it is necessary to be selective. I shall, therefore, concentrate on the essays, reviews and critical writings, since it is here that one expects to find the writer's ideas, opinions and beliefs given their clearest outline, and where the prose itself ought to create that outline. I shall confine myself to two volumes: *The English Auden*, edited by Edward Mendelson, and *The Dyer's Hand*, Auden's own collection of essays, published in 1963.

Richard Hoggart said of Auden's prose:

> When he is writing 'creatively', Auden is always something of an actor. His essayist's, critic's and lecturer's style is, comparatively, flat, rather too tightly packed, and unusually free from tonal variations. It is as if, once he is out of the 'creative' atmosphere, Auden loses his literary personality and remains erudite, intelligent and suggestive, but not very imaginative in his use of language.[2]

The implication that essay writing as an activity took Auden out of 'the "creative" atmosphere' is somewhat tendentious, since a literary essay can be as 'creative' as a sonnet. Auden, it seems, worked hard to give his prose a rhetorical weight that would in turn give permanence and authority to a range of reflections on a wide variety of topics based on his wide interests, wide experience and even wider reading, and that would also serve as a kind of magnet pulling together various conclusions on the relations between language, literature and society. Yet Auden the essayist does not compare well, say, with D. H. Lawrence, T. S. Eliot, F. R. Leavis or George Orwell, names that immediately evoke certain qualities: an impassioned anger and partisanship that drives on until the theme has been completely exhausted; original, incisive judgements of classical brevity; a hawk's eye for the meretricious, and the cogency of intelligently honest, plain speaking. With Auden, no single comparable quality stands out; we do not remember his essays as we remember those of Lawrence or Orwell, for example. What we remember tend to be particular maxims and epigrams, sentences and paragraphs—which is not surprising, since Auden sometimes favoured a dogmatic and sententious style, to the extent that some of his 'essays' are simply a loosely-connected series of random observations and aphoristic pronouncements (e.g. 'Writing' and 'Hic et Ille'; 'Making, Knowing and Judging', his Oxford Inaugural Lecture, is a belletristic ramble, self-consciously displaying the winner's obligatory urbanity and poetic qualifications). Among the few that stay in the mind as whole arguments are 'The Liberal Fascist', 'The Sportsmen: A Parable', 'The Public v. the late Mr. William Butler Yeats', 'Balaam and his Ass', and 'D. H. Lawrence', while of the short reviews, that on T. E. Lawrence, and 'Jehovah Housman and Satan Housman' are forceful, concentrated statements. Significantly, the first in this list is an autobiographical piece on a topic Auden knew inside out: the English public school; the second, as it says, is a parable; the third is in a borrowed oratorical mode; the fourth deals with a theme almost peculiar to Auden, as I shall try to show, and the fifth is on a writer whom it is much harder to be boring about than it is to be interesting.

If ordered to pick out the most striking feature of Auden's prose writings in the two volumes mentioned, I would choose the one most noticeably absent: anger. 'Noticeably', considering the writer's association with Marxism and the times through which he lived (not to mention his admiration for Blake). Of the poems in *Look, Stranger!* F. R. Leavis wrote that the irony 'is a matter of his being uncertain whether he is engaged mainly in expressing *saeva indignatio* or in amusing himself and his friends'[3]—in other words, whether he is a Juvenal or a Horace. In his prose, the fire of conviction is too often smothered by an inflammable blanket of abstract generalizing, and a Horatian equanimity that at times is no more than equivocation. For all his assertiveness (rhetorical, if not ideological), Auden is too concerned that he be seen presenting both sides of the case to be angry, too eager to reconcile dichotomies and construe a hypothetical unity out of present duality (hence the utopian impulse, the search for 'The Good Life'). The wit is more genial than mordant; 'strong' statements are often neutralized by weak digression, superficial illustration or implicit qualification. Sentences like 'A revolutionary issue is one in which different groups within a society hold different views as to what is just' and 'When an issue is revolutionary, fanatics are essential' are pointless platitudes; the next sentence—'Today, there is only one genuine [that word again] world-wide revolutionary issue, racial equality'—

is neither justified nor supported. A page later Auden affirms 'In our age, the mere making of a work of art is itself a political act'—a challenging assertion rich in implication, yet trivialized in the banal follow-up:

> So long as artists exist, making what they please and think they ought to make, even if it is not terribly good, even if it appeals to only a handful of people, they remind the Management of something managers need to be reminded of, namely, that the managed are people with faces, not anonymous numbers.[4]

(The casual tone of 'even if it is not terribly good' is particularly enfeebling.)

Sometimes Auden is the accomplished teacher and popularizer, rôles that, as a left-wing intellectual, he was not alone in being called upon to fulfil during the 1930s. We find him explaining, in the language of traditional English common sense, hard and knotty concepts for less agile minds, ostensibly in order to clarify and balance rival claims (Freud and Marx, Psychology and Communism, Christianity and Communism, etc.), but occasionally with a diluting effect, so that by making revolutionary ideas less scary, potential middle-class supporters are won over: 'No more than Communism rejects Capitalism does psychology reject selfconsciousness and reason.'[5] (The tactic of winning over middle-class support—notably the intellectuals—was adopted by the British Communist Party after the German defeat of 1933 and the switch to Popular Front policies.)

Hoggart's criticism that Auden's prose is 'too tightly packed' could also be that it is 'too clever'. The intellectual apparatus is often marshalled for very uncertain ends. The following is an example, where Auden gives, as the third kind of resolution to the problem of the environment, the proposition that

> What is, is a necessary stage in the realisation of what ought to be. This realisation may be:
> (a) Sudden and catastrophic.
> (b) A slow evolution.
> (x) Voluntary—depending on the determination of the majority of individuals, i.e. it is possible for the consummation to be rejected.

# Auden's Prose

(y) Determined—though the individual can accept or reject it; if he rejects it he joins the losing side.

Christianity is undecided about (a) and (b), but holds (y) not (x).
Social Democracy holds (b), and is undecided about (x) and (y).
Psychology, on the whole, holds (b) and (x).
Communism holds (a) and (y).[6]

Lists, numbered points, sub-headings and sub-sections are an annoyingly common feature of Auden's essays, yet despite the sub-divisions and the algebraic rigour displayed here, the reader is left dangling between permutations. The whole exercise seems to be for exhibition only.

According to Osborne,

> Those who knew him at Oxford agree on the range and volubility of Auden's conversation, or rather his monologues, for, like many of those renowned for their conversational powers, he was disinclined to converse, preferring to harangue. Like Wilde, he was a performer, though his manner was decidedly more Johnsonian than Wildean. Frequently, the ideas which he propounded with such dogmatic emphasis were simply those which he himself was tentatively exploring, trying out.[7]

Some of these characteristics persisted into the later prose. The Johnsonian manner is there in the conclusive generalizations, balanced clauses and patterned syntax. The frequency of grand openings such as: 'All poets . . .', 'In all societies . . .', 'Every poem . . .', 'Any world is comprised of . . .', 'Every work of a writer . . .', 'All works of art . . .', is high enough to give the impression of a writer with *ex cathedra* authority pronouncing eternal, universal truths. Yet laying down the law runs the risk of retort. Statements such as 'Primitive cultures have little sense of humour' and 'In all narrative art, the narration of the action takes less time than it would in real life' are not difficult to refute. Formal patterning is exemplified in: (a) 'Some books are undeservedly forgotten, none are undeservedly remembered'; (b) 'The most exciting rhythms seem unexpected and complex, the most beautiful melodies simple and inevitable', and (c) 'The ear tends to be lazy, craves the familiar, and is shocked by the unexpected: the eye, on the other hand, tends to be impatient, craves the novel and is bored by repetition.'

The balanced sentence is a form of syntactic parallelism that makes for compression. Internal cohesion is achieved by ellipsis: nominal in (a) and (c), verbal in (b). In (c) the same noun governs three verbs in each clause. This kind of parallelism is not only highly formal, but symbolically enacts the Audenesque project of unity out of duality, with a 'democratic' equality between parallel parts. The 'baroque' hierarchy of the periodic sentence, with its main and subordinate clauses, is of course more predominant, yet if Auden's prose style is characterized by longish complex sentences, cohesion is obtained by linking rather than subordinating conjunctions. The production of a 'finished' style is further aided by the relatively small number of appositional phrases, dashes and parentheses.[8] Other thoughts, afterthoughts, and the thinking process itself are either kept 'out of sight in cellars',[9] leaving only conclusions above ground, or are discreetly built into the final structure.

Auden's essays generally keep to the non-personal convention associated with the genre. Standard grammatical devices include the non-specific pronoun 'one', as in 'One can easily imagine . . .'; the pronoun 'it' as the purely grammatical subject of a sentence, as in 'It is difficult to say . . .'; the infinitive as a noun phrase, as in 'To trace . . . the influence of Freud upon modern art . . . would', etc., and the adverbial phrase 'there is', as in 'There is no reason to suppose . . .'. The inclusive 'we' is very frequent: 'Most of the literary works with which we are acquainted fall into one of two classes . . .'; 'We want a poem to be beautiful . . .'; 'When we read a book, it is as if we were with a person . . .'. The habit is annoying for those readers who are not loyal subjects of the sovereign truth being enunciated, and the qualification 'Most of us' is presumably a concession to them. The personal pronoun 'I' is either used to refer to the authorial persona conducting the discussion, as in 'There are two more points I should like to touch on', or as a hypothetical subject introduced to illustrate a point, as in

> I look down from an airplane upon a stretch of land which is obviously continuous. . . . From the same height I cannot

distinguish between an outcrop of rock and a Gothic cathedral, or between a happy family playing in a back-yard and a flock of sheep, so that I am unable to feel any difference between dropping a bomb upon one or the other.

(The passage has other, fascinating implications we cannot go into here.) In the first example, the 'I' is what we may call, following Benveniste, the 'subject of the enunciation'; in the second, it is the 'subject of the enounced'. But there are other forms of the latter: apart from the hypothetical, there is the autobiographical subject ('My first Master was Thomas Hardy.... Much as I loved him, even I could see that his diction was often clumsy'), and the opinion-holding or preference-holding subject ('. . . in literature I expect plenty of news'). In 'I mentioned Lenin. He and Lawrence seem to me the two whose lives exemplify what is best and significant in our time', there is a shift from the subject as author to the subject as opinion-holder. The third person singular, as an 'objective' form, is occasionally used to generalize from personal experience. Auden's remarks on Goethe, for example, turn out to be disguised autobiography. The young Goethe, we are told, exemplifies the type of writer who 'finds himself obsessed by certain ways of feeling and thinking of which his instinct tells him he must be rid before he can discover his authentic interests and sympathies'. There follows this passage:

> What he wrote in order to exorcise certain feelings is enthusiastically welcomed by his contemporaries because it expresses just what they feel but, unlike him, they are perfectly happy to feel in this way; for the moment they regard him as their spokesman. Time passes. Having gotten the poison out of his system, the writer turns to his true interests which are not, and never were, those of his early admirers, who now pursue him with cries of 'Traitor!'[10]

The parabolic, general case is used as a protective screen around which Auden is able to snipe back at his own pursuers. The third person plural is even more distant from the first person singular than the third person singular, and hence less recognizable as a means of covert self-revelation.

> Once upon a time we were all Falstaffs: then we became social beings with super-egos. Most of us learn to accept this,

but there are some in whom the nostalgia for the state of innocent self-importance is so strong that they refuse to accept adult life and responsibilities and seek some means to become the Falstaffs they once were.[11]

Auden's train of thought passes many stations. In 'Balaam and His Ass' there is an amusing detour in which a discussion of Jules Verne's Mr. Fogg as 'stoic saint' and type of The Punctual Man takes us past Theophrastus, Julius Caesar, the monks, St. Augustine, natural and historical time, ancient concepts of time, time as Fate or Chance, and ancient stoicism, before returning to Mr. Fogg. In 'The Joker in the Pack', there is a discussion of Iago as 'practical joker, a parabolic figure for the autonomous pursuit of scientific knowledge'.[12] Once we are onto this tack, we can pass by Nietzsche on experimental science as 'the last flower of asceticism', Iago as ascetic, Adam and Eve, Asian 'flu, human beings as biological organisms subject to scientific knowledge and control, lobotomies and sleep deprivation, psychological manipulation and advertising techniques, where 'your advertisement seems as honest as Iago seems to Othello'—but just before the essay ends, we will touch on Bacon, the gossip column, the cobalt bomb, food and sex. As Auden said in his 'Foreword' to *The Dyer's Hand*:

> Sometimes one feels cramped, forced to omit or oversimplify arguments; more often, all one really has to say could be put down in half the allotted space, and one can only try to pad as inconspicuously as possible.

The parameters of Auden's thought, which is eclectic rather than doctrinal, are essentially those of an English liberal-reformist tradition. Freudianism is tempered by common-sense rationality and the stress on individual moral choice and responsibility. The demands of the unconscious and the fantasy life are acknowledged in the therapeutic and escapist value of art: the artist 'starts from the same point as the neurotic and the day-dreamer, from emotional frustration in early childhood'.[13] Auden's Marxism is of a fairly superficial, reformist kind, a peg on which to hang the middle-class intellectual's yearning for a 'genuine community' and 'a secure place in society',[14] since the problem of 'the modern poet, as

for every one else today, is how to find or form a genuine
community, in which each has his valued place and can feel
at home'.[15] Social awareness seems to open up with the
realization that self-consciousness (the feeling that 'I am I,
and you are not I', and that 'we are shut inside ourselves and
apart from each other') is a prison, but the communal
impulse can, in certain circumstances, be a sort of death-
wish, an infantile-regressive fantasy. The 'real "life-wish" ',
therefore, is 'the desire for separation',[16] but separation leads
once again to isolation and loneliness, and for the citizen-poet
who wishes his work to have social relevance and a wide
audience, isolation is another death. The 'private world is
fascinating, but it is exhaustible'.[17] A 'purely private verbal
world is not possible',[18] since the poet's medium, language,
'is the common property of the linguistic group' to which he
belongs.[19]

Perhaps Auden's most original contribution to the question
of the relation between art and society is an implied notion of
'the society of the poem', to use Jonathan Raban's phrase.
Auden first of all rejects the agitprop function of art: 'You
cannot tell people what to do, you can only tell them parables;
and that is what art really is.'[20] The notion of art as
propaganda is based on the Tolstoyan heresy that art can
come from 'utility without gratuity'.[21] Rather, the relation
between art and society is based on a mimetic analogy, a kind
of symbolic substitution:

> When a poet is writing verse, the feeling, as it were, excites the
> words and makes them fall into a definite group, going through
> definite dancing movements, just as feeling excites the different
> members of a crowd and makes them act together. Metre is
> group excitement among words, a series of repeated movements.[22]

The analogy does not necessarily work in reverse, however:

> A society which was really like a good poem, embodying the
> aesthetic virtues of beauty, order, economy and subordination
> of detail to the whole, would be a nightmare of horror for, given
> the historical reality of actual men, such a society could only
> come into being through selective breeding, extermination of
> the physically and mentally unfit, absolute obedience to its
> Director, and a large slave class kept out of sight in cellars.

> Vice versa, a poem which was really like a political democracy—examples, unfortunately, exist—would be formless, windy, banal and utterly boring.[23]

In the essay 'Writing' the poet who writes free verse 'is like Robinson Crusoe', doing

> all his cooking, laundry and darning for himself. In a few exceptional cases, this manly independence produces something original and impressive but more often the result is squalor—dirty sheets on the unmade bed and empty bottles on the unswept floor.[24]

(Although extremely untidy in his own personal habits, Auden evidently hated to see this reflected in his verse!) The analogy is explicitly elaborated at the end of 'The Virgin & The Dynamo':

> Every poem, therefore, is an attempt to present an analogy to that paradisal state in which Freedom and Law, System and Order are united in harmony. Every good poem is very nearly a Utopia. Again, an analogy, not an imitation; the harmony is possible and verbal only.[25]

Auden is at his best, and most compelling, when he is discussing the work of individual poets such as Yeats, D. H. Lawrence, Robert Frost and Byron. The analysis of Byron's adaptation of *ottava rima* in the essay 'Don Juan' is particularly interesting. In the same essay, Auden quotes Lady Byron, who once said that Byron 'is the absolute monarch of words, and uses them as Bonaparte did lives, for conquest without regard to their intrinsic value'.[26] Auden takes up the point:

> What had been Byron's defect as a serious poet, his lack of reverence for words, was a virtue for the comic poet. Serious poetry requires that the poet treat words as if they were persons, but comic poetry demands that he treat them as things. . . .[27]

One is carried along by the argument, until the question arises: is not the essence of poetry to treat words as 'things' (i.e. by exploiting their rhythmical, rhyming, alliterative and other sound qualities)? Auden quotes an earlier version of the famous couplet on Keats:

*Second Version:*
  'Tis strange the mind, that all celestial Particle,
  Should let itself be put out by an Article.

*Final Version:*
  'Tis strange the mind, that very fiery Particle,
  Should let itself be snuffed out by an Article.

The change from 'all celestial' to 'very fiery', and from 'put out' to 'snuffed out' shows not only a sensitivity to the semantic, associative, rhythmical and sound qualities of words, but also an acute awareness of register. This may not amount to treating words as 'persons' (and one is now unsure about the whole analogy), but neither is it a disregard for their 'intrinsic value'. On the contrary, by foregrounding the materiality of the signifier, it is precisely those intrinsic properties that the poet rescues. Perhaps the Audenesque analogy of treating words as persons means, in this case, defending the rights of each individual word, whereas previously it meant forming them into a 'definite group' and making them 'act together'.

There is one recurrent theme in Auden's prose writings—it is also in the plays—that may have been insufficiently noticed, though it has intriguing ramifications. In *The Dog Beneath the Skin*, Francis risks his 'skin' to save his 'master', who is in danger of being sent to prison for not paying his hotel bills. The Abbot in *The Ascent of F6* refers to the 'blind obedience' with which others are prepared to follow Ransom. Prospero forfeits his right to Caliban's devotion, whose 'initial love for Prospero has been turned into hatred'.[28] In *On the Frontier*, however, Manners, Valerian's butler, dies of plague looking for a pot of caviare for his master. In 'Balaam and His Ass', several master-servant relationships (all male) are examined as parables of 'agape': Don Giovanni and Leporello; Mr. Fogg and Passepartout; Don Quixote and Sancho Panza, 'whose motives for following his master are love of his master';[29] and Bertie Wooster and Jeeves. In the essay on Falstaff and Prince Hal, significantly titled 'The Prince's Dog', Auden notes that 'Falstaff loves Hal with an absolute devotion'.[30] (Not cupboard love?') And there is Pickwick and Sam Weller who, 'before the story ends . . . is calling Mr. Pickwick an angel, and

213

his devotion to his master has grown so great that he insists upon being sent to prison in order to look after him'.[31] The relationship seems to be the microcosm of some utopian ideal.

Finally, in his later writings on drama, Auden reverts to some squarely conventional ideas—and misconceptions. His Shakespeare criticism psychologizes the characters of Hotspur, Falstaff, Othello, Iago and others to such an extent that imaginary situations are even found for them outside the text. They have, in fact, 'good warm red blood in their veins'. Of Desdemona, for example, he says: 'Given a few more years of Othello and of Emilia's influence and she might well, one feels, have taken a lover.'[32] Apart from their irrelevance and lack of any supporting evidence, and the fact that Auden is merely giving rein to his speculative steed, such comments assume that Shakespeare's characters have an independent existence beyond the text. That view could, of course, be debated. What is clear, however, is that the old 'sympathetic understanding' and involvement in 'character', which Auden rejected in 1935, have now returned with a vengeance. Brecht has been ditched, and Shakespeare, whose works are true for all time,[33] has taken his place: 'A play, as Shakespeare said, is a mirror held up to nature. This particular mirror [*Othello*] bears the date 1604, but, when we look into it, the face that confronts us is our own in the middle of the twentieth century.'[34] That is why Iago can happily rub shoulders with lobotomy surgeons and modern advertisers; his human nature is ever contemporary. True or not, this ignores the dramatic whole of which Iago is a part. One begins to see now why Auden, even as a practising playwright, managed to get by with so little theory. For at the end of the day, Shakespeare has said it all: a play 'is a mirror held up to nature'. It is not difficult to imagine who would have welcomed this former heretic's return to such imperishable, self-evident truths.

NOTES

1. Barbara Everett, *Auden* (Edinburgh: Oliver and Boyd, 1964), p. 31.
2. Richard Hoggart, *Auden: An Introductory Essay* (London: Chatto and Windus, 1951), p. 73.
3. F. R. Leavis, *Scrutiny*, December 1936.
4. 'The Poet & the City' in W. H. Auden, *The Dyer's Hand and Other Essays* (London: Faber, 1963), p. 88.
5. 'The Good Life' in John Lewis *et. al.* (eds.), *Christianity and the Social Revolution* (1935) and Edward Mendelson (ed.), *The English Auden* (London: Faber, 1977), p. 347.
6. Ibid., pp. 342–43.
7. Charles Osborne, *W. H. Auden: The Life of a Poet* (London: Eyre Methuen, 1979), p. 47.
8. Taking dashes and parentheses together, I find an average of one per page for 'The Poet & The City'; 0.6 for 'Balaam and His Ass', 'The I Without a Self', and 'Dingley Dell & The Fleet'; 0.5 for 'The Joker in the Pack', and an unusually high average of 3.6 for 'The Guilty Vicarage'. In the latter Auden confesses his personal 'addiction' to the detective story, adopting a less buttoned-up style, with frequent use of 'i.e.' and 'e.g.'.
9. 'The Poet & The City'. See below for the full quotation.
10. 'Writing', in *The Dyer's Hand*, pp. 18–19.
11. 'The Prince's Dog', *The Dyer's Hand*, p. 195.
12. Ibid., p. 270.
13. 'Psychology and Art To-Day', in Geoffrey Grigson (ed.), *The Arts Today* (1935) and *The English Auden*, p. 334.
14. Introduction to Auden (ed.), *The Oxford Book of Light Verse* (1938) and *The English Auden*, p. 366.
15. *The English Auden*, pp. 367–68.
16. Ibid., p. 299.
17. Ibid., p. 366.
18. 'Writing', *The Dyer's Hand*, p. 23.
19. Ibid., p. 15.
20. 'Psychology and Art To-Day', *The English Auden*, p. 341.
21. 'The Poet & The City', *The Dyer's Hand*, p. 85.
22. 'Writing' in Naomi Mitchison (ed.), *An Outline for Boys and Girls and Their Parents* (1932) and *The English Auden*, pp. 307–8.
23. 'The Poet & The City', *The Dyer's Hand*, p. 85.
24. 'Writing', ibid., p. 22.
25. Ibid., p. 71.
26. Ibid., p. 395.
27. Ibid., p. 399.
28. 'Balaam and His Ass', ibid., p. 133.
29. Ibid., p. 137.
30. Ibid., p. 191.
31. 'Dingley Dell & The Fleet', ibid., pp. 419–20.
32. 'The Joker in the Pack', ibid., p. 269.

33. Quoting the 1921 Newbolt Report, Derek Longhurst writes: '[The] sense of ideological power of culture rests on a definition of "great literature" as "timeless", "eternal", "universal" . . . and Shakespeare is used continually to prove it. Although he tells us "what Englishmen were like" at the beginning of the seventeenth century, he also tells us "what all men are like in all countries and at all times". . . . Clearly Shakespeare is seen as an *authority* on unchanging human nature; as such his work is transhistorical, and so replaces history.' ' "Not for all time, but for an Age": An Approach to Shakespeare Studies' in Peter Widdowson (ed.), *Re-Reading English* (London; Methuen, 1982), p. 151.
34. 'The Joker in the Pack', *The Dyer's Hand*, p. 269.

# Notes on Contributors

ALAN BOLD was born in 1943 in Edinburgh where he attended university and trained as a journalist. Since 1966 he has been a fulltime writer and visual artist and since 1975 has lived in rural Fife writing books and contributing features regularly to *The Scotsman* and occasionally to the *New Statesman, TLS, Glasgow Herald* and *Tribune.* He has published many books of poetry including *To Find the New, The State of the Nation* and a selection in *Penguin Modern Poets 15.* His *In This Corner: Selected Poems 1963–82* represents his best work over the past two decades; with the artist John Bellany he has collaborated on *A Celtic Quintet* and *Haven.* He has edited many anthologies including *The Penguin Book of Socialist Verse, The Martial Muse,* the *Cambridge Book of English Verse 1939–75, Making Love, The Bawdy Beautiful, Mounts of Venus, Drink To Me Only, The Poetry of Motion.* He has also written critical books on *Thom Gunn & Ted Hughes, George Mackay Brown, The Ballad, Modern Scottish Literature* and *MacDiarmid: The Terrible Crystal.* He has edited *The Thistle Rises: a MacDiarmid Miscellany* and *The Letters of Hugh MacDiarmid.* He has exhibited his Illuminated Poems (pictures combining an original poetic manuscript with an illustrative composition) in venues as varied as Boston University and the National Library of Scotland.

STEWART CREHAN, Senior Lecturer in the Department of Literature and Languages, University of Zambia, was born in 1942. He graduated from Newcastle University in 1964 and took a Ph.D. at Edinburgh University in 1970. His publications include: *William Blake: Selected Poetry and Letters* (1976), *Blake in Context* (1984) and, with Charles Sarvan, *Readings in Poetry* (1984). He has published articles on eighteenth-century, nineteenth-century and modern African literature.

ROBERT GIDDINGS was born in Worcester in 1935 and educated at the universities of Bristol and Keele. He was Lecturer in English and Communication Studies at Bath Technical College 1964–82, Fulbright Exchange Professor, St. Louis, Missouri 1975–76, and Tutor, The Open University 1971–81. Since 1982 he has been Senior Lecturer in English and Media at the Dorset Institute of

217

Higher Education. His publications include *The Tradition of Smollett* (1967), *You Should See Me in Pyjamas* (1981), *True Characters: Real People in Fiction*, with Alan Bold (1984), *Musical Quotes and Anecdotes* (1984) and several titles in the Critical Studies Series, including *The Changing World of Charles Dickens, Mark Twain: A Sumptuous Variety* and *J. R. R. Tolkien: This Far Land*. He has contributed to the *Sunday Times*, the *Guardian, Tribune, New Society, Music and Letters, New Statesman, Music and Musicians, British Bandsman* and the *Listener*, as well as to the Critical Studies volumes on Smollett, Johnson and Scott.

WILLIAM LOGAN was born, in 1950, in Boston, Massachusetts. He was raised in a Massachusetts fishing village and in suburbs of Pittsburgh and New York. Educated at the universities of Yale and Iowa, he became Director of Creative Writing at the University of Florida. In 1981–83 he lived in England as an Amy Lowell Poetry Travelling Scholar and he has received grants from the Ingram Merrill Foundation and the National Endowment for the Arts. His poems appear in *Sad-faced Men* (1982) and *Difficulty* (1984).

JAN MONTEFIORE was born in 1948. She read English language and literature at Lady Margaret Hall, Oxford, where she took her postgraduate degree. She was a lecturer in English literature at Liverpool University between 1972 and 1977, and since then has been a lecturer in English and American literature at the University of Kent. She has written articles for *Essays in Criticism, South-East Arts, Feminist Review* and *New Left Review*; she has also published a small book of poems, *In a Glass* (1979). Her book on women's poetry and feminist aesthetics appears in 1985.

CHARLES OSBORNE, author of *W. H. Auden: The Life of a Poet* (1980), came to Europe from his native Australia in his mid-twenties and has lived in London for more than twenty-five years. He joined the staff of the Arts Council of Great Britain in 1966 and became its Literature Director in 1971. He is the author of several books, including *Kafka, Swansong* (poems, illustrated by Sidney Nolan), *Wagner and His World*, and *The Complete Operas of Verdi*, which is generally regarded as the definitive guide to Verdi, and has been successfully translated into Italian. He is also a B.B.C. broadcaster on musical and literary subjects. For several years he directed *Poetry International*, London's annual poetry festival. Together with Irene Worth, Sir John Betjeman and Michael York, he performed at the 1974 *Poetry International* in *The Vertical Man*, a memorial programme

218

which he compiled from the work of W. H. Auden. His *Letter to W. H. Auden and Other Poems* appeared in 1984.

DONALD PEARCE was born in Ontario, Canada in 1917. He served as an infantry platoon officer in World War II and published a book about it, *Journal of a War* (1965). Ph.D. University of Michigan; currently teaches in the English Department at University of California, Santa Barbara; has written many articles on classical and modern poets and is the editor of *The Senate Speeches of W. B. Yeats* (1962). Co-editor with Robert Essick of *Blake in His Time* (1975), and last year with H. N. Schneidau of a collection of Ezra Pound's correspondence with John Theobold.

WALTER PERRIE was born, in 1949, in the Lanarkshire mining village of Quarter. Educated locally and at Hamilton Academy, he took an M.A. in philosophy at the University of Edinburgh. A poet and essayist, he published *Out of Conflict* in 1982; his poems appear in *A Lamentation for the Children* (1977), *By Moon and Sun* (1980) and *Concerning the Dragon* (1984). In 1984 he was appointed to the Scottish Arts Council's Scottish-Canadian writer's fellowship at the University of British Columbia, Vancouver.

MARGARET MOAN ROWE was born in Glasgow, Scotland in 1941. She grew up in Philadelphia, Pennsylvania where she received a B.A. from Holy Family College and M.A. and Ph.D. degrees from Temple University. She is an Associate Professor of English at Purdue University in Indiana and has published critical essays on W. H. Auden, L. P. Hartley, Virginia Woolf and Muriel Spark, among others. At present Professor Rowe is working on the topic of ethics and the modern British novel supported by a fellowship from the Lilly Foundation.

# Index

# Index

# Index